THE GREAT SIOUX NATION

Sitting in Judgment on America

Edited by Roxanne Dunbar Oritz

Foreword to the Bison Books edition by Philip J. Deloria
With a new introduction by the editor

UNIVERSITY OF NEBRASKA PRESS
LINCOLN AND LONDON

Library of Congress Cataloging-in-Publication Data
The great Sioux nation: sitting in judgment on America / edited by Roxanne Dunbar Ortiz; foreword to the Bison
Books edition by Philip J. Deloria with a new introduction by the editor. — Bison books edition.
pages cm
"1st Nebraska paperback printing: 2013" — Title page verso.
"Based on and containing testimony heard at the "Sioux treaty hearing" held December, 1974, in Federal District
Court, Lincoln, Nebraska"
Includes bibliographical references.
ISBN 978-0-8032-4483-2 (paperback: alk. paper) 1. American Indian Movement—Trials, litigation, etc.
2. Trials (Political crimes and offenses)—United States. 3. Wounded Knee (S.D.)—History—Indian occupation,
1973. 4. Criminal jurisdiction—United States. 5. Indians of North America—Legal status, laws, etc.
6. Sioux Nation. Treaties, etc. United States, 1868, Nov. 7. 7. Dakota Indians—Treaties. 8. Dakota Indians—
History. 9. Dakota Indians—Government relations. I. Dunbar-Ortiz, Roxanne, 1939– editor of compilation.
II. United States. District Court (Nebraska)
KF224.A484G74 2013
342.73'0872—dc23   2012050419

This Bison Books edition follows the original in beginning the main text on arabic page 9; no material has been
omitted.

FOREWORD

Philip J. Deloria

Rare are the documents that, after enduring a long reach of time, come to be seen both for their interpretive power and their historical relevance. What do I mean by that? There are some writings that offer durable, compelling interpretation. For the historian, they stand as secondary texts—that is, they are valued for their analysis, and for that reason they are not as easily seen as pieces that epitomize the moment of their creation. Other writings, of weaker interpretive power, see their analyses become less interesting with the passage of time. Often, however, such texts become more compelling as primary sources, reflections of the cultural currents of their time and place. If we no longer believe their arguments, we value them all the more for the ways those arguments open up a window on the thought and emotion of the past.

The Great Sioux Nation, published thirty-five years ago, may be one of those rare books that maintain their analytical power even as, with the passing of time, they simultaneously become markers of discrete moments in history.

Reading the book today, one cannot help but be transported back to 1977. In the layout of the text, the photographs, the style, the bold assertions mixed with uncertainties and failures of nerve and confidence, you can feel the moment, viscerally. Even the fonts used in the original edition make you think of old tribal newsletters, photocopied and mimeographed, with hand-drawn banners and headlines laid down with rub-on Letraset characters. From the vista of 2013, one realizes just how close 1977 was to the 1960s. Time unfolds. And so your encounter with the emotional feeling of 1977 can take you on a very short hop back to the feeling of 1973, and then 1969 and 1964 and maybe even the 1950s, which in turn tempt you back to the 1930s. And from there, you can almost smell the nineteenth century, the moment of our great-grandparents and beyond, and of people whose stories continue to linger in shared memories but who lived well over a century ago.

Today, the writing seems to cry out with anxieties about form and legitimacy and authority that also say something about the 1970s. The original introductions devote many words to a preemptive defense of the process through which Roxanne Dunbar Ortiz edited three thousand pages of testimony into a single slim volume. Choices had to be made. And so what was once a trial transcript was (necessarily, inevitably) altered, condensed, made readable, arranged in thematic clusters and chronological sequence. The deep question remained: was *The Great Sioux Nation* a work of scholarship? And if so, what kind? Or was it a work of popularization? And if so, then where did its authority lie?

Such anxieties were palpable in 1977, when academic ethnic studies departments—and American Indian studies itself—were both new and sparse on the landscape, when the popular success of *Bury My Heart at Wounded Knee* was strong in recent memory, and when an ethnopoetics movement insisted that oral performance (or testimony) be arranged on the page with aesthetic aims in mind. Which audiences would take *The Great Sioux Nation* seriously, and in what ways? American Indians? Academics? Concerned popular readers? As a work of testimony? As an argument for sovereignty? As a literary and performative work?

In 1978 my father, Vine Deloria Jr., would move to the University of Arizona to help start what is now an old, honored, and well-established American Indian studies program. But the shape of American Indian studies—though a field on the rise—was hardly a foregone conclusion, and the lines between academic authority, popular writing, aesthetic form, and political polemic were far blurrier than they are today. This book—slippery in its form and structure but consistent in its argument—caught that moment and takes us back to that time. Not surprisingly, we as contemporary readers find that some of the deep questions remain.

Today's readers might well ask how well the book stands as a reflection of the 1970s. The answer is, from my point of view, "extremely well"—and not simply in terms of tone and style. Here was a moment in which American Indian people were consolidating knowledge, testing the possibilities of the courtroom, and pulling together the arguments for sovereignty and cultural autonomy. All these things are powerfully reflected in *The Great Sioux Nation*. And that reflection suggests that, for all its emotional power to evoke a historical past, we need also home in on the interpretation and analysis put forth in the book.

If many of the questions remain relevant today, so too do the book's central assertions, key ideas instantly recognizable as themes that we continue to pursue, both in academic and tribal contexts. American Indian people and American Indian studies scholars have made nationhood and sovereignty central to tribal governance and to the theorization of the intellectual field. Scholars have spent the last decades puzzling out the ways oral history and tribal memory can and should appear in academic contexts, while tribes have created cultural affairs offices to handle research issues and repatriation claims. Treaties have emerged as central points for political and legal assertion, and Indian people routinely remind Americans of Article VI of the Constitution, which enshrines treaties in a privileged place in the world of American law. Colonialism has emerged as a central discourse, a way of describing the historical relationship between the United States and American Indian people. At the same time, legal activists and scholars alike have become keenly attuned to the dangers and opportunities inherent in carrying a political argument into the courtrooms of the United States. And we've come to understand in new ways the linked relation between political and cultural autonomy, the latter often viewed today in terms of language preservation and sovereignty.

All these things are found in *The Great Sioux Nation*, and in that way the book is one of a limited number of texts that are evocatively *ancestral* to the present, connecting the then and the now. What's more, the analyses in *The Great Sioux Nation* come from a range that rings familiar: the organic wisdom of Native voices blends with the voices of lawyers, historians, and American Indian political theorists. Those voices—along with the organization that structures them together into a chorus—produce a novel form of interpretive power, one that stands alongside the affective evocation that carries us back in time, perhaps a little nostalgically, to earlier moments of possibility.

What's required of the book, then, is this: a reading that oscillates knowingly between past and present, one that makes comparisons and traces historical trajectories, one that sees patterns and continuities but also perceives change, for better—and sometimes for worse. Republication of such ancestral texts always presents challenges for readers, for the barriers to this kind of reading are not trivial. May your barriers be few and your memories—whether individual or collective—be strong. And may you use this book to gain a deeper sense of the long struggle of American Indian people for sovereignty within and in relation to the United States. That, after all, was its original aim, and it remains no less pressing in the twenty-first century.

INTRODUCTION TO THE BISON BOOKS EDITION

Roxanne Dunbar Ortiz

The University of Nebraska Press, the esteemed publisher of this new edition of *The Great Sioux Nation*, also published, in 2012, *Called to Justice: The Life of a Federal Trial Judge*, the memoirs of Judge Warren Urbom, the federal judge who heard the case this book is based on. The chapter in which the judge recounts that experience, titled "Wounded Knee and the Fort Laramie Treaty of 1868," is one of the longest in the book, yet it covers only one year of his rich and complex career. The chapter begins: "At the dawn of 1974 my life was about to be absorbed by Native Americans. I could have avoided it, I suppose, but I didn't see it coming, and when I did see it, I was already deeply involved. I accepted the invitation with the expectation that I'd spend a week trying Native Americans. I stayed a year."

I could say the same myself, except I stayed a lifetime rather than a year. Immediately after the 1974 hearing I was swept into the uncharted territory of forging an international Indigenous movement. Following the publication of *The Great Sioux Nation* in the spring of 1977, the book was presented three months later as a fundamental document regarding the 1868 Sioux Treaty at the United Nations. The International Indian Treaty Council, formed in 1974 to seek international recognition for the Sioux Nation and other Indigenous nations based on treaties and agreements guaranteeing their sovereignty, worked with international human rights groups and UN officials to organize the "International NGO Conference on Discrimination against Indigenous Populations in the Americas," held at the United Nations' headquarters in Geneva, Switzerland, September 20–23, 1977. Over a hundred Indigenous representatives from the Arctic Circle to the cone of South America participated in this unprecedented initiative, triggering a three-decade process involving hundreds of Indigenous nations, communities, and organizations. This effort culminated in the landmark 2007 United Nations General Assembly's "Declaration on the Rights of Indigenous Peoples." Article 37 of the Declaration pertains to treaties:

> 1. Indigenous peoples have the rights to the recognition, observance and enforcement of treaties, agreements and other constructive arrangements concluded with States or their successors and to have States honour and respect such treaties, agreements and other constructive arrangements.
> 2. Nothing in this Declaration may be interpreted as diminishing or eliminating the rights of indigenous peoples contained in treaties, agreements and other constructive arrangements.

The Declaration was strong on the treaty issue thanks to the persistent lobbying by representatives of the Sioux Treaty, along with those of other Indigenous nations. In the late 1980s, a UN special rapporteur, Miguel Alfonso-Martínez, was appointed to study treaties and agreements between Indigenous peoples and colonizing states. The study, completed in 1999, validated the 1868 Sioux Treaty according to the Sioux interpretation. During the following years, regular treaty seminars have been organized at the United

Nations to further refine the applicable international law. The Declaration is a marker on the road to a binding international treaty on the rights of Indigenous peoples.

Contributing to the high credibility of the treaty issue was the vindication of the Sioux in their claim to the Black Hills, as guaranteed under the 1868 treaty. On July 23, 1980, in *United States v. Sioux Nation of Indians*, the Supreme Court of the United States ruled that the Black Hills were illegally taken and that remuneration of the initial offering price plus interest—over a hundred million dollars—be paid to the Sioux Nation. The Sioux people refused the settlement and insisted that the sacred Black Hills be returned to them. The money remained in an interest-bearing account, which by the turn of the twenty-first century amounted to over seven hundred million dollars, increasing every year. But the Sioux refused to take the money. They believed that accepting the settlement would validate the U.S. theft of their most sacred land. This is a profound statement coming from a people living in impoverished, colonized conditions in the richest country in the world, clear evidence of their sovereignty as a people and their insistence on self-determination.

In the decades since the publication of *The Great Sioux Nation*, American Indian studies (variously called Native American studies and Indigenous studies) programs have flourished in dozens of universities throughout North America. Native American scholars are now professors in many academic fields, including Native studies, teaching and writing invaluable books, literature, and poetry. When this book was first published, the theoretical framework of western colonialism and the United States as a colonialist settler-state was only beginning to emerge; now it is the foundational theory. Lakota scholar and poet Elizabeth Cook-Lynn's 2011 book, *A Separate Country: Postcoloniality and American Indian Nations*, is the best guide to that development.

Several books published since the Sioux Treaty hearing provide perspectives on the treaty issue, the Black Hills, the Wounded Knee siege, and Native activism in general. Two prominent leaders of the American Indian Movement at Wounded Knee published their autobiographies: Russell Means, *Where White Men Fear to Tread: The Autobiography of Russell Means* (1996) and Dennis Banks, *Ojibwa Warrior: Dennis Banks and the Rise of the American Indian Movement* (2005). Peter Matthiessen's 1983 book, *In the Spirit of Crazyhorse: The Story of Leonard Peltier and the FBI's War on the American Indian Movement*, is a meticulous history of the American Indian Movement and the U.S. government's attacks on the organization, most notably the continued imprisonment of Leonard Peltier. *Like a Hurricane: The Indian Movement from Alcatraz to Wounded Knee*, published in 1997 by Native American writers Paul Chaat Smith and Robert Allen Warrior, has already become a classic and essential interpretive work. The most comprehensive historical work on what led up to Wounded Knee is Daniel M. Cobb's *Native American Activism in Cold War America: The Struggle for Sovereignty* (2008). Lakota attorney Mario Gonzalez and Lakota scholar and writer Elizabeth Cook-Lynn published *The Politics of Hallowed Ground: Wounded Knee and the Struggle for Indian Sovereignty* in 1998, an inspired book of legal and oral histories, along with documents. Regarding the central issue of the return of the Black Hills, Jeffrey Ostler's 2010 book, *The Lakotas and the Black Hills: The Struggle for Sacred Ground*, is a thorough and useful text. Indigenous peoples' rights in international law and within the United Nations system have received considerable scholarly attention, and two collections of articles stand out among dozens of publications: *Making the Declaration Work: The United Nations Declaration on the Rights of Indigenous Peoples* (2009), edited by Claire Charters and Rodolfo Stavenhagen; and *Indigenous Rights in the Age of the UN Declaration* (2012), edited by Elvira Pulitano. The latter book contains an important article by the researcher for the 1999 UN treaty study, Isabelle Schulte-Tenckhoff, titled "Treaties, Peoplehood, and Self-Determination."

Vine Deloria Jr. and John Thorne were the main legal minds behind the strategies developed for the 1974 Sioux Treaty hearing. Both passed away in the early twenty-first century, leaving behind remarkable legacies and, in the case of Deloria, more than twenty books of literary and political genius. Both were mentors of mine and for many.

All royalties from the sale of *The Great Sioux Nation* will go to the Defenders of the Black Hills (He Sapa O'nakijin), which is based in Rapid City, South Dakota, and is coordinated by Charmaine White Face. In protecting and defending the Sioux Treaty and the restitution of the sacred Black Hills (Paha Sapa), the Defenders are also upholding Article VI of the Constitution of the United States, which asserts: "treaties are the supreme law of the land."

For dead warriors
For all our relations
and for the unborn

CONTENTS

Introduction   9

   About This Book [Roxanne Dunbar Ortiz] 10 / Indian Oral History: A Sacred
   Responsibility [Simon J. Ortiz] 14 / Sovereignty [Vine Deloria, Jr.] 16 / A Concise
   History of United States–Sioux Relations [Alvin Josephy, Jr.] 19

THE TESTIMONY

Part One: Wounded Knee, 1890 and 1973   33

   "My People Have to Be Protected" [Henry Crow Dog] 34 / Leonard Crow Dog 36 /
   Edith Bull Bear 43 / Russell Means 44 / Agnes LaMonte 47

Part Two: The Sioux Nation Before Invasion   53

   "I Am a Born Government of This Western Hemisphere" [Henry Crow Dog] 54 /
   Distortions of Indian History [Alvin Josephy, Jr.] 55 / Origins of Indian Peoples
   [William S. Laughlin] 58 / Demography [Wilbur Jacobs] 60 / The Sacred Way
   [Father Peter John Powell] 62 / Indian Political Economy [Roxanne Dunbar
   Ortiz] 67

Part Three: Colonialism to 1868   69

   "The White Folks Made a Lot of Promises They Broke" [Henry Crow Dog] 70 /
   Colonialist Programs [Roxanne Dunbar Ortiz] 71 / View from the Creek Nation
   [Phillip Deere] 74 / Indian-White Relations [Wilbur Jacobs] 79 / This Concerns Us
   All [William Bird] 89

Part Four: The Sioux–United States Treaty of 1868   91

   "Piles of Papers in the Trunk" [Henry Crow Dog] 92 / Text of the Fort Laramie
   Treaty of 1868 94 / Oral History and Written History [Roxanne Dunbar Ortiz]
   100 / The Sacred Treaty [Father Peter John Powell] 105 / Treaties Are Made
   Between Nations [Raymond DeMallie, Jr.] 110 / The Sioux Nation and the Treaty
   [Wilbur Jacobs] 116

Part Five: Lakota Oral History of the Treaty   119

   "Everything That Belongs to the Treaty" [Henry Crow Dog] 120
   Oral History 121 [Beatrice Medicine / Irma Bear Stops / Severt Young Bear / Alex
   Chasing Hawk / Evelyn Gabe / Francis He Crow / Robert Yellow Bird / Gordon
   Spotted Horse]

We Lakota Honor the Treaty 139 [John Looking Cloud / Alex One Star / Eugene White Hawk / David Spotted Horse / Ellis Head / Winnie Red Shirt / Jackson Tail / Frank Kills Enemy]

The United States Has No Jurisdiction in Sioux Land [Vine Deloria, Jr.] 141

Part Six: The Sioux Colony   147

"And I Can't Understand the Statute of Liberty" [Henry Crow Dog] 148 / The Great White Father [Wilbur Jacobs] 150 / They Got Our Warriors Drunk [Claudia Iron Hawk] 151 / Rations Not Fit for Human Consumption [Matthew King] 153 / We Had No Choice [Marvin Thin Elk] 157 / They Don't Listen [Nellie Red Owl / Reginald Bird Horse] 158 / They Are Thieves [Paul High Bear / George Gap] 160 / Dispossession [Roxanne Dunbar Ortiz] 162

Part Seven: From Victim to Victor   165

"So That They Will Go, Your Honor, Judge" [Henry Crow Dog] 166 / Nationhood or Genocide [Roxanne Dunbar Ortiz] 168 / Sovereignty [Vern Long / Francis Boots] 169 / Land Base for Native Nations [Kirk Kicking Bird] 172 / The People Continue [Madeline Red Willow] 174 / We Can Take Care of Our Own [Mario Gonzalez / Gladys Bissonette / Birgil Kills Straight] 175 / The American Indian Movement [Faith Traversie / Dennis Banks / Edgar Bear Runner] 178 / Those Who Are Left Returning [Theda Nelson Pokrywka / Ted Means] 181 / The Sacred Hoop [Lewis Bad Wound] 183 / The People Will Stand as One [Albert Red Bear] 185

Conclusion: Sitting in Judgment on America   187

"The Clock Is Marked Twelve" [Henry Crow Dog] 188 / Excerpts from the Defense Summary Argument [John Thorne] 192 / Excerpts from the Decision [Judge Warren Urbom] 197

It Does Not End Here   199

Declaration of Continuing Independence [Document from the First International Treaty Conference, Standing Rock Sioux Reservation, 1974] 200 / Indian Sovereignty—It's Alive [Larry B. Leventhal, Attorney for the Defense] 206

Selected Bibliography   217

Funeral for Pedro Bissonette, Lakota leader at Wounded Knee, killed by police. Photo by Melinda Rorick

They are taking inventory,
district court,
who are sentenced,

                white man has to take his life
                and then appeal to the Supreme Court.

There is no law
at that time

                There is,
                until this time,

there is no law.

                To make a law this time,
                this day
                at this hour,
                at this moment,
                              no fraction about it.
                —Henry Crow Dog—

INTRODUCTION

ABOUT THIS BOOK
Roxanne Dunbar Ortiz

At Lincoln, Nebraska, during December 1974, for thirteen days, the "Sioux Treaty Hearing" was held before Federal Judge Warren Urbom. Approximately sixty-five defendants, charged with criminal acts allegedly done on the Pine Ridge Sioux Reservation during the Wounded Knee siege of early 1973, moved for dismissal. The defendants claimed lack of United States jurisdiction on Sioux land under the 1868 Fort Laramie Treaty between the Sioux Nation and the United States.

The Wounded Knee siege, or "occupation," as it was called by the media, which lasted from February 27 through May 8, 1973, occurred when Sioux patriots asserted sovereignty based on the 1868 Treaty. The Treaty was the central issue in negotiations at Wounded Knee.

The Treaty Hearing at Lincoln was mainly devoted to the testimony of traditional Indians, historians, attorneys, and anthropologists. Forty-nine witnesses testified for the defense. This book includes most of the testimony of every witness, edited and rearranged topically. Contained in this compilation is probably the most complete history and analysis of Sioux culture and of Sioux-United States relations ever made available to the American public. Furthermore, the Sioux perspective through Sioux oral history forms the basis of the Hearing and of the book.

I sat through the entire hearing, as well as serving as an "expert witness." I was absorbed by both the atmosphere and by the information being presented. I participated in as well as observed the hearing. The power and wisdom of the traditional people present in the court room was nearly overwhelming. The source of the Sioux Nation was present in the Sacred Pipe. Each witness was allowed to swear to the truth on the Pipe rather than the Bible if they so chose. All defense witnesses took their oaths upon the Pipe. The court room there in Lincoln, Nebraska, felt more like a holy place than an American court of law. Since the proceedings did not require the presence of a jury, the traditional leaders sat in the jury box, sitting in judgment on America.

The issues presented at the hearing—the Treaty, sovereignty, United States' bad faith, present conditions of the Sioux, and United States government control over Indian people—are survival issues for Indian people. For a century bare survival has been the foremost issue of Indian peoples under the United States' policy of genocide. The Sioux, like other Indian peoples, are now going beyond bare survival and are asserting sovereignty which is leading to drastic changes in United States-Indian relations. The People see two roads available: Nationhood or genocide. The people are choosing nationhood.

United States' insistence on control of Indian people and Indian land is confusing to the present generation of Americans who live distant from Indian lands, and many of whom are hardly aware of the existence of Indian peoples and lands. Americans tend to see the "Indian question" as another civil rights movement. Many do not like the mistreatment of Indian people and masses of people supported the patriots at

Wounded Knee in 1973. However, the issues being raised by Indian peoples are different from the challenging and legitimate civil rights questions. The Sioux are raising the question of sovereignty, throwing into perspective the very validity of United States' political control of the continent. In asserting sovereignty, the Sioux join other colonies and former colonies all over the world who have been subjected to European and United States' colonialism, in declaring integrity as a separate Nation.

Testimony from the Sioux Treaty Hearing is presented topically and chronologically, not in the order presented at the Hearing itself. Some testimony is left in original examination form. Most, however, is edited into statements with some questions inserted for clarity. Often the attorney's question is incorporated into the response.

Many of the traditional Indian people who testified responded to attorneys' questions in typical oral fashion. Careful editing was done to preserve the style of the oral tradition.

Various decisions were required in doing the work of editing and rewriting the nearly 3000 pages of court proceedings. Several choices were possible. One choice which was rejected was the idea of editing the entire proceedings into ten or so volumes of official documents to be made available for research purposes. However, the Sioux elders expressed the need for the testimony to be accessible and available to the public and to Indian people and at a low cost.

After making the decision to produce one volume for general readership, other choices had to be made, the most critical being what to leave out and what to include.

There was no option really; the witness testimony should be included to the greatest extent possible, and all court proceedings as well as attorneys' examinations of witnesses should be excluded.

The next task was the arrangement of the testimony in a coherent form. Ideally, testimony is taken in planned order, but, realistically, witnesses must be presented with consideration of their time limitations. In the midst of the frozen Nebraska winter, at Christmastime, many witnesses could be present in Lincoln only for a few hours on a particular day. Others, unhappily, were not able to be there at all.

Gladys Bissonette, Pine Ridge; Larry Leventhal, Wounded Knee defendants' attorney; Dennis Banks and John Thomas, American Indian Movement leaders, on the courthouse steps, Lincoln. Photo by Melinda Rorick

11

Some of the testimony of the traditional Sioux people is repetitive, in response to the same questions posed, the main one being, "What is the oral history of the Treaty?" Hopefully, the repetition produces the desired effect, for repetition is an important element in the oral tradition.

The atmosphere of the federal court room was limiting on some of us who testified. The use of interpreters for many of the Sioux elders was also limiting upon natural expression. Some testimony has been rearranged in verse form, with no words changed, to capture the effect of the language in terms of the oral tradition. The remarkable testimony of Henry Crow Dog was edited into verse form by Simon J. Ortiz, whose Introduction in this book addresses the meaning of the oral tradition. Henry Crow Dog's observations and prophecies became the outline, overview, and very core of this book.

All of the testimonies of expert witnesses are summarized by the author, and edited by the witnesses themselves. Three of the longer testimonies, those of Wilbur Jacobs, Father Peter Powell, and that of the author, Roxanne Dunbar Ortiz, are divided into different parts of the book, though the testimonies were each presented as single units.

The arrangement of the book reflects my own abilities and limitations. Being an historian by profession, I found the historical and chronological order most comfortable to work with.

Vine Deloria, Jr., Simon J. Ortiz, and Alvin M. Josephy, Jr. graciously contributed to the Introduction.

The First Part of the book contains the full, unedited testimony of Leonard Crow Dog, Sioux Medicine Man and spiritual leader of the American Indian Movement. The Direct Examination by Attorney Larry Leventhal is left in to provide an example of the marked difference between the legal style of examination and the style of the oral tradition as reflected in Crow Dog's responses. The remaining portion of the first part consists of testimony related to the Wounded Knee massacre of 1890 and the Wounded Knee seige of 1973, told in the purest oral tradition style by Agnes LaMonte whose testimony remains in original form.

Part Two presents testimony by scholars which describes Indian cultures of the Western Hemisphere before the Europeans invaded. Though Sioux history is the focus, Indian cultures of North America are the subject.

The Third Part follows the movement of European and then United States powers over the continent. Testimony concerns Indian-United States relations up to the 1860's just preceding the Sioux-United States Treaty of 1868. The chapter is made up of the expert witness testimony of two historians, Wilbur Jacobs, Roxanne Dunbar Ortiz, and the testimonies of Phillip Deere, from the Creek Nation, and William Bird, Cherokee Medicine Man.

Part Four deals with the 1868 Fort Laramie Treaty between the United States and the Sioux Nation. The text of the entire Treaty is included with interpretations through expert witness testimony.

The oral history of the Treaty and discussions of the validity of oral history as compared to written history is the theme of the testimony in Part Five.

Part Six concerns colonialism, the period after the 1868 Treaty was violated by the United States, and the Sioux were defeated under the United States policy of search and destroy, massacre, and round up of people onto small, isolated reservations, disarm the people, and force them into dependency for food, clothing, and shelter. The testimony of Sioux elders as well as expert witness testimony is included.

The final Part elucidates the present situation and goals of Sioux people through the testimonies of American Indian Movement activists and Sioux elders.

The Conclusion includes excerpts of Defense attorney John Thorne's summation and excerpts from Judge Urbom's negative decision. The motion to dismiss remaining charges against Wounded Knee defendants on the basis of lack of jurisdiction was denied. Despite the denial which was expected, a sense of victory pervades, for it was the Great Sioux Nation sitting in judgment on America, not the reverse.

And, of course, the conclusion only marks the end of the proceedings at Lincoln. For the struggle continues. Larry Leventhal, Wounded Knee Defense attorney summarizes the legal aspects of the sovereignty issue. The "Declaration of Continuing Independence," a document outlining the international direction the people are taking, is the document which emerged from the First International Treaty Conference held on the Standing Rock Sioux Reservation in South Dakota in June 1974, six months before the Lincoln Treaty Hearing.

At Standing Rock the International Indian Treaty Council was formed and instructed to gain United Nations recognition and international relationships. Particularly since the Lincoln Treaty Hearing, the Treaty Council has become an important organizational direction for the Great Sioux Nation and for other Indian Nations. The Treaty Council was granted Consultative Status in the United Nations in January 1977.

American Indian Movement leaders with Marlon Brando, holding the Pipe presented to him by the Lakota, at Lincoln. Photo by Melinda Rorick.

INDIAN ORAL HISTORY: A SACRED RESPONSIBILITY
Simon Ortiz

Simon Ortiz is of the Acoma people in New Mexico. He is a writer and college instructor at College of Marin in Kentfield, California. He is author of several books of poetry and prose: Going for the Rain; A Good Journey; *and* Howbah Indians.

Indian oral history is a recognition of what has moral value. Passing on that oral history to another generation of people is an affirmation of that value. Elder Indian people say to the younger, "These things that are told to you from the past have a value that is your responsibility to carry. They not only have value because they had use in the past but you must also give them value."

The elder people say, "Respect this which has value. Respect this because it has relationship with you. Its value comes from that relationship." They mean that moral value depends on the responsibility inherent in this relationship. The whole system of life—human and non-human, physical and non-physical, personal and social—is dependent upon this responsibility. Life could not be possible without it. Moral responsibility is the ordered balance of all the myriad facets and forms and items of life. When they say, "The history of our people is sacred," they mean that the responsibility to it is sacred. A complete realization of this sacredness means that responsibility to it must be acknowledged, affirmed, and carried out fully. Therefore, the vital and necessary relationship among all things must be fully known and the responsibility inherent in that relationship must be carried out in order to realize and respect the value of human life.

Indian people must value their history. Recognition of this oral history is the truest affirmation of the moral value of our lives. This history contains within it all the struggles that our people have gone through. Therefore its continuance means the continuance of our current struggles and our lives.

Indian oral history has not been acceptable to American society not because it has been unwritten but because the Indian system of moral value has not been accepted. A value system which is based upon relationships with all things is not efficient within the workings of the American social system. A value system that is all inclusive—in the ultimate sense, speaking of a responsibility for all the universe—is unwieldy according to the precepts of the American system which is conveniently exclusive and finds useful only those parts which gain precedence and dominance over others. The Indian value system which takes into account even the most insignificant items of life, based on a shared and systematic responsibility, therefore has not been acceptable.

The leaders—educators, politicians, financiers, writers, historians, scientists, etc. of the American social system have never allowed themselves to understand Indian people's moral sense of responsibility and relationship and sharing. This ethic has always been relegated to some peculiar niche of "Indian religion" or curious anthropological data. If and when they have seriously thought about it, they have never accepted the real and material concerns which are at the basis of the Indian value system. Therefore, they do not know how this system is complementary to the creative and regenerative process of life. Indeed, they have not been able to because their system has not allowed serious consideration of Indian people's oral history.

Until the American system comes to a realization of the sacred ethic—value secured upon responsible and shared relationships—told very painstakingly in Indian oral history, it will continue to ignore everything except that which is exploitable and easily justified and its progress toward self-destruction will be steady. And so, rapidly, the immediate focus of America's attention is on survival. The winds and rivers are polluted. The mountains and plains are razed for timber and coal. The cities are choking enclaves of ghettos and industry. The American government and commercial institutions are negligently criminal. Strange religious cults are founded and cast aside. Scientists plan escape routes to other planets. Species of animals scurry for vanishing habitats. The rich and the politically powerful of American society gather behind heavy doors to plan defenses against the poor who fight conditions that stifle their lives and shorten their futures.

Ellen Moves Camp, Pine Ridge, leader at Wounded Knee. Photo by Melinda Rorick

Rapidly, the American social system and its capitalistic base is finding that continued exploitation of resources—human and non-human—doesn't work. Coal and timber are soon gone. The air and water cause cancer. Crowded cities are depressing. Institutions are unwieldy and dehumanizing. Other planets are too far away. Cults which cultivate passivity are shams. Plantlife and people compete with animals for last vestiges of natural habitats. The powerful call upon military and civil forces to protect their financial and political power, and the poor fight this power in order to have a decent life and insure a future.

Indian oral history speaks of the responsibility that must be assumed. This responsibility must be accepted and, in fact, be struggled for. This history insists that societies of human people be responsible to each other if their lives are to be meaningful and vital and to continue. Survival means, therefore, the commitment to carry out this sacred responsibility. Oral history may not have convenient formulas to efficiently carry out this responsibility but for Indian people it has been the guide and inspiration and source through which we have focused our struggle and maintained our social structure. Indeed, a study and realistic acceptance of this history can help other Americans to perceive, analyze, and re-evaluate the dominant society. It can be the vision which will insure a meaningful survival for all.

SOVEREIGNTY
Vine Deloria, Jr.

Vine Deloria, Jr. is one of the attorneys on the Motion to Dismiss in the Consolidated Wounded Knee Cases. Mr. Deloria is Sioux from Standing Rock. He is author of several best selling books, including Custer Died For Your Sins; We Talk, You Listen; Of Ultimate Good Faith; God is Red; Behind the Trail of Broken Treaties; *and* The Indian Affair. *See his testimony in Part Five.*

In 1868 the United States and the Sioux, Northern Cheyenne, and Arapaho Nations of Indians signed a treaty of peace which was considered by all a means of ending the brutal conflict on the northern plains. Less than a decade later, in November of 1875, then President U. S. Grant withdrew American troops who had the duty of preventing white miners from entering the sacred Black Hills of the Dakotas thereby initiating a war with the tribes. The following year saw those Indian nations achieve their greatest military victory at the Little Big Horn and the following year experienced the confiscation of the Black Hills and additional territory from the Sioux Nation.

For 105 years the Sioux peacefully petitioned the United States for redress from these and other grievous wrongs without satisfaction. Finally, with escalating oppressive measures being thrust upon them by the tribal government and the federal agencies charged with enforcing the law, the traditional people went to the little hamlet of Wounded Knee to protest their grievances. The tiny village was quickly surrounded by federal authorities, some military units were alerted and others sent individuals acting as "advisors" to the scene of activity, the exact pattern which the United States had used in its venture in Viet Nam. The Indians held the village for 73 days and finally signed an agreement with the Nixon administration which ended the occupation without further conflict. Nearly two hundred indictments were handed down in this incident and of these indictments only six persons were found guilty of a crime, two having pled *nolo contendere* to the charges against them.

As part of their defense, everyone indicted in connection with the occupation of Wounded Knee claimed that the United States had no jurisdiction over the Sioux Nation within its boundaries because of the 1868 treaty, particularly Article One of the treaty which made provisions for surrendering wrongdoers or providing monetary compensation in lieu of such surrender. These motions to dismiss for lack of jurisdiction were consolidated together and a special hearing was held at Lincoln, Nebraska, in December 1974 to settle the jurisdictional question.

During the course of the Lincoln hearings numerous witnesses took the stand and, whether scholar or traditional Indian, the story was the same—the United States had unilaterally violated the treaty and a major part of this violation revolved about the provisions of Article One. Even the government's witnesses were inclined to present the Sioux side of the story since the record was so clear concerning the violations. Nevertheless the court ruled against the Sioux although there was not a single item of evidence presented by the United States that it had ever legally taken civil and criminal jurisdiction over the Sioux Nation.

The case went to the 8th Circuit Court of Appeals and again the United States was unable to produce any evidence or cite any statute or treaty which gave the government jurisdiction over the Sioux. But the case had become a cause celebre and the Circuit Court refused to deal with the issue, simply noting that it was adopting the opinion of the court below. In early 1977 the Supreme Court, again looking at the evidence and recognizing the controversial nature of the legal question presented, refused to hear the case, thus foreclosing any discussion of the question in a federal court.

Judge Urbom's decision might rank among the lowest examples of morality and legal thinking in American history if it were out of the ordinary course of events in the historic relationship of the northern plains Indians and the United States. But compared with some of the evidence of treaty violation brought out in the hearings, the decision had at least a ring of compassion and human confusion which softens any harsh condemnation of Urbom.

Contained in these pages are the distilled testimonies of a number of the witnesses who appeared at the Lincoln hearings. The difficult task of editing the transcripts fell to Dr. Roxanne Dunbar Ortiz, a professor of Native American Studies at the California State University at Hayward. Working for nearly a year, she was able to bring together the major contentions and speeches of the witnesses into a consistent pattern of presentation and a great deal of credit must be given to her for this work. Some of the testimony has been compressed and some has been expanded to provide for a better articulation of the subjects under discussion. Testimony in a courtroom is much different than a prepared speech or lecture, and lacks the formality of a meeting or fireside chat. The witness can be asked questions out of historical sequence, specific points can be elaborated which have no direct relevance to the understanding of the topic, and a great deal of communication necessarily exists in the tone and quality of voice, facial mannerisms of the witness and the general demeanor of the courtroom. These elements of a trial, and the messages which they communicate, cannot be put on paper and so in some instances we have asked witnesses to revise their portion of the transcripts and attempt to use other words to communicate the meanings which were clearly communicated in their appearance in the courtroom.

What can be said of the decision which failed to deal with the basic question of Indian treaty rights? At least what can be said in retrospect? Perhaps most crucial to our understanding is the necessity to recognize the distinction that exists between the two cultures: the Indian and the European. A nameless Indian long ago remarked that "White men have ideas; Indians have visions." In this aphorism we find the clue to any discussion of what happened at Lincoln. The federal authorities, judges, marshals, and attorneys all come from a literate culture in which the most important things are items on paper. The continual rearrangement of items seems to make the extreme boundaries of thought which literate culture is capable of achieving. Thus when the traditional Indians presented testimony concerning the moral quality of the treaty and demanded that the spiritual nature of treaty promises be considered, no one on the government's side was capable of coming to grips with these kinds of issues. Law and justice became separate items for consideration and strict adherence to the law became the criterion by which the decision was made.

Even then, however, had the decision rested upon a proper interpretation of the law there is no doubt that the Indians would have won easily. Numerous Indian Studies and political science classes have analyzed the Urbom decision and have walked away in a stupor at the inability of the judge to follow simple lines of reasoning or to draw the proper conclusions from the evidence which was presented. One famous remark made by Judge Urbom, to the effect that he had to consider the fact of witnesses who did not appear representing some alternative interpretation of the treaty, must someday be enshrined in the halls of confusion and irrationality. But all of this confusion stemmed from the political nature of the trial. Obviously if the Lord Himself had testified it would not have made much difference since the potential explosiveness of the decision—that the Sioux might be a quasi-independent nation inside the United States—was simply inconceivable and unacceptable to the administration in power and the society which it represented. Sometimes the incredible nature of truth makes falsehood acceptable and thus it was in this case.

If, however, the Indians have visions, and contain within the oral tradition a wholistic view of reality, why could not this viewpoint have been expressed in legal terms? Morality, as such, has a proper function in arbitration wherein each side presents both legal and moral premises, reasonings, and contentions and where the task of the arbitrator is to find that strange and unique combination of morals and laws which will resolve the dispute under consideration. A federal court is not designed to decide either moral or legal issues. Rather it is an arena wherein parties contest, in an intellectual and rhetorical "trial-by-combat" for a victory. The Indians, coming to court to contend essentially legal and moral issues, did not conceive of their role as adversaries nor of the proceedings as an effort to make points against the other side. They were concerned that the whole story of their suffering emerge. It did emerge, as Urbom's rather sentimental reference discloses, but it did not carry the day against the determination of the judge to exclude the same from consideration.

Where does this story now go? The Sioux have been in court on the treaty of 1868 since 1920 without any redress. They have suffered the indignity of seeing various federal courts skirt the issue of their treaty through various devices of rhetoric and strained logic. Perhaps no faith in the judicial proceedings has existed for a long time now for it is only when they have been forced into federal court, as happened at Lincoln, that they came to testify. Federal authorities continue to point to ill-conceived decisions such as Urbom's and maintain that the issue has now been decided and that the Indians must abide by the decision. But any fair reading of the transcript will reveal that the issue was very skillfully avoided and cannot be morally considered *res judicata* by any means. Pending a radical uplift in American conceptions of morals and justice, however, it cannot be conceded that the issue is closed, for few political leaders will dare to open the case for fear that the story will emerge to haunt their careers.

This book records what the Sioux people, the scholars and the attorneys for the Sioux attempted to bring to the attention of the federal courts, the administration of that year, and the American people concerning the nature and status of the Sioux Nation. Sovereignty exists as much in the hearts of people as in the ability of a political group to use military force to maintain itself. If the Sioux people have been the first victims of the American oligarchy of wealth and privilege, the average citizens will be the last and most oppressed victims of this group. Thus if reading this book produces only sentimentality and sympathy the presentation will not have done its job for in a real sense everyone is a member of the Sioux Nation, a victim rather than an oppressor.

But if the moral issues raised by the Sioux people in the federal courtroom that cold month of December 1974 spark a recognition among the readers of a common destiny of humanity over and above the rules and regulations, the codes and statutes, and the power of the establishment to enforce its will, then the sacrifice of the Sioux people will not have been in vain.

CONCISE HISTORY OF UNITED STATES-SIOUX RELATIONS

Alvin M. Josephy, Jr.

Mr. Josephy is Vice President and Editor in Chief of American Heritage Publishing Company which publishes American Heritage Magazine *and* Horizon Magazine. *Mr. Josephy is author of* The Patriot Chiefs; The Indian Heritage of America; The Nez Percé Indians; *and* Red Power. *See Mr. Josephy's testimony in Part Two.*

The following is an historical background to give perspective to the point of view of the Sioux Nation of American Indians of the Dakotas with regard to their current claims of sovereignty and complaints of broken treaties and present-day repression by the Government of the United States.

The tens of thousands of people who came to be known as Sioux Indians were among the original inhabitants of North America, organized into numerous autonomous groups that were allied, were culturally similar and interrelated, and spoke slightly differing dialects of the same language. Their spiritual and governmental values and structures of society had evolved through thousands of years and were satisfying to the people. They governed themselves; they managed and controlled their own affairs; and they neither required the assistance of outsiders, nor menaced others.

The first white men from Europe who intruded into their villages were French missionaries and fur traders from Quebec and Montreal, who in the 1600's imposed themselves on Sioux peoples living in Minnesota, trying both to wean them away from the spiritual beliefs of their fathers by Christianizing them, and to enroll them as allies in the fur trade against the British from Hudson Bay and various other Native peoples whom the English were already aggressively exploiting as procurers of furs. The English soon also made their appearance among the Sioux, and the white men's imperialistic rivalry for control of the continent harmed all the Native Americans, including the Sioux—seducing and forcing Native groups into roles as armed auxiliaries in the white men's wars, introducing alcohol and disease, and corrupting societies with European materialistic traits. The Sioux nevertheless successfully maintained throughout the period of French and English disruption their own sovereignty, independence, and traditional values and ways of life.

After the transference of the so-called Old Northwest and Louisiana Territories to the new government of the United States, American fur trappers from St. Louis began to meet groups of western, or Teton, Sioux, including Oglalas, Hunkpapas, and others, along the Mississippi and Missouri rivers and in present-day Minnesota, Iowa, and South Dakota. During their passage through Sioux lands in 1804, Lewis and Clark reported such a meeting.

The following year, on September 23, 1805, Lieutenant Zebulon Pike made the first American treaty with a group of Sioux Indians in the vicinity of present-day Minneapolis, Minnesota, purchasing two tracts of land in that area for a military post, and asserting "the full sovereignty and power over said districts forever." The agreement neither intended to assert power over the Sioux people, nor said so, and the treaty itself was never officially proclaimed by the President of the United States. American ability to implement the treaty was negated by the fact that, in reality, the British presence was still too strong in the area—a situation underscored when, during the War of 1812, the British effectively barred Americans from the upper Mississippi and middle Missouri rivers. During the conflict the British again tried to enroll groups of Sioux people into fighting their wars for them—this time against the Americans.

After the war, the British disappeared, and American officials, beginning on July 19, 1815, and continuing through the 1820's and 1830's either journeyed into Sioux lands—or brought members of individual Sioux groups to St. Louis or Washington, D.C.—to sign certain treaties, thought up, desired, and written by the Americans and, through one means or another, imposed on the Sioux peoples to make possible the American policies of western land acquisition and exploitation. These policies, first enunciated by Congress during the Federalist Administration of George Washington, envisioned the payment of the national debt and the expenses of the government by the sale of western lands—which would be procured by purchase from the Indian tribes. Almost from the start, however, it was clear that the Indians did not wish to sell their lands, and beginning in 1790 bribery, deceit, fraud, and armed force were all used to dispossess the tribes and move them westward ahead of the advancing white land speculators and settlers. Thus, military force was used under Generals Harmar, St. Clair, and Wayne to seize present-day Ohio and much of Indiana from Indian owners. President Jefferson encouraged a speed-up of the process of driving all Indians out of the East and across the Mississippi River, giving license to such unprincipled agents as General William Henry Harrison to use bribery, to make Indian negotiators drunk, to forge their marks, and to use individuals with no authority in order to produce treaties that ceded land to the Americans.

The first treaties with the Sioux—who lived in lands beyond the immediate need of the westward-moving whites—were to procure their friendship, rather than their lands. The initial treaty, that of July 19, 1815, was signed with one group of Sioux who had been in contact with the British, rather than the Americans, during the War of 1812, and was merely to establish "perpetual peace and friendship" between those Sioux and the Americans. The document stated that the Sioux of that group placed themselves "under the protection of the United States, and of no other nation, power, or sovereign, whatsoever"—reflecting the Americans' principal aims of preventing the Indian signers from becoming allies in the future of any potential enemy of the United States.

This wording and similar phraseology in other treaties is important to present-day Indian peoples in at least two respects. First of all, the wording itself—aside from how it was conveyed to the Indians, and what they understood it to mean—obviously conferred on the United States no authority, or sovereignty over the Sioux group. It was, as stated in its preamble, a treaty of "peace and friendship" between two independent parties met on equal terms. Secondly, white historians, when reviewing treaty documents made with Indians, have been derelict. Victims of ethnocentricity, they have viewed the written word from the point of view of the white men who wrote it, but, in general, have failed to question how it was communicated to the Indian who did not speak English, or spoke and understood it faultily; what the Indian understood that it said; how the Indians among themselves reacted to it; what replies and objections the Indians might have made; how the white men treated those replies; and how the treaty was finally signed, and by whom.

Thus, the written words of a vast number of Indian treaties, including most of those made with the Sioux, are deceptive, hiding the facts that, again and again, a white man's "gist" rather than the full treaty was spoken, not read, to the Indians; that the "gist" was often deliberately false or misleading, hiding or distorting what the words of the treaty actually said; that the communication was made to the Indians by an interpreter, often a Frenchman or halfbreed faulty in English or the Indian language, or both, and sometimes by a man who had had trouble with the Indians, wished to see them harmed, and played mischievous tricks in his role as interpreter; that frequently the actual Indians with authority to speak, and sign a treaty for their people, refused to do so, and the Indian signatures on a document were those of individuals who were bribed, or gotten drunk, or who had no authority to sign for their people, or are actual forgeries, placed on the document by the white negotiators after the treaty meeting.

All these ramifications to written treaties, ignored by whites, have become clear to Indians in recent years, as they have begun to examine the documents for themselves. From their own oral accounts, they know their own people's understanding of the treaties as it was handed down to them, and they know, as well the individual accounts of false treaties secured by episodes of white men's bribery, deceit, forgery, and military force. But, adding substance to what they know from the records of their own people, has come the modern research and scholarship undertaken in claims cases, and by present-day historians, examining the records of the white man himself, in the American National Archives and elsewhere, revealing the letters, diaries, and official reports of negotiators who boasted in detail how they cheated the Indians in the treaty sessions.

Against this background, history records the following early-day treaties made between individual Sioux groups and United States negotiators: at St. Louis, on June 1, 1816, a treaty of "peace and friendship," confirming to the United States any cession of land previously made by these Sioux to any other European power (there were no such cessions), and acknowledging "the protection of the United States"; in 1825, four treaties by different groups of Sioux, including the Oglalas and Hunkpapas, of the middle Missouri River and South Dakota, acknowledging the "protection" of the United States, regulating trade with Americans, providing for the punishment of the "misconduct" of either whites or Indians in their relations with each other, and, in one of the treaties, promoting peace between the eastern Sioux of Minnesota and Iowa and their Indian neighbors. Although the latter treaty, signed at Prairie du Chien on the upper Mississippi River on August 19, 1825, has the Indians acknowledging "the general controlling power of the United States," it is questionable if the Indians had any clear conception of what this might signify. At any rate, the Indians by that treaty did not surrender sovereignty, nor did the United States assume any authority or "control" over the Indian signatories.

By the 1830's, the Western, or Teton, Sioux, including the Oglalas, were engaged in trade relations with American fur men throughout the northern plains, from the western side of Iowa almost to the Rocky Mountains. Their peoples composed groups that exercised all the independence of free peoples. At the same time, Sioux groups in the East, in Iowa and Minnesota, under the pressure of advancing whites, began to make treaties that ceded homelands and hunting grounds in that part of the country. In two very large cessions, in 1851, the Eastern Sioux peoples ceded a great amount of land in Iowa and Minnesota, reserving for themselves a small area mostly along the Minnesota River. In that same year, at Fort Laramie in present-day Wyoming, the Western, or Teton, Sioux, designated as the Dakota Nation, and including the Oglalas

21

and other groups of Sioux who lived on the plains, signed a treaty, along with many other plains tribes, agreeing, at the behest of the white negotiators, to permit the U.S. Government to establish roads and military and other posts "within their respective territories." The Government requested this treaty council in order to acquire a right-of-way for a route for white settlers who were crossing the plains to Oregon and California. In an effort "to safeguard" the route from friction between the travelers and Indian peoples whose lands they were traversing, the Government in this treaty induced the tribes to designate their respective homeland territories, promise not to war upon each other, and stay away from the white travelers. Despite the fact that the white travelers were already utilizing the Indians' hunting grounds and chasing away and depleting the buffalo herds on which the Indians relied for sustenance, the different tribes, including the Sioux, gave peaceful right-of-way to the travelers through their lands in that Fort Laramie Treaty on September 17, 1851. The treaty in no way implied a surrender of sovereignty or other authority by the tribes to the U.S. Government. In fact, the treaty several times referred to the tribes as "Indian nations" and in one article stated that the "principals or head-chiefs" of the respective "nations" will conduct "all national business" for the individual Indian groups.

In 1858, a series of treaties in Washington, D.C., with groups of Eastern Sioux brought from Minnesota and western South Dakota won more cessions of land from them, formalized the lands left to them as reservations, and stipulated the details of relations between them and the American government, placing some of their affairs in the hands of government agents of the Office of Indian Affairs of the Department of the Interior, and providing for allotments, the paying of annuities, the building of roads and posts on their land, the educating of their people, trade relations, and so forth. Though no mention was made of surrender by the Indians of their sovereignty, the treaties opened the door for the unilateral assertion of complete authority by the Office of Indian Affairs agents over the destiny and daily life of those Indians. These treaties, however, did not relate to the Western Sioux. In Minnesota, the treaties soon led to tragedy. Thousands of newly arrived immigrants to the United States, mostly of Scandinavian and German background, moved onto the ceded lands and were soon oppressing the Indians and threatening the lands the Indians had kept for themselves. The conflict became intolerable for the Eastern Sioux, and led to a short, but violent, war in 1863, which resulted in the death of many of the Eastern Sioux, as well as settlers, the seizure of more Sioux lands in Minnesota, and the driving of most of the Sioux people westward, out of Minnesota, by the United States Army.

The Western Sioux, meanwhile, retained their sovereignty and independence in their homeland, which included all of present-day South Dakota west of the Missouri River, part of western North Dakota, and large areas of eastern Montana, Wyoming, and western Nebraska, and which was centered on the Black Hills of South Dakota, which were considered the sacred heartland of their lives, lands, and culture. Within a short time after signing the Fort Laramie Treaty of 1851, however, the Western Sioux began to come under great pressure and provocation from white travelers through their lands. Aggressive acts against Indians by intolerant and racist whites on the Oregon Trail led to increasing friction, which was made worse by impulsive, glory-seeking military officers of the army. Troops began to chase and hound Sioux groups indiscriminately, and then fall on unsuspecting villages of people who have been uninvolved in conflicts. Indian men, women, and children were massacred by General Harney and others. The Indians were forced to fight back to survive what became a genocidal war of extermination against them on the central plains. In the mid-1860's, warfare was constant between the various plains peoples, including the Sioux, and troops.

The conflicts interfered with the routes that whites were now using through Indian lands to travel to Colorado, Montana, and the Far West, and in 1865, unable to break the Sioux militarily, the Government sought peace and held a series of treaty meeting with groups of the Teton Sioux at Fort Sully in present-day South Dakota. The purpose was principally to induce the Sioux by treaty, rather than by armed force, to abandon their central plains lands to the white travelers and homesteaders and move north onto reservations in South Dakota. The treaties made at Fort Sully are among the principle examples of documentary evidence in conflict with the Indians' version of what they were told, and what they understood. The words say that the various Dakota (Western Sioux) groups, including the Oglala, the Miniconjou, the Brule, the Two Kettle, the Sans Arc, the Hunkpapa, the Blackfeet Sioux, as well as two groups of Yanktonai "Acknowledge themselves to be subject to the exclusive jurisdiction and authority of the United States."

The Indians state categorically that this was never communicated to their negotiators or their people, and that the Sioux, still free, independent, and strong—in fact, negotiating from a position of strength—would never have agreed to such an acknowledgement of surrender of their sovereignty. The evidence of history, and of later events, supports their assertion. The two interpreters at these meetings, Zephier Recontre and Charles Degres, were illiterate, could neither read nor write, and were deficient in communication with Indians, as well as the whites. They were tools and partisans of the chief white negotiator, General H. H. Sibley, of whom they were frightened. It had become policy at that time, moreover, for white negotiators to put down in words whatever they wanted to say—sometimes after the treaty meeting was over—and then tell Washington that the Indians had read the wording and had agreed to it. On occasion, the lie was revealed, to the great embarrassment of the government, when Indians were brought to the East, had the treaty wording read to them by Washington officials, and then revealed that the wording was all new to them. In the case of the treaties at Fort Sully in 1865, the Indians understood that they were merely to assert that the troops would stop making war on the Indians. Promises were made of material assistance to Indians who wished to locate permanently as farmers on tribal land, and in the case of one group, a reservation was delineated on the Missouri River, over which, once again, the government gradually and unilaterally assumed dictatorial control over the Indians' lives. Hidden in the treaties, also, was a commitment by the Indians to "withdraw from the routes overland already established, or hereafter to be established through their country"—a patently deceitful clause, designed immediately to force the Indians to abandon their lands along the Platte River Basin, but ultimately giving the government the right to slice through Sioux lands anywhere they wished. This clause was not communicated to the Indians, and if it had been told to them, it would not have won their assent.

The Oglalas and other Teton groups returned to their lands, only to be faced by a new white assault in 1867 and 1868, when the United States Congress, now in the hands of corrupt Radical Republican bosses, made collusive deals with promoters of the Union Pacific Railroad and western mining interests, giving away Indian-owned land as "grants" and making other commitments that trampled unconscionably on Indian rights. New rights-of-way were required for the transcontinental railroad, and for a wagon road from the Oregon Trail through Sioux hunting grounds to the mines of western Montana, and when the Indians balked at being pushed off their lands, troops were ordered to drive them off. When the Army began to build forts along the so-called Bozeman Trail in Sioux country, the Sioux resisted, finally ousting the army in a series of victories under Red Cloud. In defeat, the army, under General William Tecumseh Sherman, met with the leaders of all groups of Western, or Teton, Sioux at Fort Laramie on April 29, 1868, agreeing to abandon the proposed Bozeman road and the forts that had been built along it, and promising to keep troops and other white men out of the Indians' country, to leave the Indians at peace, and permit them to remain in the Platte River Basin, where they hunted and traded at various posts.

This is what was told to the Indians by the deceitful interpreters, Nicholas and Antoine Janis, and what they understood, but, again, the wording of the treaty went further, including provisions that Red Cloud and the other signers later insisted were never read to them. The wording established all of South Dakota west of the Missouri River as a guaranteed reservation for the Sioux, and acknowledged that other Sioux lands—in western Montana and Wyoming—were "unceded" Indian land, in which the Sioux and Cheyenne could continue to hunt without white interference. Agencies would be established on the reservation, and Indians would go and live at them. (This implied that the Indians could be ousted from the Platte River area.) The designation of the Western Sioux lands as "unceded," as distinct, somehow, from the South Dakota "reservation," was legally meaningless, and reflected a confused attempt to create a basis for later fraud.

Soon after the signing of the treaty, government troops broke it, ordering all Indians out of the Platte Basin. When the Indians resisted, war broke out again, and the troops steadily forced the Indians northward. By 1870, the government, at the request of corrupt Congressmen, were also trying to drive the Sioux out of the "unceded" lands of Wyoming and Montana. The Sioux resisted there, also, and Red Cloud went to Washington and New York, revealing to startled audiences of reformers, church leaders, and others that he had never before heard of most of the provisions included in the Fort Laramie Treaty of 1868. The revelations embarrassed the administration and the Radical Republicans in Congress, who themselves were soon to become exposed in the great Crédit Mobilier scandal that revealed their collusion in giving Indian land to the Union Pacific Railroad promoters. Enmeshed as the principal thieves behind this new deception of the Sioux were such men as Vice President Schuyler Colfax, Speaker of the House James G. Blaine, the Secretary of the Interior, and many Senators and Congressmen, including the future President James A. Garfield (who also forged the name of the leader of Montana's Flatheads to a treaty robbing that tribe of the Bitterroot Valley in western Montana).

The scandals led to a so-called "peace policy" and "reform" by the government, which were a sham, and visited more harm on the Indians. A Congress, smarting with anger against the Indians, dropped all pretense of recognizing the Indian groups as free, independent people, enjoying sovereignty, viewing them, instead, as subject peoples, whom the U.S. Government could conquer and rule as it saw fit. There would be no more treaties, since they implied agreements with nations that enjoyed the right to speak and deal for themselves. As a token of "peace," the government, in the only episode of the joining of church and state in the history of the United States, turned over every reservation to a different church, giving the church administrators, now become agents as well as educators of the Indians, complete freedom, with army support, to Christianize the Indians and turn them into white men, using any form of punishment and oppression they deemed necessary to accomplish this goal. With extreme ruthlessness, under the guise of charitable reform, the government unilaterally began robbing sovereignty from whatever Native peoples still possessed it.

For a time, Sioux power kept the white oppressors at a distance. But the new Government policy opened Sioux lands to a new wave of uninhibited plunder of Indian property. Again, corrupt members of the Grant administration and of Congress made personally-enriching deals with the notorious banker, Jay Cooke, turning over 47,000,000 acres of land grants, including Sioux reservation and hunting lands, to his Northern Pacific Railroad. The railroad's survey parties were accompanied through the Sioux lands by General Custer, who was in league with the criminal Secretary of War, William Belknap, a grafter who would eventually be driven from Grant's Cabinet in disgrace for a corrupt deal with an Indian trader. The Sioux, often led by Crazy Horse, tried to drive Custer and the railroad builders from their lands. The violations of the 1868 Fort Laramie Treaty were finally climaxed by a deliberate intrusion by Custer into the sacred heart of Sioux country, the Black Hills themselves. Flaunting the treaty, every right of the Sioux, and the objections the Indians made to this act of aggression, Custer announced to the world that he had discovered gold in the Black Hills.

Inevitably, a gold rush started, and white miners overran the center and the most holy portions of the Sioux lands. When the Sioux tried to drive them away, the government, in another unconscionable action that violated the 1868 treaty, attempted to force the Sioux into ceding the Black Hills. The 1868 treaty had said specifically that no "cession of any portion or part of the reservation . . . shall be of any validity or force . . . unless executed and signed by at least three-fourths of all the adult male Indians, occupying or interested in the same." No Indian, much less three-fourths of the Sioux people, was willing to sell the Black Hills at any price, and the frustrated government now ordered all Sioux to evacuate the area and go and live at the agencies on the reservation. The White man's greed and immorality at this time can only be understood by recognition of the complete moral collapse that was going on in Washington at the time of the Grant administration and the worst Congress in American history. The entire American nation was being plundered by collusion between industrial robber barons and politicians who were without conscience.

The results of the unabashed policy of Indian robbery and suppression are well known. The Sioux resisted giving up their lands; a huge army attacked the Sioux; one part of it, under Custer, assaulted a Sioux and Cheyenne village at the Little Bighorn River. Custer's defeat, trumpeted by the politicians as a "massacre," led to a determined war of annihilation against the Sioux which ended in the survivors being herded into the agencies and punished on their own lands as "hostiles" and prisoners of war. Patriotic leaders of the Indian resistance, including the great Oglala hero, Crazy Horse, were murdered. Behind fences of wire, the Sioux groups were beaten and starved into submission. There reservations were turned into concentration camps, and a brutal policy of forcibly stripping them of their traditional ways of life, standards, structures of society, spiritual beliefs, and cultural values was inaugurated under the administration of a dictatorial and tyrannical triumvirate of government agents, Christian missionaries, and soldiers. The policy was to beat the Indian-ness out of the Sioux, turn them into compliant whites, push them eventually off their lands and into white society. Those who resisted were to die out. Either way, the Indian would become "the vanishing American." There were to be no more Indians, no more Sioux. Trying desperately to survive, many Sioux embraced spiritual beliefs, which the white man called "the Ghost Dance." Viewed as an obstacle to the forced assimilation of Indians, these beliefs were proscribed, and Indians practicing them were treated as "hostiles." Sitting Bull was murdered, and the religious movement was all but destroyed in a harsh military oppression climaxed by the hideous massacre of some

300 Sioux men, women, and children at Wounded Knee in 1890 by vengeful members of Custer's old military unit, the Seventh Cavalry.

The Sioux did not die out. In 1882 and 1883, the Government unilaterally imposed on them the present-day reservations, forcing various members of each group of Western Sioux to sign "agreements" (treaties were no longer allowed) that established the reservations, turned over to the U.S. enormous portions of Sioux lands, ended the large "reservation" created by the Treaty of 1868, and opened the way for the allotting of the new reservations into small plots of land to be distributed among individual Indians. These agreements were responses to the political pressure of the large number of white immigrants who were pouring into the Dakotas and demanding Indian land for their own homes, farms, and ranches, and for rights-of-way for roads and various means of transportation and communication. The newly arrived whites were among the most vicious enemies the Sioux had ever encountered, many of them bigoted and racially intolerant to the near-pressure of Indians, whose lands they coveted. Under the influence of these "bonanza" farmers and the equally-aggressive poorer settlers, the government merely confronted the beaten, demoralized, and captive Sioux with documents and said, "sign here," again violating the 1868 Treaty, which had said that three-fourths of the adult males would have to sign any new cession of Sioux lands.

During the following fifty years, the Sioux, who had never given up their sovereignty, were subjected to a forced assimilationist policy, administered by government agents and missionaries. The allotment policy, formalized by the passage of the Dawes Act of 1887, created a built-in obstacle to the economic development of the people. Robbed of their old ways of securing a livelihood, nothing viable was offered as a substitute—only minimum levels of subsistence rations (often withheld as punishment) and agricultural and stock-raising programs that inevitably failed because of government ineptness and corruption. The lot of the people became increasingly desperate, as revealed finally by the Meriam Report in 1928. The Indians were literally consigned to starvation, disease, poverty, and death by a country of white conquerors who wanted to know nothing about them, and by a government that was waiting for them to think, act, and live like whites, or die off. The U.S. Government had stripped them of their lands and freedom, and ruled them absolutely through the boss-ridden mechanism of the most corrupt and inefficient bureaucracy in the federal government, the Bureau of Indian Affairs. In 1924, the Congress, without consulting the various Indian groups, made the Indians citizens of the United States—a move that, in many respects, was a travesty, since it did not confer on the Indians the right to self-government, or any of the other civil and political rights, enjoyed by all other American citizens. On the contrary, it further fastened a dictatorial hold over the Indians, by implying that, as citizens of the United States, they could no longer think in terms of possessing the sovereignty of free and independent peoples, which had been taken from them.

Under pressure from reformers, the Indian Reorganization Act of 1934, attempting to lighten the economic burden of American taxpayers, who were still paying for appropriations for Indians who had not disappeared, tried to cope with some of the root causes of the social and economic ills on the reservations. Various economic and cultural bows were made in the Indian direction to try to restore their morale, but a new system of government was instituted that was to lead to new difficulties. Again unilaterally, the American government imposed on the Sioux reservations a uniform governmental system, modelled not on traditional forms which would have been familiar to the Indians, but on the white men's own government—a system of tribal councils, headed by executive officials who were members of the tribes. The people found this system strange, and in a large measure were unable to support it. New institutions rapidly deteriorated into governments of a class of reservation professional politicians, who hungered for the favors and salaries of their positions. Since the Bureau of Indian Affairs gave up none of the important governmental functions on the reservation—including that of veto power over all financial matters—the Indian tribal council governments were purely accommodating rubber stamps for the white bosses in the agencies' offices—with no more power than that of honorary Native legislatures under the thumb of governors in the British colonial system. Even worse, as the Indian political leaders worked more and more at the direction of the Bureau of Indian Affairs and other white governmental functionaries on the reservation, they lost all sense of responsiveness, and of accountability, to the people, holding themselves responsible, instead, to the agents of the Bureau of Indian Affairs. In time, the tribal governments—far from offering the people a protective and democratic self-government—degenerated at worst into gangster-like cliques, riddled with nepotism and petty graft and supported by the Bureau of Indian Affairs and both Indian and white police forces, and at best into quiet, ineffective, do-nothing bureaucracies that lived off governmental salaries.

Today, on some reservations, the Indian governmental apparatus—usually dominated by those who are most assimilated and, quite often, by those of least Indian blood and Indian cultural heritage—are willing tools for the Department of the Interior's modern-day role of bringing about corporation termination—selling and leasing Indian resources to the large conglomerates of coal and mineral exploiters, home development builders, and other aggrandizers of Indian property. On other reservations, the tribal governments, supported by the Department of the Interior, have become little more than self-enriching tyrannical dictatorships, victimizing the people by illegal elections and brute force of private police units.

In recent years, the excesses of these governments, together with the continued desperate economic and social conditions of the people; the unabated prejudice, discrimination, and violence visited against the Sioux by the white population of South Dakota; the Bureau of Indian Affairs' stranglehold over Sioux life; and the indifference of the rest of the American population have contributed to the growth of a genuine liberation movement among the Sioux, aimed at achieving honest, accountable governments of their own choosing, which through traditional Indian means and methods would carry out meaningful policies and programs for the people's economic welfare and, by reasserting and reclaiming a sovereignty they never gave up, would restore dignity, self-government, and hope to the long-oppressed Sioux Nation.

This Sioux movement, supported and aided by other Indians through the American Indian Movement, has been violently resisted by the American Government, through the Department of Justice and the Department of the Interior, which built up and supported the brutal and undemocratic "front" government of Richard Wilson on the Pine Ridge Reservation in South Dakota, where the liberation struggle has been most widespread and successful. Likening the new Sioux patriots and their AIM supporters to the Black Panther movement of the blacks, and failing to see the deep and widespread cultural, religious, and political roots of the new Indian struggle as a unique national movement of all Indians for freedom, the Department of Justice, through the FBI, has waged a blind and ineffective reign of terror against the Indians, on and off the Pine Ridge reservation, using every method it employed against the Black Panthers, ranging from wiretapping and frameups to ambushes and assassinations. Such confrontations as the occupation of the vicinity of Wounded Knee in 1973, desperate attempts by the Indians to focus world attention on their grievances and plight, have been part of a struggle in which the FBI and its instrument, the false government of Richard Wilson and his U.S. Government–financed storm troop units of "goon squads," continue to arrest, beat up, and murder many Sioux patriots.

At the root of this American Government-supported violence and intimidation against the Sioux is an unspoken, but very real, government determination not to lose control to the Indians of the increasingly valuable Indian lands and natural resources, including water, mineral, and timber rights. The American Government for a decade has spoken of "giving" self-determination to the Indian tribes, but no meaningful step has been taken in this direction, nor will it be taken as long as Indians own any land or natural resources. More and more, American industry and finance covet these resources, anxious to acquire them on their terms, and national policy dictates, through the Senate and House Interior Committees of Congress, the Office of Management and Budget, the White House itself, and the Department of the Interior, that the Government be in a controlling position to make these Indian assets available to the white private sector on terms satisfactory to the whites. Under such conditions, fraudulent governments like that of Wilson at Pine Ridge must be sustained as willing accomplices of the government and the whites, even if only to lease out Indian-owned grazing land to South Dakota white ranchers at criminally-low rates that cheat and defraud the individual Indian owners. This situation, rampant at Pine Ridge, reflects the wholesale exploitation of the Indian peoples, which still keeps them oppressed, powerless, and in the throes of poverty.

Nevertheless, despite the terror and the efforts of the Department of the Interior and the Department of Justice, as well as of Congress, to ignore the dictatorship and killings at Pine Ridge, and the continued suffering of the Sioux people under an exploiting, colonialist government, the struggle goes on, inspired by the examples of the Sioux patriots of the past who fought and died for their people. The Sioux Liberation Movement, composed of Sioux people of all ages, men and women, youths and elders, holy men and modern-day warriors, is sustained by right and justice. Blood being shed by the Sioux patriots today will not be in vain. History and the future are on their side.

THE
TESTIMONY

Citation of Testimony in Order of Appearance in the Text

WITNESS	APPEARANCE IN TEXT IN ORDER OF APPEARANCE	APPEARANCE IN COURT TRANSCRIPTS
Henry Crow Dog	Introduction, Part 1, 2, 3, 4, 5, 6, 7, & Conclusion	pp. 1241-1255
Leonard Crow Dog	Part One	1314-1336
Edith Bull Bear	Part One	299-308
Russell Means	Part One	1279-1913
Agnes LaMonte	Part One	1385-1409
Alvin Josephy, Jr.	Part Two	259-297
William S. Laughlin	Part Two	210-251
Father Peter Powell	Part Two and Four	23-96
Roxanne Dunbar Ortiz	Part Two, Three, Four, Six and Seven	376-479
Phillip Deere	Part Three	1256-1279
Wilbur Jacobs	Part Two, Three, Four, and Six	712-921
William Bird	Part Three	1369-1374
Raymond J. DeMallie, Jr.	Part Four	1172-1235
Beatrice Medicine	Part Five	924-1045
Irma Bear Stops	Part Five	704-707
Severt Young Bear	Part Five	548-589
Alex Chasing Hawk	Part Five	1077-1080
Evelyn Gabe	Part Five	1063-1076
Francis He Crow	Part Five	636-654
Robert Yellow Bird	Part Five	1338-1348
Gordon Spotted Horse	Part Five	628-635
John Looking Cloud	Part Five	1237-1239
Alex One Star	Part Five	1134-1137
Eugene White Hawk	Part Five	1123-1126
David Spotted Horse	Part Five	515-518
Eillis Head	Part Five	1336-1337
Winnie Red Shirt	Part Five	1094-1095
Frank Kills Enemy	Part Five	1138-1141
Vine Deloria, Jr.	Part Five	97-286
Claudia Iron Hawk	Part Six	1126-1133
Matthew King	Part Six	480-544
Marvin Thin Elk	Part Six	1050-1062
Nellie Red Owl	Part Six	589-593
Reginald Bird Horse	Part Six	595-618
Paul High Bear	Part Six	1045-1050
George Gap	Part Six	1091-1093
Francis Boots	Part Seven	363-372
Vern Long	Part Seven	1081-1087
Kirk Kickingbird	Part Seven	308-363
Madeline Red Willow	Part Seven	698-703
Mario Gonzales	Part Seven	1352-1359
Gladys Bissonette	Part Seven	1096-1123
Birgil Kills Straight	Part Seven	654-674
Faith Traversie	Part Seven	1378-1385
Dennis Banks	Part Seven	1147-1164
Edgar Bear Runner	Part Seven	1360-1368
Theda Nelson Pokrywka	Part Seven	1142-1147
Ted Means	Part Seven	674-694
Lewis Bad Wound	Part Seven	618-627
Albert Red Bear	Part Seven	1164-1168
John Thorne	Conclusion	1626-1810

THE UNITED STATES DISTRICT COURT FOR THE DISTRICT OF SOUTH DAKOTA

UNITED STATES,

                Plaintiff,

       v.

CONSOLIDATED WOUNDED KNEE
CASES,

             Defendants.

)
)
)
)
)
)
)
)
)
)
)
)

CR. 73-5019

TRANSCRIPT OF THE TRIAL

ON THE

MOTION TO DISMISS FOR WANT OF JURISDICTION

Before

The Honorable Warren K. Urbom, Chief Judge

U.S. District Court for the District of Nebraska

Lincoln, Nebraska

THE FIRST DAY:

MONDAY, DECEMBER 16, 1974

Indian Witnesses To Be Most Important—Thorne

By GORDON WINTERS
Star Staff Writer

The most important witnesses at the hearing on the Fort Laramie treaty of 1868 will be Indians, telling what the treaty means to them, the chief treaty defense attorney said Sunday.

John Thorne, of San Jose, Calif., speaking at a rally for treaty supporters at the Nebraska Student Union, said Indians from the Pine Ridge Indian Reservation in South Dakota will relate the oral history of the treaty signing handed down from their ancestors.

"For the first time Indians are going in a white court, before a white judge, under white law and unfortunately with a white lawyer, and tell what the treaty means to them," Thorne said.

"It's high time white people find out what the treaty says and how we have violated it."

What the treaty means, Thorne said, is that Congress cannot pass any laws which affect the Sioux Nation with which the treaty was made.

No Right

Because of that, Thorne said, the United States government has no right to try anyone for the events of Wounded Knee, 1973.

That claim is the heart of the "treaty defense." The hearing on the defense begins Monday in U.S. District Court in Lincoln with extraordinary measures being taken to accomadate spectators in a second courtroom which will be wired for sound from the courtroom where the proceedings will actually take place.

Thorne said that he is "very worried" about what's going to happen in that courtroom tomorrow" because he is asking a hard thing in the white man's system.

Marshall Decision

Thorne said that Judge Warren Urbom, a federal district judge, is being asked to overrule a Supreme Court decision on a previous treaty written by legal giant Chief Justice John Marshall in 1823.

Marshall's decision, Thorne said, was that the United States does not have to honor treaties with Indians because "might makes right." That decision, Thorne said, was one of the most "degrading, dehumanizing, immoral and unjust decisions ever made."

Although the issue will not be dealt with directly in the treaty hearing, Thorne said the most important section of the treaty deals with the land set apart for occupation by Indians.

"One of the ideas we must get out of is the idea that we gave them this land," Thorne said. The treaty set apart about the western half of South Dakota for the Sioux.

What the Sioux did in the treaty was reserve that land as their permanent home and gave white men the rest in exchange for the provisions of the treaty, Thorne said.

That land, Thorne said, must be returned immediately to the Sioux.

The cost of the return would be about what the U.S. spent in one year in Vietnam to kill and maim other human beings, Thorne said.

Another speaker, American Indian Movement national chairman John Trudell, told the crowd of about 200, mostly Indians, the treaty was broken for 100 years before America began talking about its validity.

When Indians were herded onto reservations in the 1860's, Trudell said, it created the illusion the "war was over."

"But the war is not over and will never be over until we have justice," he said.

PART ONE

Wounded Knee
1890 and 1973

Henry Crow Dog, Rosebud. Photo by Melinda Rorick

MY PEOPLE HAVE TO BE PROTECTED

The Great Spirit has taken care of us,
                          but
the white folks say
                we are going to take care of you.

                And they rid of all the buffalo.
                They try to get rid of the elks
                and deer
                and that family,
                        but
they couldn't do it.

Still we have to get permits
to do this. We had no permit at that time,
                            Same
with Indians. You couldn't catch an Indian,
not today.
                You have to release yourself
                or you have to do something to get release.

I have to have protection
I want protection.
My people have to be protected.

So my grandfather made a sign,
>   the justice,
two horns,
two eyes and one mouth.
>   One mouth,
>   One language.

I don't have to write a language to get to Heaven.
Afterall
>   this is myself.

I thank the coming foreigners,
the immigrants, when they come here.
This is safe place,
>   they come here,
>   they want to make it safer.
As we go,
>   according on the highways today,
like in this, what we are here,
>   in Lincoln,
>   Lincoln, the name
of that president,
>   here today we want to settle things.

So we have to have good emancipation.
So let's get together and settle right
>   so that
we will get along after we walk
out of this household.

My grandfather says
>   there will be somebody coming.
>   They are coming.
>   They are going to do some wondrous thing.
>   So you are going to see them.

(From the testimony of Henry Crow Dog, Lakota elder and spiritual leader from Rosebud Reservation.)

LEONARD CROW DOG

Leonard Crow Dog, spiritual leader of the American Indian Movement, is the son of Henry Crow Dog.

Mr. Crow Dog, where do you reside? [Larry Leventhal, Defense Attorney]

In the Rosebud Reservation.

And are you Lakota?

Yes, I am a Lakota.

Do you hold any position of responsibility with your people?

As a spiritual leader.

What are your duties as spiritual leader?

First of all, I never was in a white man's school. I can't read, can't write, so the only thing I could have is that knowledge that grows with me by the universal, the university of my life. So since I was a spiritual man, of the many many things that I choose, I choose my Indian people who I represent in a spiritual way.

And you have served in this position, then, since you were quite young?

The spiritual power was given to me on the day I was born.

With the Lakota people, is the spiritual part of life incorporated in the entire concept of life?

The spiritual power is not like the white man religion. The Indian life is nature. It grows into the human being who develops into the whole universal cycle that is used in the spiritual world.

Is the spiritual aspect of one's existence and of Lakota life, then, incorporated within the nationhood of the Lakota nation?

The generation of what it represents.

So in other words to understand the Lakota Nation, one must understand the spiritual beliefs and spiritual practice of Lakota people?

The spiritual practice, we don't practice. See, it grows into the human being.

So there is an identity with the individuals with the spiritual life?

The nature identity is born into the human red man and the Red Nation.

You have taken your oath on the Pipe, and you have indeed administered the oath to several of the witnesses. What does the Pipe mean to Lakota people?

We call it the Sacred Pipe first of all. Not only the Sioux people, but the Red Nations calls it the Sacred Pipe. But the white man called it the peace pipe. And then he couldn't live by what he said was the peace pipe.

What is the significance of the White Buffalo Calf maiden in the deliverance of the Sacred Pipe?

White Buffalo, the sacred White Buffalo Calf means we are the Buffalo party, this generation. The white man, the government has the democratic party, the republican party. We are the Buffalo party of the Red Nation. The government hasn't understood that this is the Red Nation's continent, this western hemisphere.

When you identified the Red Nation, what do you mean?

When I am talking about the Red Nation, I am talking about the Red Indian Nation here, the Lakota Nation and various other tribes.

What is the significance of the four directions and of the four colors of mankind?

Eons ago, we didn't use the four colors. Just lately, perhaps a hundred years ago, we have been using the four colors. A long time ago, in our grandfathers ways, they used one color. The tree of life, the cedar, the grain of the plain, the grain of the red power among the Indian tribes.

But we used the four directions, the four winds of the earth. The whole universe, the whole world is on a space. And by that, we Indian people pray in the four winds of the earth.

What is the sacred hoop?

Nobody can say where the sacred hoop ends. So we use the word unity. We call all, "My relation."

Does the unity also express itself in a relationship to the earth and to animal and plant life in the universe?

Yes. All four-legged animals that live on this Mother Earth here in this continent work with the Indian relation to the power.

What is the significance of Mother Earth?

First of all, we walk on silver, gold, all the elements you see today. We know all that, like in the testimony that has been said, we never rape our Mother Earth. The Earth is sacred to us. That's why we have the Buffalo party, that's why we have the White Buffalo Calf.

Indian people have that power to use, but today what has the government done to us who, over many, many years of our generation of Indian life, knew what was Indian? Who is Indian? And who can tell when and how this Indian man or the generation was born in this western hemisphere. Who knows? — only the Indian generation knows.

Today we have a mother for the cow of our generation. We used to have the buffalo of our mother's respect, but now we have difficulty with the whole system of this government.

Is there a distinct Lakota way of life which is practiced today?

Long time ago, they called us savages and many other names. But now they can't find any other word, so they call us militants and renegades. But we are the Dog Soldiers Society. The chiefs and headmen, the traditional and adult society. The American Dog Soldier Society.

What is the role that the chiefs and headmen play?

They are the people, the headmen and chiefs, who decide all things for the Indian tribe. He wears the sacred bonnet. The government put it as a "warbonnet." That's why my father, Crow Dog, when the government said to him, "Crow Dog, you will wear the warbonnet"—and the government said to Red Cloud, "You are going to wear the warbonnet"—Crow Dog said, "No, I do not. If you call it warbonnet, I will not use it. I will use my two feathers." So Crow Dog did not. Why?—the word, "war," it means broken treaties today.

What role do the headmen play within the Indian nations?

The headmen, they decide upon matters of the bands of their tribes, of the Indian nation.

Who are the traditionals?

The government of the whole universe of the Indian people, the nation.

And what is the role that the Dog Soldiers have traditionally played within the Lakota Nation?

We are the good people. We are the evidence of this whole western hemisphere. We are the landlords, and we never made no promise to no other country. The wives and the Dog Soldier Society was organized—the first time the treaty was made—against the bad men among Indians. Now, the government is the bad man today; it has broken the treaty today of our lives.

What is the Winter Treaty?

The Winter Treaty is the Pipe that we Indian people have, our generation. It symbolizes a generation of the Indian people, the language that we speak. We speak three languages. We speak the adopted language, the English language. The white man has been with us close to so many hundreds of years, and he couldn't speak our language so he used Indian interpreters. And then we have the sign language and the solemn language. We speak these languages. But only Indian tribes know that, see.

Have you through these various languages received the oral history of your people?

Yes. We, the grass root people, what you might call the traditional people, still exist the Indian life of our people.

As a spiritual leader, do you have a special responsibility in conveying and passing on the oral history of your people?

Most of my duties, what I do, are to perform sacred ceremonies among many tribes. It's unity, united together. The fire is one. Any tribe uses fire and cedar and tobacco.

Do you find then that among the various Indian nations on the North American continent that there is a like respect for Mother Earth as is present in the Lakota people?

The whole continent was given to us, this whole western hemisphere by the Great Creator. In some statements they use God, but I always use the Great Spirit, the Earth Maker. The government should see with its naked eye. Our land has become concentration camps or whatever you call them—reservations.

In your role as a spiritual leader, do you pass on these beliefs and practices and talk to people about them and practice them with people that you have been testifying to?

Most of my spiritual experience that I have I tell the various tribes. I think I represent close to eighty-nine tribes. We are all united together teaching the ways. We socialize ourselves with the bird called Eagle. And the earth, the sacred water. They are all sacred things that evolve, that the Creator made in this earth. It does not belong to only one nation, but it belongs to human beings that live in this world here.

Perhaps you could identify several of the ceremonies which you have spoken of generally. What is the purpose of the sweat lodge? And of the Sun Dance? What is the Yuwipi ceremony?

The sweat lodge is of the purification of the Mother Earth. The Sun Dance, we had before even the seven days the white man brought. Before the seven days of the religious Christianity, we had the sun. We have the Sun Day. We have the biggest Sun Day. The Sun Dance. But there has been a lot of misinterpretation there.

The Yuwipi is one of the original ceremonies that was given to the people. Nobody knows how old that ceremony is, but it's been handed generation to generation. Various tribes have that ceremony, and it is sacred to Indian people, very sacred.

In receiving the oral history of the Lakota people, whom have you spoken to and gained this knowledge?

Most of my spiritual experience is the spiritual. It is spiritual; it doesn't come from the human. It all comes from the spiritual power. I can't read, can't write, but what makes me speak English? What makes me speak this adopted language? Sometimes, I give myself a psychiatric checkup on why I speak, why I do these things, and why I represent these good people who I represent.

What role does oral history, the traditional words and wisdom, play in the life of the Lakota people today?

Today the federal government doesn't understand. We have headmen like the chief, the headmen and the traditionals. The traditional people and the headmen, what they do is respect, respect the earth, respect the generation of this whole continent. That's why we recognize each other. We shake hands not only on Sundays; we shake hands. If we see each other in a few years or a few weeks or a few days, we shake hands. Why? Because we know the love of this generation.

Have the various treaties which the Lakota people have entered into formed an important part of the oral history of the Lakota people?

Since I was born, the only thing that I really heard about was the Black Hills and the 1868 Treaty. I never for a second thought myself that I was going to testify against the federal government of our nation about the 1868 Treaty.

You mentioned earlier the Winter Treaty. Would it be correct to say that this is the first treaty that the oral history relates.

Even before the white man came to this western hemisphere, we had the oral history of our generation, called the seven fire places. We Indian people had that, and it is the Winter Count. It formed into this teepee, the greatest church. All these other churches were not here. The greatest church we have is our teepee and the sweat lodge. Before there was any treaty.

But since the first treaty was made, many many treaties have been made by the federal government. How? Who is right and who is wrong today? How soon? We don't have any lawyers. We don't have any professors. The white man with his knowledge and his brains, he can see he is violating all the treaties. We used to be warriors and hunters, and now we hunt for education and knowledge.

To make sure that I have this clear, the Winter Treaty was, as I understand it from your testimony, not a treaty with the white man but more of a spiritual commitment by the Lakota people—is that correct?

That is the dome of the continent, the Winter Count, but none of the professors or lawyers don't know what the Winter Count of Indian generations is. It's still standing today. That's why we speak our languages.

Mr. Crow Dog, as a spiritual leader do you receive your information and guidance from various sources?

Whenever I go into a ceremony I do experience the ceremonial advice from the spiritual. And the traditional people, they give me advice. I will take that. I will take that oath to respect.

When you receive information in a spiritual capacity from various leaders, is that information similar to what is known as oral history?

That is what it is, the oral history of our Indian people. It is born with us, the generation.

And you have had the experience of speaking with tribal elders and speaking with your grandparents and other elders as to the history both spiritually and historically of your people?

Yes, historically and spiritually, I speak with the traditional and headmen. A few years ago and lately, I have been visiting most of the traditional people across the country, visiting various tribes.

Because of your unique role, then, would I be correct in saying that this is what you meant by saying that you—at least in part—received this information spiritually because everything you do in that way is a spiritual act?

Everything that symbolized whatever the traditional people and headmen told me

Leonard Crow Dog, A.I.M. spiritual leader. Photo by Michelle Vignes

about the treaties are the pictures of what I've seen. It does mean something to our Indian tribes.

And you have heard from the traditional people and from some of the elders the oral history or the descriptions of the signing of the Treaty of 1868?

We knew—like what I said a few minutes ago—what really brought attention. Did we make any treaty with another country? No. We were here. That's why we never made any treaty with other countries. It's what the government has done to us, what the government has done to Indian tribes.

He brought his Bible and everything in violation of thou shalt not steal and thou shall not kill. Now what he did in 1890 at Wounded Knee is what he did to various tribes. See, he's living a lie, and I am sure the government eye acknowledges that.

We see now. We know. We already were civilized. We could not live the civilization of his government. We have our own Indian government that we live nature by. We do something like materialistic things too. We do that, but we balance all things together as one. That is a unique organization of our oral history of our generation.

Did the preservation of this Indian form of government play a role in the intention of those who signed the Treaty of 1868?

Most of the chiefs at the time who made the interpretation when the headmen and chiefs signed the Treaty of 1868 knew it.

Mr. Crow Dog, is there an oral history that you have knowledge of which indicates what the Lakota signers of the 1868 Treaty thought at the time of the signing?

The signing of the Treaty, the people, the traditionals, the headmen, are the chiefs of the generation who have been holding to their generation for many, many years now, and the people understand. We do know now of our generation.

Is what you are saying that your oral history does say that there were certain intentions and certain understandings on the part of the Lakota people who signed the Treaty?

Our oral history is something that you have to know. We never had a second thought that another country was going to come here and sign a treaty with us. The Indian generation, we thought, was going to be here alone.

Your oral history, then, does tell you something about what was in the minds of those who signed the Treaty and what the Treaty was supposed to say and do?

Yes. The Treaty today is the foundation on which the Indian people now stand. We made a stand. It's what traditional people think today of the 1868 Treaty.

What did the chiefs who signed the Treaty understand it to be?

Well, at that time, our chiefs stated not to violate what the government has violated today.

What were the understandings that those chiefs had that would not be violated?

The Chiefs, who spoke in turn at various times there, said what could be said. But it's not stated in the Treaty of 1868 what some of the traditional chiefs did say.

Is it conveyed through your oral history?

It should be.

And what is that?

We speak the Lakota language, the Sioux language. Today we speak the Lakota language and hundreds of years ago we spoke the Lakota language. Some words were used that are not used today, and it's never been written into the Treaty.

When the Treaty was signed, did the Lakota people who signed the Treaty ever believe that they were giving up any sovereign rights?

We are the nation. We are nation before even the government. Before we signed any treaties. We are nation.

Was the understanding, then, that the nation would continue?

The nation would continue. Why we were put here on this continent.

Was it the understanding that this nation would have control over those things that happened within the territory that was guaranteed to the Sioux nation?

The territory, what they now call Indian reservations, whatever they call them now today, the Sioux nation did not understand. We do understand now.

The white man, the government couldn't speak our language. If he could have

41

spoken our language, we could have made a true negotiation in signing the real state of the Treaty instead of what has happened—the violation that we live today.

But, we are Nation.

What are some of the violations, as you understand it through your oral history, that have been committed by the United States?

Just like the bad men among Indians, the bad men among whites of the 1868 Treaty. Can the government see with his knowledge that he made a violation? Violation at Wounded Knee? He made a lot of violations. Only thing is, he made one mistake when he gave us the knowledge; so now we anchor the knowledge and we are going to use that. We are using it today.

You referred to bad men among the whites and bad men among the Indians—were you referring to Article 1 of the 1868 Treaty?

Many years ago we didn't have bad men among Indians. Just since the government, whites come in here, then we started getting that way.

Is it your understanding that that article preserves the sovereignty of the Sioux nation in dealing with Indian people and gives the Sioux nation a choice of how to deal with Indian bad men?

If anything happened in our tribes and our Sioux people, we let the traditional people and headmen decide. And then whatever was decided, the Dog Soldier society went into the session to deal with whatever was going to be done. But we never had a death row in our Indian history.

Are you familiar with the provision in Article 12 that speaks of the necessity of receiving three quarters of the adult male Sioux signatures in order for there to be certain changes, in order for there to be a new treaty that would effect certain rights given by the Treaty?

Never been. Once they signed the Treaty, the majority of the people knew that it would be changed, but the Indian council never act on it. See, we honor what the government say. So we don't violate it. The session still exists and the Indian council is still here today.

Does the three quarters have any special significance in Lakota history and culture?

Just like the white man, just like these three doors here on the left side here, white men have three things, Father, Son, and Holy Ghost. We Indians have that power too. That's why we use the fourth thing, the one major and three other parties. The fourth is the one that's going to organize the chief and the headmen. That's why we use the sacred bonnet. One feather right in the center of the bonnet.

And that symbolizes the same type of ratio that's in the Treaty?

It symbolizes to our generation.

Is it your understanding that the 1868 Treaty was signed through the use of the Sacred Pipe?

The reason they used Red Cloud's seal when they made the 1868 Treaty was to seal and to honor with the Sacred Pipe. That's why we use the Pipe here. Why? We could have used the Bible, but the violation of the federal government—we couldn't do that.

Does the use of the Pipe, then, in the signing of the Treaty indicate that the Indian people who are signing the Treaty are pledging themselves to honor and to abide by it?

Keep the home fire burning to our generation and to the sacred lodge.

42

EDITH BULL BEAR

Edith Bull Bear is 86 years old and does not speak English. Her testimony was interpreted by Severt Young Bear.

I was three years old at the time of the Wounded Knee massacre of 1890. We lived south of Wounded Knee, and my father was involved at Wounded Knee. The people were getting ready for the Ghost Dance at Wounded Knee. They were surrounded by troops of the United States government. My father was wounded by the troops at Wounded Knee. He was shot in the knee and his horse was killed.

The people were getting ready for the Ghost Dance at Wounded Knee. They were surrounded by troops of the United States government. My father was wounded by the troops at Wounded Knee. He was shot in the knee and his horse was killed.

We moved to Pine Ridge village and my father was arrested and taken prisoner. He was taken prisoner for seven years. When my father was taken prisoner, there were several other men with him. They made him stand in water and they tried to drown him. There were many other hardships the prisoners had to go through.

After he got out, he was taken by Buffalo Bill's Wild West Show and he travelled all over the world with the Wild West Show.

My grandmother told me about the 1868 Treaty. She always talked about the Treaty. From what she said, I learned that the government made a lot of promises it kept for only two years. After that, a lot of the promises were broken.

We were supposed to receive payments from the Black Hills plus payments on the killing of our buffalo. For the buffalo, we received about ten dollars every spring around May. This I knew we received for at least three years. After that we never received any payments.

The Treaty said that the land belonged to the Indian alone, not to white men. There was not supposed to be liquor brought on our land. But they brought liquor to our country and they got Chief Red Cloud drunk and they made him sign the Treaty.

The land was never given to us. That belonged to us already. White people weren't supposed to come into our country but even with that in the Treaty they still came in anyway. Look at us, your people are sitting where our land is. The only purpose they came into our land was to take our land, and they are still coming in.

Before the coming of the white men to our country, whenever we made a promise or made a deal with someone, we respected and honored the word of that promise. But after this, the Indian people recognized that we lost all of this because of the influence of the white people.

I was born in Rosebud territory, but I am a Sioux Indian, a Lakota. There is no difference between us—the Rosebud Oglala and the Pine Ridge Oglala. We are Lakota, and whenever we see each other, we shake hands. We are happy to see each other. We traded our best horses with each other. That's our way of life.

43

RUSSELL MEANS

Russell Means, Oglala from Pine Ridge and American Indian Movement leader at Wounded Knee, 1973:

I was fortunate the first five years of my life because I was brought up by my grandfather, my mother's father who was Yankton Sioux. Up until I was five years old I had no contact with white people. My grandfather told me a lot of things about the traditional way of life. He would take me out in the country on long walks. He would talk about the trees, all of life, how important they are.

After I entered the white man's schools, I lost contact in large part until I joined the American Indian Movement. I have had four and one-half years of college. At one time all I wanted to be was a tax accountant because I figured that is where the money was. But through the courtesy of Dennis Banks and Clyde Bellecourt I joined the American Indian Movement.

We asked ourselves collectively, "What is an Indian?" Based on our collective experience, we went back to our old people on the reservations, not only in South Dakota but in New York, Canada, Hopi, to the Crows. We asked and we are still learning.

I understand this: I understand that every living thing comes from one mother, and that is our Mother Earth. It has been said by the old people that only the white man rapes his mother. I have been in West Virginia; I have been in Montana and in the state of Washington. I have seen. But if all living things come from one mother as has been told to me, we are all relatives. We are all brothers and sisters. That includes every living thing, the green things, the winged of the earth, the four legged, the things that crawl and swim, the mountains, the streams, the rain, the clouds. I have been told by Matthew King who has been told by his grandfather that the tabernacle for the American Indian is the universe.

Because all living things are related we must respect one another as we would our own blood relatives. Treat them with the same kind of respect and reverence. At first I questioned this, but they proved it to me, the old people. They said that if we are all related, then look around you. A tree, one tree in the four seasons, one small cycle in the total cycle of life can tell you how to live your life, how to live with yourself, with your family, with your community and with the world at large, in four seasons.

My grandfather said when I was five years old, "Grandson, you are about to enter the white man's world now. I want you to remember a lot of things." One thing stuck in my mind all through—when I was on skid row, when I was in college. "Remember one thing, the white man has got no eyes and he has got no ears," he said. I see the white man chop down a tree without a prayer, without a fast, without any kind of reverence. And here the tree can tell him how to live, and so can the spider and the snake and the raccoon and the bear and the salmon and the eagle. The white man has a law about endangered species. I think they should pass a law about endangered species according to human life, because over fifty different peoples have been eradicated from the face of the earth on this continent.

We built our civilization from what we learned from the green things, from the eagle, and from all of life, all our relatives. They taught us and that is how we built our civilization. Then we have people tell us we are primitive savages. I am not a savage and my grandparents are not savages nor are my ancestors. Who dropped the bomb on Nagasaki and Hiroshima? Through the American Indian Movement I have come to realize the value of what my ancestors have told me, the value of being Indian, the value of believing what I am Indian for.

The 1868 Sioux Treaty is the epitome of the wisdom of our elders. Look at every provision. Why are we sitting here today if not for their wisdom and they are supposed to be savages. They provided for education; they provided for food; they provided for our rights—our human rights. Everything in that treaty, our elders, our "savage" elders, provided for us, and we live by that treaty today.

Russell Means, American Indian Movement leader at Wounded Knee. Photo by Melinda Rorick

I went to Wounded Knee only because of that Treaty. All the negotiations with the government negotiators who came in and out, was always about the Treaty. The first night we were in there, we send out a copy of the 1868 Sioux Treaty to the FBI and said that was why we were at Wounded Knee. Then came my trial in St. Paul. People have died for that Treaty—before, after and today. People are in jail now because of that Treaty.

I really have nothing to say that is original. I am only a mockingbird mouthing what I have been taught.

When I was a little boy, once I was listening to a radio show about Custer. This was during World War II. My grandmother came and turned off the radio and said, "Wait a minute; let me tell you." And she told me how we let Custer come in even though we had the 1868 Sioux Treaty. We let Custer come in once, come into the Black Hills. According to my grandmother, at that time we did not have the understanding of gold as the white man did. When Custer came back a second time, he came hunting for us, not gold, and he attacked us in violation of the 1868 Sioux Treaty. So we gave him a sensitivity training session, the ultimate sensitivity training session. The might of the United States indignation rose up and we ended up with the 1877 Agreement.

I know that in 1871 Congress passed a law that there would be no more treaties with Indian people. The 1877 agreement was not a treaty according to the laws of the United States. It does not bind us. It does not bind the people who were inside Wounded Knee in 1890 or in 1973.

The 1868 Sioux Treaty affirmed our land, and nobody can come on to it unless they have our permission.

Wasicu is what we call white people. Literally it means "fat-stealer" or "stealer of the fat." There was a time when we had never seen a white man. We used to hang out our meat to dry. Every morning, some of the meat would be gone, the best part with the fat on it. The village got worried about it, so they asked the boys to watch. The young boys saw this real pale thing with a lot of hair on it. It came out of the bushes and took the meat. When the young boys told the older people about it, they would not believe them. So they put some soldiers out to watch. The soldiers saw the same thing. They laid a trap. That is when they started saying, "We have got to catch the *Wasicu*, the fat stealer."

We are still waiting on that promise when we stood down our arms on our own country, under our own Treaty. We have subjected men and women and old people to these courts because we believe that somewhere, sometime, some place, this country is going to have some integrity and honesty in its dealings with Indian people. I will probably die chasing after that integrity and honesty. So be it.

AGNES LaMONTE

Agnes LaMonte is an elder of the Lakota, the Oglala people of Pine Ridge. Her son, Buddy LaMonte, was shot during the Wounded Knee occupation of 1973 by Federal Marshalls. She tells how she saw the events of that time:

I was raised by my grandparents. My grandfather and other old chiefs would come together and talk about the Treaty ever since I was knee high to a grasshopper. They wanted to get back the Black Hills. My grandfather passed away without seeing it done.

They would smoke the Pipe. We honor our Pipe. A lady brought the Pipe to the people so they would know the Great Spirit. When we pray we do not pray for anything that is bad. We pray for peace, love, joy, and happiness. We want peace.

My grandfather always talked about this 1868 Treaty. In Indian they say *The Treaty*, but they mean the 1868 Treaty. My grandfather said, "Someday, that's going to end. In the way the white people are leasing the land, we're leasing it to them, and someday we're going to get it back. But I don't know about these little children. They might not see that."

"And the Black Hills," he said, "that was ours, but the white people lease it, too. They want to lease that so we lease it to them. We didn't want to lease it, but one chief made a mistake."

Nowadays, the tribal councils get a big board together and make resolutions and they don't let the people know what's going on. Well, it's just like when Chief Red Cloud got with the white people and they got him drunk.

"So how did he sign his name," I asked, "if he never knew about writing or anything?" The whites claimed that he signed his name.

My grandfather said, "He said he signed his name, and so that's how we're leasing the Black Hills to them. They say they got Chief Red Cloud drunk on fire water so he signed that to them. If he hadn't done that we'd still have ours but that's what he done."

And my grandfather spoke of the Pony Claim, and I asked, "What do you mean by Pony Claim?"

"Well," he said, "you know, they took our horses away from us and we didn't have any more. This Treaty of ours and it's going to be up soon, and I don't know what's going to happen. They might take it away from you little children so when you grow up your grandchildren will know this."

That's what he told me. That's what he told us. In the long run our Sacred Pipe will help us to win our Treaty, and we honor our Pipe.

I remember a lady was talking about some drunks who were raising cain. I said, "Never a time as far as I remember did the Indians ever fight like that. They didn't get drunk. They loved one another, even the early white settlers, they got along. Nobody got drunk, going from house to house fighting." I said, "They all loved one another. They all helped one another. They share their food with one another. They never asked to be paid back for a loan or favor. But now it's up today. There's hatred amongst the people. They hate one another on account of the Chairman, Dick Wilson."

The Pine Ridge people demonstrated for the impeachment of Wilson, but they didn't get anywhere. Then they organized a civil rights next, but still could not budge him from his chair because he got away with a lot of money and he does not want to get caught.

One evening I went over to the Calico Hall where they were supposed to have a meeting and powwow. They talked about how they could not do anything, so then they decided to call on the American Indian Movement people for help to remove Wilson. My boy was in it.

The next evening I went and they were still there. There wasn't any dancing and I asked when they were going to start. They said they were not going to. My daughter came and told me to go home and take care of the kids, that they were going to Porcupine. They all lined up in cars. The traditional men were having a meeting some place nearby and they came back and said it was time to go. I did not know where they were going. They all got ready. As they went I could see a whole streak of red lights going south. I thought they were all going for a dance or something.

I didn't go right home. I went by the police station in Pine Ridge village. There was a car stopped there with two women standing there. I stopped by the stop sign and the women came over and said, "What's going on?" That was Chairman Wilson's wife. "What's going on, all these people are going by, going east?"

I said, "I don't know, that is what I'd like to know, and I'm going north."

I left and when I was home about an hour later the news came on and they had taken over Wounded Knee because of the chairman. It went on and on, and they were all right. The first thing you know there was a bunch of Federal Marshalls come into the dormitory where I work. They all had these blue jump suits on and they had guns.

United States Army at Wounded Knee, 1973. Photo by Michelle Vignes

We put them up in the dorm. We moved out our little boys into the next dorm, doubled up.

We were giving lunch there for the boys and I was making fried bread. One of the Marshalls came over and said, "Say, lady, do you have a recipe for this?"

"No, I don't have no recipe, but when you eat this, why, you be lively."

So he said, "Oh, well, I better try one."

"What purpose are you here, are you Marshalls?" I asked.

"Well, I don't know, but it's an order that we had to come." He said they were afraid that A.I.M. people would take over the agency.

I asked, "What are they going to take over, what is there to take over? It's not like D.C. There's nothing here and it belongs to the Indians. What they're going to take is done gone. There's nothing here."

48

"Well, that's the order we got."

So it went on and on and then the marshalls went to Wounded Knee. Then they came back, and I asked, "Where did you guys go?"

"Wounded Knee."

"What for?"

"Well, that's the orders we got so we went to Wounded Knee and we thought we'll get them people out of there."

"Well, I don't know, I don't think you can. They are there for some purpose. They asked for their Treaty and they want to remove this chairman. But I think he's under the U.S. Government and that he's got you guys in here with guns."

"Well, I really don't know," he said.

It went on, and the first ones left and then the second bunch came in. They all looked tough to me, but I wasn't scared of them. So I asked them why they come. They said, "Well, we come here to protect the building, the Bureau of Indian Affairs building."

"There's nothing to protect, the Bureau of Indian Affairs building," I said. "Probably, you can protect Wilson."

And he never said nothing, but I was right. He was protecting Wilson and the Government.

It went on and on, and the first thing you know, I'm on the outs with my supervisor. To this day. He wouldn't look at me. He won't speak to me. He called the workers down to his office, so I went down in there just to hear, snooping around. A guy said, "I want you, all you people to get down there, you workers, to get down there and sign up at the Mills Hall to go to Wounded Knee."

I stood there and listened to them and they all walked out and went down to register. They are the goons now of today, those who registered. They left and they came back. Then the first thing I know the next day they had their guns. One lady came and told me, "You know what, under that employees-used-to-be building, they are hauling guns out of there, loading them up in vans and police cars. What's going to happen?"

I said, "I don't know. I was working."

First thing you know, why my supervisor came out with a black hat. He never did wear a hat. I thought he looked like a drug store cowboy the way he dressed or a Montgomery Ward cowboy. He had a gun coming out and he pointed up in the air. He put his gun in the car and took off to the east. He's the guy who won't face me today. He's scared of me. I wanted to say something to him so bad.

I told my daughter, "Even Christ forgives his enemies on the cross."

She said, "I'd forgive them but I'll never forget what they done."

Later on they all went down in there and they all had guns, even women had guns, the goon women had guns and helmets on. I don't know if they knew how to shoot or just tried to scare the people. One morning they said they're going to get them out of Wounded Knee at 6:00. They said they were going to mow them down if they couldn't get them out of there.

Well, I prayed with my Pipe that nothing will happen to them because little babies, children, and young people were in there. I kind of got shook up over it, but again I thought, "Oh well, they're not going to do it."

The first thing I know they opened the road block and that's the time I went in. I loaded my car with food and clothes, aspirins and what not for my grandchildren. Whatever they needed I took in. It seemed like people in there were happy. They were milling around.

Then there was the time they shot that Marshall. I asked my son, "Can't you come home?"

He said, "I don't know."

"Well, why don't you come home one night anyhow and get cleaned up and put clean clothes on and come back?"

And he said, "No, I'll think about it."

So I went home and the next day I came again.

"Just go home and bring me some chow," he said. My son was a big eater. When I came back, why, he said, "No, mom, I cannot leave because it's not right for me to leave my sister and my little nieces and nephews. My nieces, they're girls, and why should I leave them and go home and be out there while they're in here fighting for their rights?"

"Well, at least you can come home one night?"

"No, I don't think so. I'll tell you, I'm here for one purpose," he said."Remember that, don't forget it, and Dicky Wilson is not going to get me out of here alive. But, mom, we're going to win, so just remember and pray for us and we're going to win."

So I left.

Dick Wilson and his outfit, they were going east one morning. Oh they were going to just get them out of there. They were just going to mow them down, so they went, but they didn't make it. They couldn't do it. I don't know why they couldn't do it.

These Marshalls, this second bunch, was in there. They were FBIs. After I noticed they were all FBIs, I didn't have no faith in the FBIs anymore because they lied to me. They were there in the dorm and they had guns, and they had whiskey. Our little boys are from about six or seven years old in the school. They are really nosey. You know, these little guys would go see why those FBIs were in there. They'd sneak in and they'd say, "Mrs. LaMonte, there's some guns in there. There's some guns in there and there's some shells in there and there's some whiskey in there."

I said, "You stay out of there." They even had dogs, police dogs, the FBIs. I don't know where they put those dogs, but those were the two nights that I was off duty. I thought if I was there on duty and I saw those dogs in the dorm, I would chase them out of there. They have no business of being in there.

And that's what happened. First thing I know they all went into Wounded Knee. The day before they killed my son, my nephew, Cut Grass, came to see me. He had trouble with his wife, and he came. He was really feeling bad. Just then, one of my granddaughters was going back to Wounded Knee. They would come in and out. I don't know how they did it with all those FBIs, Marshalls, B.I.A. cops, goons, 82nd Airborne, but I don't know how they came in and out. Anyway, we made packs for them, whatever they could carry—food and clothes for my son, the three girls and my granddaughters.

My nephew asked, "Where are they going?"

"They're going back into Wounded Knee," I said. "They're taking food and stuff back in there."

My nephew said, "Well, they are girls and why should I be sitting here. I'm going with them."

So I made a pack for him. I took them over in the afternoon. I took them on the north side of Wounded Knee. They sat there and waited until dark and they went in. I prayed for them and I sang a song that people sing when the enemies are around coming for them. With that song, the enemies couldn't come even if they have three or four guns. So I sang the song for them and I thought, "Well, I will just wait."

"Do your best to get back in," I told them. Some little hungry children were in there. I left and came home.

My nephew, Cut Grass, wasn't in there very long when he came to court here. The FBI really worked on him. He wasn't in there very long. They go in though. On the way they got lost and gave the howl or whistle that let them into Wounded Knee. It's our belief, our spiritual belief, that they were being guided through into Wounded Knee. They got in Wounded Knee at dawn and they walked in front of the 82nd Airborne where they were camping, but no one was up. The Great Spirit held their eyes closed so they didn't see them. So they walked right in there.

After they distributed their food and stuff, I guess they went to bed. They slept because they had walked all night. Some time then my son got killed. Oh, the FBIs were liars. They told my two granddaughters, my daughter and my son in law and my nephew and my niece, they told them if they walk out with the body they're not going to touch them, that nothing would happen to them. And that they could take the body back to Pine Ridge village. So they got ready and walked out with a stretcher and put my son's body in the van.

When they came out, the FBIs came and they slapped handcuffs on the girls and my nephew. Instead of letting them follow the body back to Pine Ridge, they stuck them in jail. I called my grandson at Wounded Knee, told him that they threw them all in jail, put them behind bars. I got back from work. At the jail, they were all standing looking out of that cage and the welfare was going to take the baby away. My daughter went down there and took it away from them.

We got to see my son lying in a room. There were some Marshals there. We waited for the pathologist to get there, waited and waited for day and night, the night and the next day and the next evening he got there. One of my girls said, "That guy is here now. Come on, let's go down there."

Wounded Knee cemetery, site of the mass burial of Lakotas killed in the Wounded Knee 1890 massacre by the United States cavalry, where Buddy LaMonte is buried. Photo by Melinda Rorick

So we went down in there, all down in there, and I got to see him.

I said to the pathologist, "You got to see his wound?"

He said, "yes."

"Well, tell me what kind of a bullet they used on my son."

"I cannot do that because if I do I have to tell another story."

To this day I'm after that pathologist. I walked out, and he was just going to shove the body back, but my daughter went and pushed the door open and we went in. We followed him out back upstairs and in the elevator. He wouldn't tell because he was working under the Government. He's under the Government work. He's not going to tell what happened. But after we saw the wound, we knew it was a Howard rifle. And I know where the shell is through the spiritual way. I know where it's at to this day.

And that's how my son got killed.

My son didn't do anything wrong. All the people in there they didn't do anything wrong to anybody. They didn't shoot at anybody to kill. But all those FBIs, B.I.A. cops, Marshalls, the goons, and 82nd Airborne were there. For awhile there was a patrol, border patrol there.

Last summer some people, tourists, were at Wounded Knee while I was there visiting my son's grave. They asked me where Wounded Knee was. "Right here," I said, "This is the church that burned down. The goons burned it down because there's a lot of evidence in that church. It's full of holes. It's just like a honeycomb in there. The people were in there so they shot at them. So this is it," I said. "And down the hill you can see that house over there. It's burnt down, and that church over there, that's where the people stayed. And this, all of this hill around here was where they surrendered, a handful of people."

"My," one woman said and she cried, "how cruel they can be."

And I said, "Yes, the people are fighting for their rights. They're fighting for their Treaty. They want that Wilson to be removed from his chair, but he wouldn't do it and the Government helped him."

Wilson called D.C., called Nixon for help, told what his Marshalls and FBIs and goons were doing to the people. All that time Nixon was the headman. He knew but he didn't do nothing. They said they would help, but they never did. After we found out that the Government had Wilson by the neck, we knew that was why they didn't do nothing. Now they are trying to kill our people who were down in Wounded Knee.

I thought it over, about the first massacre in 1890. My mother was twelve years old and she was right in there. She used to tell us what happened. She said they surrendered to the Government like that, and they took all their weapons, whatever they had. When they got through then they started shooting them, little babies on up, women, men. She showed me a spot where they couldn't get one man. They just jump all over the hills after him. Just about the time that he got to the top of the hill, I don't know how many shots, but they took a lot at him. There was a marker there and somebody took it away. How well I remember that.

In that massacre, they went and they killed my mother's uncle and aunt right there. She was packing a baby, but the baby didn't get killed. They took the baby and took it to the day school in Manderson. They went to these white teachers with the baby and said, "When it's all settled down, we'll come back after the baby." About three years later they went after their nephew and the teacher's wife cried because she was well attached to that little boy. So my grandfather said, "Well, what do you think, lady, he's well attached to these white people, and he's an orphan. They give him a good home and maybe he'll have a good education, so why not let them have him?

So they did, and his last name is Miller. He's a doctor, but I don't know if he's still living or not.

I never had given it a thought that someday this would happen here again and my son was going to be next, lying in the Wounded Knee Cemetery. Before this happened he liked to joke. They were sitting around and he said, "If anything happens to me," he said, "bury me here in Wounded Knee." And he laughed. Later on he said, "Things are getting tough, I see, so if I get killed, I don't want to bother my people so just bury me in the bunker. That's where I want to be, fighting for my people. I don't want to go out of here, out of Wounded Knee. I want to be buried right here."

So that's where we buried him. My mother's uncle and aunt are buried there from the 1890 massacre.

I told the tourists, I said, that I never thought that my son would be next, that he would be lying here. And I don't know why the Government had to shoot my son. I said to them, "He didn't do nothing. He was just walking when they shot him."

PART TWO

The Sioux Nation
Before Invasion

I am a born government of this western hemisphere —
that's chief interpretations—and interpret
                                        the life
of the civilization of this western continent,
physically
and spiritually

The interpretation and the knowledge,
                                        physical
                                        and spiritual

There are four races:
                        white,
                        black,
                        red,
                        and yellow.
This time
            I say   prayers,
                        prayers and prayers
                        and prayers.
                        The Great Spirit is first,
Not us
or any one of these races.
We belong to one corner.

And at that time
                        my grandfather,
he was given the sergeant major,
and he was a soldier
                        and he is akicita
and he had to take care of   what the chiefs
                                        and what the elders said.
He want to have obedient
                        of the Great Spirit
                        and obedient of the welfare
                        and the humanity
                        of the Lakota,
                                        because
they are Wolakota.
                        They call them Tetons
                        People in the center,
                        people of this western hemisphere.
So what you have to speak
to this universal language.

We are   Lakota,
            Ikchewichasha
            aboriginal.
                                        —*Henry Crow Dog*

54

DISTORTIONS OF INDIAN HISTORY
Alvin M. Josephy, Jr.

About twenty-five years ago when I first began to meet American Indians and talk with them and listen to their particular view of things, I began to realize that we had not been getting accurate information. Right from the very beginning, we had a history that was self-serving for our purposes. It is quite logical that history does serve the purposes of a people.

When I went to school, we had a regular formula for learning history. The curriculum presented, first, the "Age of Discovery" with Columbus' arrival and then the period of colonization across North America. It came to me as a shock, even before I was interested in Indian history, to realize there had been Frenchmen far into the interior of the continent before the English establishment of Plymouth and Jamestown. Later on I was shocked to realize that the Spaniards had been in the Southwest much earlier also. It depended where you got this history, whether you were born in California and got the California version, or another.

Nevertheless, none of the non-Indians were getting an objective perspective of Indian-White history similar to that which an American might give to both the French and Germans if he wrote a history of the Franco-Prussian War. I was particularly concerned that almost everything that was in print was distorted. Indians were defamed or overlooked completely, totally ignored. My friend and associate, Arthur Schlesinger, Jr., who won the Pulitzer Prize for the book, *The Age of Jackson*, never mentioned, for instance, the Trail of Tears of the Cherokee Nation, or John Marshall's decisions concerning the Cherokee. Indians were completely left out of that book.

The most noted historians influence the writing of secondary history, the history used in college classrooms. They also influence the run of the mill historian who prepares history for high school and elementary school. After I was being published, historians would call me and say they were working on a book and had to say something about Indians. They asked me to help them fill in the material they needed. It did provide me with an opportunity to do a little educating.

There has been a distortion of history and the use of half history, just telling history with blinders on. There has been defamation of the Indian people.

With the Kennedy assassination, there developed a great interest in this country concerning violence. Being with American Heritage Publishing Company, I became interested in the whole question: Is the United States more violent than other countries? Out of that interest I began to realize that the first contact between Europeans and Indians on the Atlantic Coast was violent. The early patterns set were the patterns that persisted as settlers moved west.

The settlers had an education from their birth, from their own people and books as to what an Indian was, how an Indian would behave. In the 1840's, people who moved West from the East and had never seen an Indian had preconceived ideas about what they would experience when they arrived in Indian territory. They expected violence. It is obvious that violence was not strange to either the Indian or the settler. The differences lay in the extent and the nature of violence and what motivated the violence.

Indian warfare was totally different from European warfare. Indians rarely fought all-out, total wars against others. Wars were motivated principally by raids and feuds, and fights ended quickly with little loss of life. There was rarely anything like the encirclement of towns and settlements such as occurred in Connecticut and Rhode Island where entire Indian villages were surrounded and everything was burned and every living thing was cut down. In one such episode, six hundred men, women, and children were massacred as they tried to escape. In this way the Pequot Nation was almost destroyed by the English; Indians were regarded by their Puritan attackers as the children of Satan, justifying their extermination.

Out of that kind of no quarter total war came all the hostilities and all the ferociousness that later characterized border warfare in the East and then on one frontier of colonization after another. The Indians learned, in other words, that it was all out war against them, and they had to respond or perish. The narratives of the wars against the Pequot show that the Indians were shocked, horrified at this kind of warfare which was being conducted against them.

The people who came as settlers to America, the early settlers, had a very recent tradition of religious wars among themselves in which there was great hostility and extreme barbarism in Europe. The wars of "the reformation" preceded by the Crusades were accompanied by extreme violence.

Before Europeans came, Indian people regarded peace highly. Peace had a very important role in the structure of their societies. It was not that they were absolute pacifists or refused to fight. For instance, the Pueblos and Hopi had reasons for being peaceful and living a peaceful life, not being aggressive and belligerent. Yet they could and did fight in their own defense when they felt their societies were threatened.

There were what anthropologists call "warrior societies," in which warfare, in Indian terms, had specific social functions. People also had feuds and there were aggressions, but they were qualitatively different. Often such hostility would end for a time for peaceful trading, then flare up again. Or it might be just one small group that would carry on a feud with others of another group. Some large nations carried traditions of hostility against each other, such as the Chippewa and the Sioux. But they were capable of truce and peace and a different kind of warfare.

Scalping was not originated by Indians. Poachers in England had their ears cut off. Europeans had the habit of taking parts of the body in war. The Dutch gave rewards for Indian heads even before there was open warfare in their area of colonization. Indian heads were put on pikes there very early, but people got tired of lugging in the heads so soon they just brought in the scalp to show that they had killed an Indian.

Great civilizations existed in North America prior to European arrival. The "Mound Builders" of the Ohio Valley, for instance, flourished about two thousand years ago. Villages existed all over the Northeast and a network of them stretched into the Plains. Commerce bound villages together from the Rocky Mountains to the Atlantic Coast and from Canada to New Mexico. The villages and the artistry of the people required an advanced ability at organization. I find nothing "primitive" in these societies.

In Mexico, agriculture began about nine thousand years ago and gave a foundation for the rise of fantastic civilizations ranking with Greece and Rome. There were rise and falls of civilizations here as in Euro-Asia, and they left legacies to the people. Teotihuacan was probably the greatest city in the world in AD 500. It had 200,000 population, and was eight and one-half miles in area. It was the center of a huge civilization.

The distortion of Indian history has worked very badly against Indian people themselves. It has given them a sense of shame in their heritage, with children exposed to distorted material. They have had no feeling of self-identity or anything but shame for their background, for their own people. The distortions have worked on non-Indian people to keep them uninformed about the American Indian and disinclined to gain information. It has created stereotype thinking and has really been the single biggest cause, in my opinion, of the blocking of beneficial Indian legislation. If the constituents of a congressman have certain feelings or opinions, they bring their influence to bear on their representatives and often it is opposed to Indians.

I was educated in the East, and practically no impact about Indians was made on me. When I was a child, I saw a book about an Indian Chief, but such children's books were idealistic versions of the Indian. After that the only exposure I got was inferior information about Indians—that Indians were in the way, like trees to be knocked aside. Indians were not presented in realistic terms as humans. By the time they mention Custer's defeat, well—that is about the last reference to Indians in a school textbook.

From the very beginning of the European colonization of North America, I think they have followed a policy of divide and conquer. History shows that. Columbus used the first Indians he found against other Indians and Cortez did the same in Mexico. The Pequot War is an example. The English used Mohigans to aid in wiping out the Pequot. Then on the Plains some Nations furnished scouts for the United States Army. I think it was an attempt to use one nation to do the dirty work against another. The policy of the United States government has always been to secure the western lands and to pacify the area so that it could be colonized.

There obviously is a Christian element that must be grasped in the study of relations with the Indians. There are many strings that have to be pursued to understand the relationship between Indians and whites, such as the rise of an economic system in Europe before the time of expansion, the rise of nation-states, the feudal system. These facets fed into what made a settler at Plymouth behave as he did behave in contact with Indians. Christian attitudes that came from the background of Christian history had an important impact on relations with Indians.

The religious wars in the sixteenth and seventeenth centuries came close to being wars of extermination in Europe. That was a pretty violent history and many hundreds of thousands of people were killed. Some nations did not survive as nations because their independence was taken, such as Ireland.

Quite often Indian people thought they were superior to the settlers who were coming here. Indian people viewed themselves as a people, a good and strong people. They liked their way of life and this was their country. Here was an outsider coming in. The Indians would treat with him, talk with him, but very often had a feeling ranging from patronization to contempt for the settler coming.

In regard to sovereignty, Indian people managed and ran their own affairs. No one did it for them. The Sioux had the concept of sovereignty when they treated with the United States. The Sioux did not give up any sense of sovereignty in any of the treaties they made with the United States.

ORIGINS OF INDIAN PEOPLES

From the testimony of expert witness, William S. Laughlin, Chairman, Laboratory of Biological Anthropology, Department of Biobehavioral Sciences; Professor of Biobehavioral Sciences at the University of Connecticut. Dr. Laughlin received his Ph.D. at Harvard University.

I am concerned with human evolution and with population variation and with population history. My primary focus has been on the origin of man in the Americas and the movement of people from Siberia to the Americas. I have been working on such studies since 1938.

All the emigrants into these continents came from Asia and more precisely from Siberia. They came across the Bering Land Bridge which formerly connected Siberia and Alaska, then moved down all the way into South America. There were no people here before the Indians arrived.

The most conservative estimate of when the migrations began is 15,000 years ago. There were probably at least three separate migrations, all of them small. I would estimate that the migrations occurred over a period of two to four thousand years. Then the Bering Land Bridge was submerged. That cutoff date, some 11,000-10,000 years ago, is clear.

The people who migrated had to adapt to every ecological zone—high altitudes, dry deserts, jungles, river conditions, arctic cold. In this way they performed one of the most interesting and significant experiments in human evolution, genetic and cultural. People from one continent successfully going to another continent and occupying every ecological zone is significant.

In every case they had to solve the problems of what foods were edible and how to get the animals in a systematic fashion. Hunting, it should be noted, requires childhood training in observation and animal behavior. Hunting as a way of life is a complex integrated biobehavioral system, and not simply a subsistence technique. Therefore, they had to have adequate social organization to solve the economic and territorial problems. Agriculture was developed first in Middle America and spread. All the major items of civilization—monumental architecture, the concept of zero, mathematics, astronomy, writing—were present without external intervention—the entire inventory of what constitutes civilization.

Corn, potatoes, varieties of beans, these and many other plants were Indian inventions. No place else in the world has the plant, maize, been developed. However it was done, the Indians went from whatever the predecessor of corn is to a plant that now exists. Its development was around 4,000 years ago or more.

Major architectural achievements began over 2,000 years ago and reached an apex around 400 A.D. Large civilizations with complex systems of trade over large areas existed. Pyramids which are of similar complexity to those in the Middle East, to which they are not related, were built. There are astronomical observatories with sight-lines for observing planets and the timing of planetary movements. There were many interesting forms of architecture; several kinds of house styles were developed.

In the Southwest, the people used adobe and stone. In the Southeast, some houses were built on elevations with ingenious interlocking devices for holding them together. The Eskimos invented the snowhouse, the winter house called an igloo. On the West coast, some amazingly large houses, often over a hundred feet in length and of quite massive and ingenious construction were built. The Plains people devised teepees which are very artful and workable housing, practical for their use. In the Northeast, the long houses were developed. These housed hundreds of people in some cases. Suitable housing was always developed.

Europeans found it difficult to believe that the Native people, the people they encountered were equal to them. They thought that the trigger or the impetus or stimulus for Native development came from somewhere else. The most logical place was the Middle East, where European influence had originated. So they reasoned that Indians were of the tribes of Israel. I think there is a tendency to explain away the autonomous achievements of American Indians by assuming that somebody else was responsible for them.

The Sioux shared the knowledge of other Native nations here. They had a basic knowledge of astronomy, where planets were, and used this knowledge for travel.

The living Sioux Indians are demonstrably and clearly related to earlier Indians who were here in the United States many thousands of years before any Europeans arrived anywhere in the Americas. The incontrovertible evidence is seen in a great many physical traits of the teeth and the skeletons. The genetic continuity between the living Indians and their antecedent populations is firm and it is demonstrable with the highest level of scientific proof.

DEMOGRAPHY

From the testimony of Wilbur R. Jacobs, Professor of History at the University of California, Santa Barbara. Dr. Jacobs is author of numerous books and articles on Indian-white relations, including Dispossessing the American Indian, *Scribner's, New York, 1972.*

Recently I published an article, "The Tip of the Iceberg, Pre-Columbian Indian Demography and some Implications for Revisionism," on aspects of Indian demography which will help to bring about revisions in historical writing. (*William and Mary Quarterly*, 3rd Series, XXXI, No. 1, 123-32.)

Ideas about Native American populations in 1492 have been drastically revised. Formerly, up to about ten years ago, we thought that there were about one million Native people in North America and about eight to twelve million in the whole western hemisphere. Now, the most recent estimates are that there were as many as 100 million people in the western hemisphere in 1492 and that ten million of those lived in North America. Twenty-five million occupied central Mexico. Eight million lived on the island of Hispanolia (modern Haiti) where they perfected the domestication of food plants to the extent that they had a greater yield per hectare than comparable fields harvested in Europe in 1492. Everywhere native people developed a life style to support larger populations through the discovery and domestication of food crops (maize, beans, melons, squash, cassava and other crops) supplemented by protein obtained by fishing, hunting, and by gathering foods from wild plants.

As a result of the European invasion, millions and millions of native people died. Smallpox was the worst killer along with measles and other viral diseases. There were also epidemics of typhoid, typhus, influenza, and at a later date, diphtheria and venereal disease.

The Native American Indian population in the Americas before the invasion was thus greater than all of Western Europe. Several leading writers and scholars have contributed toward establishing the new demographic figures. Among them are Henry F. Dobyns of Tucson and three University of California, Berkeley faculty—Woodrow Borah and the late Sherburne F. Cook and Carl O. Sauer. These scholars made detailed studies of Indian depopulation in certain areas of the Western Hemisphere including New England, California, central Mexico, and Haiti. By the use of logarithmic formulas, Spanish population accounts (tribute records and similar documents), and other data, resasonably accurate population appraisals can be made. This is a very complex field of research and demands the highest skills in quantitative mathematics, medicine, ethnology, and archaeology. Anyone who questions this data must himself delve into these special fields.

I have made some evaluation of these studies. My own work has primarily been in studying extant records of Arawak Indians and by analyzing depopulation patterns of Indians in North America and aboriginal people in Australia. My conclusion is that the new estimates are correct, and that we must now cope with the fact that millions and millions of Native people died as a result of European contact. This is probably the worst demographic disaster in world history.

These large populations before the coming of the white man had organized themselves for mutual protection and to make the best use of the land. These Indian societies were primarily religious societies. Religion was an overriding factor in the life style of Indian peoples' political groups. Various Indian nations in the Americas recognized each other as distinct nations, very much as European nations identified themselves as nations. They respected each other's boundaries, negotiated treaties with each other, and they maintained a cultural and linguistic identity. At the time of the Columbian exchange between Europe and the Americas there were a series of distinct, self-governing Native American societies in the Western Hemisphere that have many parallels with the nation states of Europe.

Christian missionaries have been an important part of the genocide committed against the Indians. Photo by Michelle Vignes

THE SACRED WAY
Father Peter Powell

From the expert witness testimony of Father Peter John Powell, St. Augustine's Indian Center, Chicago, Illinois. Father Powell holds the degree of Doctor of Divinity in sacred theology. He is also a Research Associate of The Newberry Library, Chicago.

My scholarly studies have centered upon the recording of the sacred ceremonies and history of the Cheyenne, who are my own people. I came into these studies through the study of the Lakota sacred ways, which I have studied both in pre-graduate and post-graduate work.

I first began my pre-graduate studies in 1941, among the Dakota in South Dakota, on Crow Creek and Lower Brule Reservations. Later I was adopted as a son by the One Feather family of Pine Ridge Reservation. Since 1955 I have been involved in scholarly studies at the request of the Cheyenne priests and holy men, and the Chiefs and leaders of the military societies among the Cheyenne. I record Cheyenne history against the background of the Cheyenne sacred ceremonies.

I have been instructed in the Cheyenne sacred ceremonies as a Sun Dance priest. In 1971 I was the first non-Cheyenne invited to accompany the Keeper of the Sacred Arrows, and three other holy men, for the sacred four day fast on Noaha-vose, the Sacred Mountain. The Keeper of the Sacred Arrows is the greatest holy man among the Cheyenne people.

I found my way into the Catholic priesthood, Your Honor, through the study of the Lakota sacred ceremonies. This was many years ago, when I was still a very young man. It was through the study of the Lakota sacred ways that I became convinced of two things. First of all: that the Lakota people, my own Cheyenne people, and Native American people as a whole, were the most naturally spiritual people of any people in the world. Secondly: that Lakota history and Lakota life can only be understood within the context of the sacred ceremonies of the people themselves. Every act (in the sense of a formal agreement or treaty) that has been accomplished between the Lakota people and the United States; every act of a formal nature made by the Lakotas with any other Indian nation, has its true context within the sacred ceremonies of the people themselves.

From my study of the Lakota holy ways, I also found a further vocation within the priestly vocation itself. My recognition of the holiness that underlies the Sun Dance, the holiness that underlies the sacred ceremonies as a whole, made me realize, in a personal sense, that the only way I could understand mankind as a whole, the only way I could truly understand Plains Indian history, was to know and to be a part of the sacred ways of these people, the Cheyennes and Lakotas. Now, after twenty-one years in the priesthood, I still believe these people to be the most naturally spiritual people in the world.

Both the Lakota and the Cheyenne consider themselves to be "The People." The implication of that designation is that the whites, the *wasicus*, were (and are) something less than people, something less than human beings. Traditionally, this is so because the *wasicu* way of life was not (and is not) lived within the context of the Sacred Way that is the Lakota way of life. Traditionally, because of this lack of "humanness," whites did not have use of or occupancy of the Earth, the Mother of the People. Thus, the right of the Lakota to occupation of their lands is a sacred right. And not only is it a sacred right; but it is also a sacred obligation. The Lakota and Cheyenne people are among the most civilized people that one could imagine. These were people who, at the same time in their history as the Fort Laramie Treaty, had discovered what other Americans are only discovering at this time: that is, the true relationship of man to his environment, the relationship of man to creation.

The Lakota people, at the time of the Fort Laramie Treaty, had developed one of the most beautifully thought-out governmental systems possessed by any nation in the world. The men who constituted their legal system were the Council Chiefs, the headmen (or chiefs) of the warrior societies, and the members of the warrior societies themselves. All possessed their respective responsibilities in tribal government. The balance of power was closely defined; and the roles of the Chiefs, headmen and soldier society members beautifully interlinked.

The Council Chiefs possessed the final authority. These Chiefs were the peacemakers, and, ultimately, the peace-keepers among the people. They had been chosen Chiefs because they best represented the ideal of what it was, and is, to be Lakota. Most of the Chiefs had been great warriors in their younger years. However, even more important was the fact that they were pre-eminent among all other men for their wisdom, compassion and generosity. Generosity was considered the paramount virtue among the Lakota people; and it is considered the paramount virtue to this day. Thus these Chiefs, the Council Chiefs, were the men who best represented the essence of what it is to be Lakota.

The Chiefs then, were those wise men who ruled the people and who had the final say in the relationships between the people and their government. However, rather than use the word "rule," I should say that the Chiefs were the men who both led and served the people. For the Chiefs were, and still are, not only the leaders of the people, but also their servants. Rarely did a Council Chief seek to impose his own personal will upon the wills of his followers. Instead, ideally, he was the man who carried out the collective mind, the collective wishes, of his people. Ideally he was the wise, compassionate, generous leader who was willing to give all that he possessed, his life included, for the good of his people.

Working in a close, but subordinate, relationship to the Council Chiefs were the headmen of the *Akicita* or warrior societies. These were the men of action who carried out the directives of the Council Chiefs. They, and the men in their respective societies, were the guardians, the protectors of the people. The *Akicita* also served as camp police. At the time of the tribal hunts, the Council Chiefs appointed them guardians of the buffalo herds. Thus the *Akicita* regulated the activities of the hunters during the great tribal hunts, so that all families might have an equal opportunity to obtain a good supply of buffalo meat.

Thus, even though white authors often describe the Lakotas as being a warrior people, nevertheless it was the Council Chiefs, not the warriors, who governed the people. It was the men of wisdom, generosity, and often holiness as well, the men who represented the essence of goodness, who actually governed the people. Ideally, then, it was the Council Chiefs who gave the orders, and the warrior society headmen and members who carried out these orders as they affected the lives of the people as a whole.

These people, the Lakotas and Cheyennes, were a people whose theology, whose government, whose relationship to the environment was far advanced over that of the whites who first made contact with them. Ideally, then, it was the Council Chiefs who gave the orders, and the warrior society headmen and members who carried out those orders as they affected the lives of the people as a whole.

These people, the Lakotas and Cheyennes, were a people whose theology, whose government, whose relationship to the environment was far advanced over that of the whites who first made contact with them. Ideally, I believe that this still is true today. And I believe that it is time for whites to turn to the Lakotas, to my own Cheyenne people, and to Indian people as a whole, not only to learn what the relationship of man to his environment should be, but also to understand the very nature of man himself.

Let me stress that in Lakota life there is no difference between the sacred and secular as presently exists in Anglo-American life and learning. For the Lakotas and Cheyennes all creation is sacred, all creation is filled with supernatural life. Among my own Cheyenne people, when the Mazheono, the Sacred Powers, appear to men they assume forms that human beings can recognize. Thus the Sacred Powers may appear as animals, birds, or natural forces; or occasionally they assume the form of a man or woman, his or her body covered with sacred red or yellow paint. The point is that the Sacred Powers assume these natural forms so that they, who are spirits, may appear in forms that human beings can both recognize and understand. For the Lakotas and Cheyennes, your Honor, this is a sacred world, a world filled with supernatural life and power. The Earth, the Mother of the people, is, of course, a living supernatural Person as well. Thus to give up their tribal land, to give up their holy way of life, would mark the end of Lakota or Cheyenne existence as the People, as human beings. To give up the Earth, their Mother, would also cut them off from Wakan Tanka and from all the Sacred Powers, whose spiritual presence fills all creation with supernatural life.

Animals are respected not simply because they are living creatures, possessing special powers and attributes of their own; but, more important, they are respected because the Sacred Powers often choose to reveal themselves in the form of animals. For example: the buffalo is a sacred animal, not only because of his own great power; but more especially because Wakan Tanka, the Great Mysterious, has chosen to reveal one aspect of His own infinite power under the form of the buffalo's power. The Great Mysterious also reveals His generosity through the buffalo. For the buffalo generously provides the people with food, clothing and shelter. Thus, before the extermination of the great herds by the white hunters, the buffalo provided the people with everything they needed for life. Life without the buffalo was unthinkable for the old-time Lakotas; and to this day, the buffalo's supernatural power remains to be drawn upon by the individual who asks for that power through fasting and prayer.

Thus, the buffalo was approached in an attitude of respect and prayer. Before the great tribal hunts were begun, prayers were offered by the holy men, as well as by individuals among the people themselves. After a hunter killed a buffalo, he usually offered a prayer of thanksgiving, both to Wakan Tanka, Who gave the buffalo to the people, and to the buffalo himself who had given up his life so that the people might eat and live.

The sacred Sun Dance was, and is, the great central act of worship of both the Lakota and Cheyenne people. From the Sun Dance lodge sacred power flows out upon the world, power to bring new life to the world and to all creation. This holy power not only renewed the buffalo herds; it also drew them in close to the people, so that the people always would be able to obtain food for life. Thus, the buffalo plays a majestic role in Lakota life. For Wakan Tanka has sent the buffalo to the people to show His own generosity; while at the same time, the buffalo is himself one of the Supernatural Beings, sharing in the power of Wakan Tanka Himself.

Life is sacred. Life is to be respected. It is not to be destroyed wantonly. When it is destroyed, it is for the purpose of bringing life and sustenance to the people. As I said before, animals are manifestations of the supernatural Beings and supernatural life that fills all creation. Thus, our Lakota and Cheyenne people did not kill game wantonly. Game was killed primarily in order to bring sustenance to the people. It was not killed for the sheer joy of killing, as white hunters all too often kill game today.

Reverence for life, supernatural life, characterizes the Lakota and Cheyenne attitude toward creation.

At the time of the Fort Laramie Treaty, it is doubtful that any of the Teton Lakotas, the western Sioux, could write their own language. The one thing that approximated written history in traditional Lakota life is the Winter Count. The Winter Counts were the painted buffalo robes, kept by the historians among the Lakota people. Each winter a small painted scene would be added to the robe, as a reminder of the most important event of that year. The Winter Counts were, and are, important records of the great events of the past. However, most of the past was preserved in the memories of the people themselves, especially in the minds of the tribal historians. For the historians were the men recognized as possessing the best memories among the people. The position of tribal historian was one of great respect. I have been told by old people that the tribal historian was second in importance only to the great holy men of the people. For the tribal historians were the preservers of sacred knowledge too. What they retained in their minds, and in their Winter Counts, were the most important events in the history of their people, a history shaped by Wakan Tanka and the Holy Powers themselves. Thus, for the Lakotas and Cheyennes, their history is, indeed, sacred history.

Disciplined people live by rules, and the Lakotas traditionally were, and are, among the most disciplined of all people. Once again, the rules they live by derive their origins from the Sacred Powers and the sacred ceremonies. When the White Buffalo Woman appeared, bringing the seven holy ceremonies to the Lakotas, she taught that the people must live together in peace. They must live together in purity of mind. They must live together, loving each other as brothers and sisters.

The White Buffalo Woman also taught that the Lakotas must live together thinking in terms of sharing what they had with other people, rather than thinking in terms of accumulating wealth, as whites often do. Generally speaking, there was no such thing as the accumulation of vast wealth among the Lakota or Cheyenne people. Generosity was the paramount virtue among our people; and the Chiefs were the men pre-eminent in showing forth that generosity.

The needs and rights of the tribe came before those of the individual, important as individuality was to the Lakotas. During the seasons of the great summer and winter buffalo hunts, single hunters or bands of hunters were not permitted to hunt by themselves, for, in doing so they might stampede the herds, impeding the ability of the entire tribe to gain enough meat to feed all the people.

Here, again, the warrior societies moved into the picture. Their responsibility was to see that no one slipped off to attack the buffalo individually. If anyone did so, the warrior society members possessed the authority to whip the offender, to tear apart his tipi, or to shoot his horses. They had this authority because this offense was a flagrant violation of the unity that bound the members of the tribe together, a unity holding that all the people must have an equal chance to obtain enough food.

An individual, then, was not supposed to put his needs before the needs of the people as a whole. There is a fine interbalance of individual freedom and Chiefly authority among the Lakota people. The Council Chiefs, who are at once the leaders and servants of the people, appointed the warrior society that patrolled the village and the buffalo herds prior to the great tribal buffalo hunt. The headmen and members of the warrior society carried out the Chiefs' orders, stopping and punishing any individual who might try to kill his meat before the others. Rarely did individuals attempt to do so anyway; for the members of the tribe tried to act as one family, taking the needs of all the members into consideration. In Lakota thought, it is always fitting and proper to put the needs and the rights of the tribe first. For, in doing so, the individual man or woman is acting as a human being should act. He or she is functioning as a true member of the People.

INDIAN POLITICAL ECONOMY

From the expert witness testimony of Roxanne Dunbar Ortiz, Cheyenne from Oklahoma, Professor of Native American Studies, California State University, Hayward. Dr. Dunbar Ortiz holds the Ph.D. degree in History from UCLA, Los Angeles.

Native peoples are referred to as "savages" by Anglo-American writers. "Savage" does not necessarily refer only to violence. Europeans were not opposed to violence. Most references to savagery I have found were made in the context of observing Native land ownership and land use concepts. Indians were "savage" because they did not want to be homesteaders, because they opposed private ownership of land.

Europeans, Christians had an idea that they had originated in a Garden of Eden where everyone shared and shared alike, no one starved, everyone was provided for. Europeans believed that Indian people were living in that imaginary primeval state.

Before Europeans arrived, there was no lack of necessities for Indians. Their social structures were built around human needs and human relationships and the preservation and reverence for all life. The Europeans thought that in overcoming their own imaginary Garden of Eden stage, they had somehow advanced and were "civilized."

I see the European rise to power, the rise of economic class structures, of private property, as a definite setback for humanity. It will take a long time to repair the damage that has been done with that development. The social institutions that developed with European colonialism and which have been imposed on Native peoples all over the world, as well as on the majority of their own people, are backward and anarchic.

Colonial institutions are contradictory to the development of well-balanced social institutions which control relations among people. The European concept of the nation-state, the concept of national sovereignty came about with capitalist economic development. The Indian concept of sovereignty was and is qualitatively different. The Sioux say, "This is our country." To the European, that would mean something with a hierarchical political system and power in relation to other countries.

What basically constitutes a nation is a common language, a common land base, and a common culture. That is all. That is sovereignty. The social organization of peoples vary. Native governments varied from the huge Iroquois Six Nations Confederacy to the autonomous Pueblo city states.

Europeans have in the past centuries of capitalist development and expansion twisted the concept of sovereignty to define it as empire rather than cohesive cultures. They have set up certain definitions that apply to themselves, such as the right of discovery or conquest, and then apply it to others and say that is not a nation because they have military and economic power over them.

Generally, anthropologists hold that Indian people adapted themselves to their surroundings, calling to mind some sort of primitive idyllic existence. That partial truth is misleading, for Indian people formulated certain ways of being, based on traditions, practices over centuries. For Indian peoples, the concept of being the same yet different is perfectly natural, whereas with the European something different means something inferior or superior.

There are many different ways of living for Indian nations. Among the Six Nations, the people built large collective lodges and were farmers. They produced a great surplus. Each family did not have a granary and farm their individual plot like the Iowa farmer. That is inefficient and wasteful. There was no waste. There were collective granaries and equitable distribution of food.

From history books, one gets the impression of the squalid, dirty Indian camps of the Plains. In fact, after the armies and settlers destroyed the herds and carried on continual warfare in order to subdue the Plains Nations, there was starvation and deprivation, but not before. The Plains Nations had developed intricate social organizations which dealt with every facet of being.

The variety of life styles in the Western Hemisphere is very different from fairly homogenous Western Europe or the United States today. Despite the variety, certain basic aspects were very similar. One similarity was the concept of land and natural resources and the whole integral universe. Another aspect was the importance of the individual and the community. There was no dichotomy. What was good for the community was good for the individual and what was good for the individual was good for the community. Individual creativity flourished. For an Indian, to be isolated away from the people, was worse than death. In fact, among some Nations, the most extreme punishment for wrongdoing, was banishment for a specific period. That was the worst punishment possible.

The Sioux had a common land base, culture, tradition, and language. They are often referred to erroneously as "nomadic." This term is deceptive. The people had summer and winter homes, and moved in relation to the herds in a definite pattern and in a very organized way. They established encampments. Their land area was recognized by surrounding nations who did not encroach upon it without the Sioux' permission. They knew exactly what their land base was and is. United States authorities had a hard enough time recognizing the collective permanent Pueblos of New Mexico, but to recognize the kind of land holding and social organization of a hunting society was beyond their ability.

Some areas used by the Sioux were shared with other nations, but only with very clear agreements. There was not the concept of ownership, but rather the importance of the relationship. Peace between nations and the preservation of the herds was the foremost consideration. They knew the land, every inch of it. I doubt that the Rockefeller family or other wealthy land owners, who claim more land than the whole Sioux nation ever did, know every inch or even a part of their claimed land. For some such, they have never set foot on the land they lay claim to.

The buffalo had certain established migration patterns which were seasonal, so the Sioux moved in relation to the buffalo. The buffalo was the basis of their economy. Not only the meat for food, but every part of the animal was used—for clothing, housing, utensils, and ceremonially. There were buffalo in other areas than Sioux territory. There were millions of buffalo all over the whole western plateau and plains of North America, but the particular area of use for the Sioux was the Northern plains.

PART THREE
Colonialism To 1868

THE WHITE FOLKS MADE A LOT OF PROMISES THEY BROKE

I didn't go through education,
but the spirits speak to me,

        and maybe
        anyone of the ladies
        and gentlemen
        of this court

would have in that education
of that knowledge.

        So let yourself grow—
        your hair grow

But white man came
and say
      be civilized
so they cut my hair.

        Civilization
        why civilization?
        I get a lot of problems.

It is not me
I told the Great Spirit
it is not me.
        The white folks,
        the white folks
make a lot of promises
they broke.
        I didn't tell nobody,
        Your Honor, Judge.

               —*Henry Crow Dog*

COLONIALIST PROGRAMS
From the expert witness testimony of Roxanne Dunbar Ortiz.

There were no Native American Studies programs when I went to the university in the 60's. I pursued studies of conquest and colonialism. I was most interested in finding out exactly what occurred historically in the conquest and colonization of Indian people. I also wanted to find out just what the United States government is, how it was constituted, how other colonial powers had formed themselves. In the Ph.D. program in History at UCLA, I chose four major fields: History of Spain and Spanish conquests in America; Latin American history; United States history; and European intellectual history. I studied the European world view.

I learned how Native peoples of the whole Western Hemisphere were conquered by colonialism. I wanted to find out what the future of Native peoples might be in light of colonial control. I did some comparative studies with other colonized Native societies—African nations and other non-European peoples who had been conquered and colonized during the past five centuries. I had to create my own comparative studies, applying developed theories of history to Native peoples. I did not find anthropology useful because I wanted to understand the political and economic realities. Anthropology largely takes Native cultures out of the context of colonialism.

After a time, some patterns became clear to me. First, colonialism has something to do with a certain period of human history. I developed an overview of history in terms of this being a time of European conquest and consolidation of power. Secondly, all the people who have been colonized by the European and United States powers are now in the process of overthrowing colonialism. An historical process is at work and Indian people of the Western Hemisphere are part of that process of decolonization.

Doing comparative studies broadened my view of what had happened to Indian peoples historically. I did a study of a Virginia slave plantation, for instance. It is an in-depth study of one family over five generations, a wealthy slave plantation with six hundred chattel slaves, African slaves. There I saw how the importation, deculturation of African peoples was accomplished. This particular plantation became a slave-breeding plantation, dependent upon the sale of slaves in the cotton belt, after about the third generation. They bred slaves as cattle are bred. The family who owned the plantation and the slaves was one of the most prestigious colonial and then American families, among the "founding fathers" of the United States. Understanding this origin of the United States gave me a new perspective. I looked at Africa itself, where African nations have been revolting against European colonialism, uniting with each other, forming new nations. I could see then the projection of what is possible for Native peoples of North America, of the Western Hemisphere.

The most thorough study in colonialism I have done is a case study of a particular area, northern New Mexico. I chose that area because the people there experienced two colonial powers—Spanish and the United States. What I found was a great many

71

differences between Spanish and United States colonial programs, but also similarities in terms of how colonizers operate, how they settle colonists on the land who then fight to keep that land, acting as a buffer, a policing agent for the colonizing power.

The myth of the wild frontiersman who could not be controlled by the central authority is revealed. Rather a conscious policy of conquering, subduing, and controlling Native people may be seen. Colonial policy brought settlers to America, and some were even forced to emigrate.

In New Mexico, the land was occupied by the Native "Pueblos," and their land base was greatly diminished under the Spanish, as were their numbers. Then when the United States entered and claimed the area through the conquest of northern Mexico, the Native people came under United States colonialism. There as in other areas of colonization, the United States pursued its policy of settling newly claimed areas, under the rules of the Northwest Ordinance of 1787 which set up methods of colonizing subdued areas.

With United States colonization of New Mexico, most of the land of the former Mexican citizens and Pueblo land was taken, leaving small holdings. Once state government was established, control of the water supply was taken. Sacred lands, similar to the Black Hills of the Sioux, were taken. In cases brought to the Supreme Court, the Court claimed lack of jurisdiction to settle the question under the *Treaty of Guadalupe Hidalgo* between the United States and Mexico. The Court asserted that Congress has treaty making power and the Court cannot settle political questions.

In looking at other areas of colonization, I see the same pattern—taking of the land by force of violence; removal of the Native economic base; intimidation of the Native people with police power and the bureaucratic structure which keeps Native people in a constant dependent relationship with the colonizers.

In the Spanish conquest areas, however, there was a different program for land control than under United States colonialism. The Spanish continued to follow the Roman legal code which recognized land use primarily, not land ownership. This is an important issue in the Southwest. The Spanish granted land use rights, grazing rights, and aboriginal claims. In some ways the land base, the economic base was not disturbed. The Native people remained economically self-sufficient, and supported the Spanish bureaucratic elite. The Native people were colonized in political terms in being forced to learn Spanish and forced to at least superficially practice Catholicism. Other Native peoples in the surrounding area—Navajos, Apaches, Comanches, the Hopi—were never conquered by the Spanish. There was constant warfare in the two centuries of Spanish domination of the Southwest, and many of those Native people were taken as captives when individually captured. These captives were the people who came to comprise the "Spanish" villages of northern New Mexico, detribalized Native people—*genízaros.*

The economy of newly established "Spanish" villages was similar to that of the Native Pueblos—self-sufficient farming and stockraising. Only a handful of Europeans ever settled in the area, until the United States took over. Spanish power in the area was curbed by resistance. The Spanish entered the area in 1598, but in 1680 the Pueblos led detribalized Natives, mulattos and Mexican Indians brought to the area by the Spanish as workers, to revolt and drove the Spanish out. Spanish presence was eliminated for twelve years. They returned with limited power. The Pueblos maintained a certain amount of power in relationship to Spanish authority. They were not completely colonized until the United States came in and took away the economic base, forcing the people into dependency. This has been the United States method of colonization and control. The means has been massive influx of settlers.

72

The central issue of colonialism is the relationship of Native people to their land base. The Spanish and then the independent Mexican government recognized community land use instead of private ownership. When the United States came in it made all the land public domain open to homesteading, except for small irrigable plots which became useless once water rights were lost to the Native people. The United States did not allow the practice of community control and use to continue, but rather divided the land into 160 acre plots and opened it to homesteading, bringing Anglo-American settlers in. Then the large stockmen, railroads, and land-dealing entrepreneurs bought up the homesteads. Today most of the land in New Mexico is "owned" by a few wealthy businessmen. These methods are the United States' unique contribution to the development of colonialism.

I have been studying American law in order to better understand the Anglo-American concepts of property. I have found that English and European traditional law also has a concept of land use, of common land. But capitalism, particularly United States capitalism, has brought the division of land for sale and settlement, making of land a commercial commodity.

The thrust of United States economic development, which came to dominate in North America, concerned land—a conscious policy of taking the land from Native people, colonizing the people into a state of dependency, placing settlers on the land to defend their self-interest, drive away or kill the Native people. The final stage has been, in this century, to remove the settlers themselves from the land, so that corporations and the United States government control most of the land directly.

United States political leaders knew they had to destroy Native cultures in order to get the land and its resources. They had no need for Indian labor for they decided very early to import African slave labor and white indentured labor. They wanted Indian land. They saw that the strength of Native resistance was the land base and the collective bond that provided the stimulus for resistance. Genocide, cultural and physical, became the primary policy of United States colonialism in North America.

Indian people, Indian leaders did not well understand the profit motives of the capitalists. Until Tecumseh in the early nineteenth century, colonialist motives were not clarified, and by then the United States had mobilized colonial institutions and power to the extent that Native resistance became survival-, not victory-oriented. Tecumseh's analysis of United States colonialism is the basis of contemporary Native nationalism.

VIEW FROM THE CREEK NATION
From the testimony of Phillip Deere, Creek Nation, Oklahoma:

From the early dawn of creation we were known as *Este-mus-asa-so-che*, and later on in years for short we became *Mus-ko-ke*, and when we were in contact with foreign people, they called us Creeks.

I am a medicine man. I am in some ways familiar with the traditions of the Lakota, and have had occasion to discuss with Lakota people their oral history as relates to the 1868 Treaty between the Sioux and the United States. We Creeks, too, have always used the Pipe. The Pipe is sacred to us.

The history of treaty making, not only with Lakotas but for all Indians, is well understood to recognize nations. It is well known throughout the whole country that a treaty was not to be broken, and it was our understanding it would not be. Provisions of treaties were misunderstood by Indian people. The only thing that was understood was the land part of a treaty, such as boundary lines. Same way with the Lakota people. They understood that this piece of land was to belong to them, "as long as the sun rises, and the river flows, and the grass grows," that this land was going to belong to the Indian Nation.

In the Lakota Nation, the sun was going to rise on Lakota land, and it was going to set on Lakota land. That is the same understanding that my people had. Though we were not in contact with Lakota people, we understood the same thing. Then the treaty making days were here, that was our understanding. There has been a misunderstanding there. The white man looks at the treaty in one way, and the Indian looks at it in another way. When we mention, "as long as the sun rises, and the river flows, and the grass grows," what does the white man think when he hears that? What does the government think when he hears that? Indians have a different way of interpreting that.

As you know or everybody knows that this was said orally, before even a treaty was signed. It may not be in the treaty, but this is well understood by the Indian people what the meaning of this means. We Indian people closely relate to nature. Sitting here, you are looking at that sun, you are looking at that grass, you are looking at that river that flows. That was the understanding we have always had. Without anyone telling us, this was our understanding that we are part of the nature.

Anytime the government broke and violated the treaty, to this day, an Indian walking down the streets of Lincoln is looking at the sun. He is looking at that grass. He is looking at that water that flowed. That was our understanding when we made treaties with the United States government.

My interest in the Fort Laramie Treaty is nothing different from any other Indian treaty. It promises in there that a certain tract of land belongs to this Indian, and that they would govern themselves, they would live traditionally, separate from the white man's ways. This was clearly understood, even from the very beginning when we first contacted the European people. It was well said that there are two canoes. We ride in one canoe, and the European people ride in another. This means that one person

74

cannot ride in two canoes. We have our own way of life. We have our own tradition that we are going to live. We had our own government. We had our own way which we cannot compare to the system of the white man. Therefore, it was well understood by my brothers in the New York state when they presented the two-roll wampum belt to the first settlers. That also told them that there are two ways of life, and that one man cannot live those two lives. They have to stay on their side and we stay on our side.

My people made a treaty with the United States in 1790. I am a descendant of those people who made this treaty and I have a tribal ground that was set up since times immemorial. After the treaty signing, we got the same promises as the Lakota. We clearly understand that these treaties were violated.

Phillip Deere, Creek, American Indian Movement leader at the First International Treaty Conference, June 1974. Photo by Michelle Vignes

By the acts of Congress from time to time, we have found that grass failed to grow, rivers stopped running, according to white man's ways. We are believers in the truth. Once we make a promise we want to keep it. We had laws here, but none of our Indian people ever stood behind bars. Every nation has some type of law. Indian people had law, our own Indian law. Majority rule does not have any meaning to an Indian. A leader, a person holding position did not have to have the majority vote in the Indian way. There was no such thing as election. Different nations had different ways. Yet, they still did not have this majority rule. Most Indians became tribal leaders, earned their leadership. Some leaders became a leader by birth, which means when I say by birth, no man has the power to give you so much authority. You are born with it, which means there is only one which causes this woman to bear a child. There is only one that causes you to live which no man can say is wrong. If I am born, according to my clan, to be a leader, that I cannot help. I have to hold that position. That is how strong the Indian people believe in their traditional ways.

Some treaty signers might have been the rightful people to sign the treaty. Others, I would say, were not the proper people to represent the people, according to the Indian way. Everything in the treaty was not supposed to be one sided. It was supposed to go equal. But in later years we found out that there may have been some provisions of that treaty that could even change the treaty in which without the consent of the people, laws have been passed.

There was a time, when they signed a treaty that nobody, no country, could pass the law on that nation of people. They governed themselves. They run their own government. They made their own rules. They followed their own system of government which means that we could not get over the fence and we could not be equal to the foreign people that we were in contact with, the people that we made agreements with. It was agreed and it was our understanding that we would govern ourselves. We would be independent, separate from this new nation. That was the understanding of the Indian people.

There were more than three hundred nations living here within the present boundary lines of the United States and there never was a nation that went to another nation and tried to govern them. Every nation governed themselves. This was thought to be understood before a treaty was even made. The Six Nations believed in the two roll wampum. The Five Nations believed in the law of love, peace and respect. I do not like the term, "Five Civilized Tribes." The entire United States only knows one civilization, which means that the Indian people are not civilized people. They are considered as savages by law until we accept their type of civilization. So when they say "Five Civilized Tribes," it is only a short word telling the people that they accepted the white man's ways.

If the whole world understood the law of love, peace, and respect, it is my firm belief that we would be a lot better off. This was the natural law of our people. No other law can replace it. Not even a treaty can replace it. This was mentioned many, many times before the treaties were signed but our people were in a lack of understanding what that treaty provided for. The only thing that we were told, that we were going to have a certain piece of land where we could live and govern ourselves. Other provisions of the law we did not understand. If my ancestors had understood it, they wouldn't even have signed it. The treaty signers, the first ones were traditional people. If they knew what was in there, they may not have even signed it. If they knew what was meant in that treaty, they would have been in disagreement but they didn't know.

Indians did not know what the Interior Department was and as late as 1916, my own people went to Washington to see the Commission of Indian Affairs and came back and reported that they had seen the President of the United States. That shows how much they knew about the Interior Department and the Bureau of Indian Affairs and the government officials. That these Indian people did not know, with the lack of understanding, they were taken advantage of.

All the treaties, you will see, beginning from early times, none of the Indians could speak English enough to understand. So the leaders of these people had to put down their x mark showing that they couldn't read or write English. Therefore, the treaty was not understood by the Indian. All these years, even this very minute that we are in court, we are in court here because we don't understand these treaties. Not the way the government has explained it to us now. We don't understand it. Congress passes a law yesterday, and it becomes effective the next two years. The full blood

Indian will not understand it until that law is enforced on him. That is where we stand today. The mixed blood, they may understand it, but that is not the kind of people that the government dealt with from the beginning. The Indian the government dealt with had his own culture, own language, and was not interested in the value system of the white man because they are related to the Mother Earth. The creation is more important than all the gold you can find, all the oil wells that you can have. The land is the most important thing to an Indian. If gold was important, different nations would have fought over Black Hills, but they did not.

When I talk about Indians, I always explain myself. I am talking about Indian's Indian, not the white man's Indian, not the Indian that the white man made an Indian. I am talking about the one who understands the tradition, his custom, his language, understands the Indian ways. He is the Indian to me and the one who holds on to his Indian ways, and still has all the love for nature and the Mother Earth, this is an Indian. When the Indian picks up the white man's way, forgets that the earth is so sacred and that all life has been derived from this Mother Earth, when he forgets that, I don't even place him as a white man. He may be even worse than a white man whenever an Indian does that. I am of this earth. My ancestors came out of this earth. When my mother brought me into this world, no one else can claim her my mother. I claim her my mother because I came out of her. The same thing with land to an Indian.

We are the evidence of the western hemisphere. We have every bit of our love to go to our Mother Earth and the nature from which we derive. Christianity is something else which was brought on us. A lot of us believe in it. We understand it. We know what is written in the good book, but our religion, we hold fast to because it is nothing but the Indian's right that he obey the Great Spirit. There is no such thing as a Sabbath day for an Indian. Every day is holy. Every time he rises in the morning and sees the sun come up, he is thankful for that sun to come up. Moon, the stars, everything that your eyes can see is respected by Indians every day of life.

When our people made treaties with the government, they are believers in the truth. They trust one another. We Indians don't have to have witness, for our word is good, and it has always been that way. Being friendly to a person, it has always been known that this Indian will do anything for you if he is your friend. He is the one that will stick with you and he will not break that. We took it that all people lived that kind of a life and that they all believed that way. My ancestors who first signed the treaties thought that. In order to show us that they are friendly, they came to my people.

This is something that doesn't even look important, but this little piece of metal here took the land of Georgia, Alabama, and parts of Mississippi. This was given to the Indian people, especially some of the leaders of the nations, those that they understood to be the leaders were given to them. Later on a piece of paper given to sign gave away land, portions of land, and continued to go on until time came that the Removal Act was passed and that they had to move into the now known Oklahoma. The same government that is today was existing then when this happened. The same government dealt with the Lakota people, and how many such things as this was given to them. I heard their testimony of buffalos vanishing. In exchange for buffalos, they were given cattle. How many times, when naturally we had them for thousands of years before the white man came here. This cow giving thing, the annuities, was not an everlasting one, when nature could provide for us. How could any man come and replace what we had?

What can the government do to erase their guilt of massacre such as Wounded Knee? Like my own people who were hurt so much, the Massacre of Sand Creek, people that were driven from their homes, barefoot in snow, bleeding, dying, freezing, how could anyone heal that scar that the Indian person has in his heart? How much government money would it take to heal that scar that I have in my heart? The descendants of Wounded Knee, how would they ever be healed of that scar? No way. There is no money that would take the place of the lives that were lost in Wounded Knee. In our modern times, our Indian people still believe in their treaty, and that this treaty was violated.

What other ways do we have? What must we do? I have sought legal channels. I am not an attorney, but I am well acquainted with my own Indian land laws, and I find there is no legal way for my people. There is no legal channel. There is no place for us to be called equal. Citizenship was passed on us, therefore, they tell us the treaty making days are over. Twenty point solution papers which concern the treaties were presented to President Nixon who rejected them. But we take it they are still treaties because they are under a solemn guarantee. These treaties still yet exist. You can erase it by another law, but by the Indian's heart that treaty is still there because that was the true belief that the Indian had, that this land would belong to us. It would remain here as a nation, that we would govern our own selves and we would live as we pleased.

If we could live like the white man, we would not have even made the treaty. There would have been no need for a treaty. All we had to do was jump into your boat and go down the stream, but we couldn't. This was well known when we first met the European people and that is how come we had a treaty.

Now we have been told several times that we cannot negotiate on treaties, that we can't talk about treaties. To us if there isn't treaties, there isn't a United States, because it took treaties to make such a big nation as the United States. If it hadn't been for treaties, there might not have been any United States. By one treaty after another, land was turned over to them, and it became a big nation.

I say that we believe in the truth and it appears that this has nothing to do with the Lakota people, but it still has something to do with treaty making. Lakota people are my brothers. They are my kind, and I have every right to speak up for him, also.

INDIAN-WHITE RELATIONS
Wilbur Jacobs

This discussion on Native-white relations came as a response to a series of questions leading Professor Jacobs to tell of his research and its bearing on historic contacts between Native peoples and whites.

One of my most recent investigations was a comparative study of the impact of European frontiers upon Australia, New Guinea, and North America. This analysis revealed what happened to Native peoples as Europeans invaded their territories and converted land areas to missions, farms, ranches, mining claims, and towns. I visited Indian reservations, aboriginal reserves in Australia on the mainland and on islands, and the interior Sepik River towns in the rain forests of New Guinea. Some Native peoples have survived the invading frontiers of Europeans and some still maintain a degree of sovereignty over their own affairs.

When I edited the letters of Francis Parkman, author of *The Oregon Trail*, I traced Parkman's journey of 1846 from Independence, Missouri, to Fort Laramie and into the basin of the Medicine Bowl where he lived with the Oglala Sioux people. In preparing to edit the book I talked with modern Sioux people and studied ethnology, archaeology, and Sioux history. I was especially interested in the nineteenth-century Sioux because Parkman was one of the first to compare the Sioux to other Indian peoples as a scholar in comparative ethnology. He studied the Sioux of the 1840's in order to understand the life style of the Iroquois of the 1640's. It was important to me as a specialist in early American and frontier history to understand Parkman's methods. I could then appreciate his intimacy with the Sioux people and see parallels between his accounts of Sioux culture and his portrayals of other Indian life styles.

However, I have become a Parkman critic because of the racist themes that appear throughout his history, *France and England in North America*. At the same time Parkman, sometimes called America's greatest historian, did give his readers an understanding of American Indian heroism in resisting the white advance. It was through study of Parkman and his writings that I came to have a deep appreciation of the richness of Indian culture, the differences and similarities between such Indian peoples as the Sioux and the Six Nations Iroquois. This experience enabled me to see more clearly the way in which European frontiers altered native cultures in various periods of history.

We can, for example, now discern in the history of the United States distinct patterns of Indian-white relations which heretofore have not been fully recognized. These patterns of contact and withdrawal are also found in history of Native-white relations in the Pacific Islands, in New Zealand and in Australia.

In the first stage of white contact friendly relations very often developed with whites because of Native hospitality and gifts offered by whites. We find evidence of this in our very early records, from the accounts of Columbus, and the early settlers at Jamestown and Plymouth colony. Traditional customs of sharing and kindliness to newcomers among Indians was often misinterpreted by whites unaccustomed to Indian ways of thinking and acting.

The friendly atmosphere soon disappeared when Europeans sought Native land and often took it by force. A second stage in these relationships emerged as an era of conflict, disputes and open warfare. The strongest of the tribes sometimes were able to hold back the white invader for many years. As late as 1750 the Six Nations Iroquois held the balance of power between France and England in North America. By sheer military power, by diplomacy (a policy of neutrality), the Iroquois maintained their land base, their paramount role in the Great Lakes fur trade, and their cultural integrity. Less powerful tribes were easily overwhelmed by waves of European settlements, especially along the Atlantic Coast.

As this second era gradually comes to a climax (an era of several decades or as long as a half century), a third stage becomes evident as Native people are engulfed by a sea of white invaders. First came the explorers and missionaries; then the traders, miners, agricultural settlers. These are followed by railroads and pockets of urban civilization. It is in this period, the third stage, in which Native people often develop a scorn for their own customs in an era of depopulation and despondence. Some scholars have written about a process of deculturalization that takes place when Christianity is introduced. Traditional life styles at this time may almost completely disappear. For instance, the Chumash Indians of California, who occupied the Southern California coastline from San Luis Obispo to Malibu Canyon, virtually disappeared. The Franciscan Fathers, with the encouragement of the Spanish Crown, forced the Chumash into a mission labor force. Instead of learning to be Spanish Catholic farmers, the Chumash became victims of forced labor, inadequate rations, harsh treatment, and disease which finally killed nearly all of them. (Sherburn F. Cook's book, *The Conflict Between the California Indian and White Civilization* gives the details on California native depopulation causes.)

Many native societies had great difficulty in surviving at all in the wake of the European invasion. Take, for example, the Arawak of Haiti. We estimate now that the population of these people on the island of Haiti was some eight million in 1492. By the 1600's the population of Native people here was reduced to zero.

For those aboriginal societies who somehow survived the onslaught a fourth stage is discernable. Among Indian people it is sometimes called a Native American renaissance. This kind of rebirth of Native culture is especially evident among the Sioux today (as in this courtroom) in whom we can see vigor and pride in cultural traditions. We can observe the rebirth, or renaissance very clearly in the cultural history of the Six Nations Iroquois, especially the Seneca, with the emergence of the prophet Handsome Lake about 1800. We now study the Iroquois in terms of their civilization's decline and rebirth as does Anthony Wallace, the anthropologist, in his fine book, *Death and Rebirth of the Seneca*. Thus this fourth stage in the history of Native-white relations is oftentimes the era of cultural rebirth in which Native people unite and turn again to the tribal inheritance as a source of inspiration.

In studying Native-white relations, I have found that the cultural identity and even the physical survival of a tribal people is closely associated with possession of their landed heritage. To the extent that tribal societies maintain physical possession of their land, they survive as a cultural entity. They have an identification with the past that is linked with the land. Those tribal peoples in this country who have been dispossessed have had enormous difficulty in maintaining tribal traditions, although many of them have struggled valiantly and continue to do so.

In terms of Native-white relations in this country, there were two methods of exterminating Indians. One was to kill them outright and the other was to take away their land and in the process of doing that, to take away their food supply. My conviction is that the physical dispossessing of the American Indians is very closely associated with the whole question of the survival of the American Indian people and the cultural inheritance of Indian people is tied to the land.

I have analyzed patterns of dispossession that were established in the early period and set a precedent for the dispossession of the Sioux at a later date. One of the Chapters in *Dispossessing of the American Indian* shows how the first Indian boundary line was established as a result of the British proclamation of 1763, how that boundary line was extended to include the northern frontier and southern frontier, to separate white civilization from Indian civilization. The Proclamation line did represent an attempt by the British government to provide a sanctuary for Indian people, but it was regarded with hostility by colonial land speculators such as George Washington. That boundary line was a precedent for establishing another boundary line at the Mississippi River in 1830 for the removal of woodland peoples. The boundary line idea was eventually extended to separate Indian people further from white people by the creation of the reservation system. The arrogant white assumption that Indian people should be separated from white civilization by a boundary line provides an understanding of the origins of the reservation system.

The separation of whites and Indians was a concept supported by early presidents including George Washington and Thomas Jefferson. It was later implemented by Andrew Jackson. And the concept was partly responsible for setting up boundary lines for reservations in the 1840's and 1850's. The idea of blocking out the Sioux behind the boundary line of a large reservation resulted in the Sioux Treaty of 1868.

One of the basic attitudes that Anglo Americans and Europeans developed over a period of years was that Indian people, as evidenced in their unique method of fighting and making war, were treacherous and unreliable. Europeans who fought with armies marching against each other in full view did not understand the value of Indian methods of self-defense such as camouflage and surprise attack. Eventually the United States military leaders took up the Indian commando style of fighting. Roger's Rangers, late in the colonial period, were carbon copies of the best woodland warriors.

Largely as a result of Indian techniques of making war, there was a misconception of Indian chiefs as underhanded, treacherous leaders. For example, Plymouth Colony, very suspicious of King Philip, demanded that he disarm his people and put himself at the mercy of Plymouth authorities. He refused to do so because he regarded himself as an independent leader of the sovereign Wampanoag Nation. Although the whites shed the first blood in King Philip's War, he was regarded by New Englanders as a treacherous conspirator. The role of treacherous conspirator is given to almost every one of the great historic Indian chiefs.

As a result of the ugly stereotypes of Indians that Americans came to have, we find that oftentimes there was support for wars of extermination. This was especially true during the colonial era when overkill of Indians was justified on the basis of conspiratorial tactics used by skulking tribesmen. Several of the seventeenth century Indian wars carried on by the Puritans and other colonists were wars of extermination. Indian people along the coast lived in villages with stored up food supplies so it was relatively easy to carry on scorched earth wars to wipe out town after town of native peoples.

As the colonists moved into the interior, the survivors fled before them. Now the whites met powerful inland confederacies who often adopted members of those tribes that had been defeated. The inland tribes, east of the Appalachians had the great American forest at their back and could easily live by hunting, food gathering and fishing if their corn supplies were destroyed. The result was that the whites turned to the expedient of treaty making in the eighteenth century. The alternative of making treaties with Indian tribes (some of whom were allied to the French during the period before 1763) was a necessity. These powerful inland woodland tribes such as the Cherokees, the Iroquois, and the Chicasaws could not be conquered or dispossessed. Yet there was still the tendency to treat with Indians as potential conspirators. Pontiac's uprising, even to this day is called a "conspiracy."

When the whites reached the Great Plains, they confronted the Sioux. These people, like the powerful inland peoples, at first could not be dispossessed. Nor was there any way of exterminating them except by killing off their food supply, the buffalo, and certain American military leaders advocated just that policy. Meanwhile, as with the Cherokee at an earlier period, the treaty-making tactic came into existence.

There are few examples in all this treaty making that Indians were regarded as heroic leaders rather than as treacherous negotiators. The point I make is that historically there was a refusal to recognize Indian noble qualities of leadership involving personal qualities of generosity, courage, hospitality, kindness, integrity, honor, intelligence, perception, and greatness. The noble "savage" was a myth. This is an idea perpetuated even today by writers in American literature. And in history there is only recently a tendency to give more space in recognizing the outstanding qualities of leaders such as Tecumseh or Pontiac. These were great Indian leaders because they understood and perceived the extent of the damage that had come to their people as a result of contact with whites. This was undoubtedly one of the reasons that they were convincing leaders among their own Indian people.

Although there always were the Indian haters in our society, we should also keep in mind that there were also many Anglo-Americans who appreciated the finer qualities of Indian character. There were also whole segments of American society that objected to harsh treaty terms given to Indians and other injustices they suffered.

One such sympathetic white writer has said that no people in the world understand their true national interest better than Indians. I agree. And we should point out that in the treaty negotiations Indian people constantly sought peaceful solutions to disputes and conflicts with whites. Indeed, many of the treaties had their origin in overtures from Indians who had a sincere hope of keeping the peace. Throughout our history of Indian-white relations we have often overlooked the great tradition of peacemaking and peacekeeping among Indian peoples.

One reason for our neglect of this aspect of Indian culture is that the Anglo-American people and their leaders have had very little knowledge of the principles by which Indian people governed themselves. Indians were regarded as savages, as survivors of a kind of savage life that whites had overcome in the past. This attitude, of course, gave strength to the idea of removing savages from the path of civilization's progress westward. I call this the historic conquistador attitude. It is associated with our "conquest" of the continent. There is thus reason to believe that the conquistador outlook has resulted in the maltreatment of Indian people and in the destruction of many of our resources. As a consequence of our preoccupation with development and progress we have not understood American Indian views on conservation and protection of the environment. We have had no real appreciation of the Indian concept of mother earth.

Indian community occupation of the land as opposed to white division of land into areas of private ownership has been another source of misunderstanding. Very early white colonials in America questioned Indian rights to the land (which was held in common). Of course Native people never accepted the white concept of fee simple title to the land. Land, as Tecumseh regarded it, was like air and sunshine and could not be sold by individuals to the whites.

The Indian conception of the land was tied very closely to their physical subsistence from plants, wildlife, streams, and ocean beaches. The natural source of food was not to be destroyed. Environmental concern among Indian peoples was a part of their religion.

Major tribes of the California area, sometimes mistakenly called "digger Indians," moved in triblets from area to area (traditional hunting and food gathering areas recognized for individual tribes) to take advantage of natural produce including nutritious roots which were dug from the ground. The triblets were on the move during specific seasons of the year. In one season these Indians lived by the seashore and harvested different types of shellfish. During another part of the year they lived in forested territories and hunted deer. And in a different season they roamed in an area where rabbits and other small animals could be caught and where various types of roots, berries, and nuts could be gathered. In a very fragile semi-desert area they lived without disturbing the ecological balance. They lived this way for centuries, exercising a type of population control, so as not to kill off their source of food supply. And they numbered in California as many as 300,000 the greatest population density north of the Valley of Mexico.

These things were never really understood by whites in our history. They tended to see Indian communal land ownership as a parallel to communal land ownership advocated by radical leaders in Europe. After the Marxist revolts in the 1840's, there was a tendency to associate Indian lifestyles with communism.

American frontier ideas of progress have been partly conditioned by several influential writers. One of these, Frederic Jackson Turner, wrote an essay in 1892, called "The Significance of the Frontier in American History." This one essay caused a virtual rewriting of all American history textbooks. In a sense, Turner echoed frontier attitudes of white people. That is perhaps why his work had such an impact upon historical writing. Turner perceived the attitudes of white pioneers. The gist of the interpretation is that American attitudes of self-reliance and self-government are associated with the pioneer advance as it moved westward from the Appalachian frontier to the Mississippi Valley and to the Pacific Coast. The prosperity of America, the high standard of living, is a result of the gifts of unlimited land, unlimited resources, and this has given America a higher standard of living.

There is much truth in the Turner Frontier Thesis, but it is, in many ways, a white racist interpretation of history because it portrays Indians as mere savage obstacles to the westward movement of white civilization. Indians are viewed in this concept of westward advance as forcing pioneers to consolidate together for military defense. Out of this "togetherness" grew institutions of self-government. The interpretation of Turner's also tends to discount the role of Mexican peoples in the development of the American Southwest, and offers a complete misunderstanding about the role of black people in our past. The interpretation, however, still persists, especially the frontier-sectional argument that the history of America is largely the history of compromise and rivalry between the larger American geographical sections or regions. It appears in almost all our college history textbooks.

Basic to the theoretical scaffolding in the Turner frontier theory is also conquistador attitude. This was the attitude of many of our leaders in westward expansion. The "savages" were in the way of the whites as they moved west. Not unexpectedly, many of our leaders were hostile to Indians. Senators like Thomas Hart Benton exhibited a particularly anti-Indian posture. Benton wrote and talked enthusiastically about American expansionism. He seemingly regarded Indians as nonpersons.

Pioneer Americans and their representatives in Congress have historically held the idea that it was their manifest destiny to occupy this continent and that somehow the Christian religion and Protestant American Christianity ordained this. It was their destiny to own this vast land and it was their God-given right to move across the continent from sea to sea.

This frontiersman outlook toward the land, its resources and Indian people has been a vital part of our justification for taking over a large part of North America. And Americans have been historically wasteful in the utilization of the continent's resources. Today we are concerned about energy conservation because of a history of careless and wasteful consumption of our landed wealth. The pioneer asked, "why should I do something for my descendants; have they done anything for me?"

The philosophy of exploiting Indians and our natural wealth throughout our history, was tinctured by a religious outlook of pious justification for our actions. We sometimes linked the Christian religion to God-given natural rights for each Yankee individual.

The great English philosopher of the seventeenth century, John Locke, associated ideas of property ownership with agriculture. The concept of natural rights, life, liberty and property (Jefferson later changed property to the pursuit of happiness in the *Declaration of Independence*) has been incorporated into the Constitution of the United States. These were sacred, natural rights for all citizens. The exception was Indian people.

Indians were regarded as nomadic, that is, Indian people were viewed as non-agricultural peoples, and therefore could prove no evidence of land ownership. The idea of dispossession, then, was given a certain pious Christian impetus through the sacred doctrine of natural rights.

We are not always aware of the fact that Native American virtues are echoed in some of our hero figures in American literature and in motion pictures. The figure in James Fenimore Cooper's novel, Hawkeye, is as much Indian as he is white. The reason he is admired is because he has all the virtues of a great Indian warrior of the woodland area. Mountain men in American history are regarded as heroic because they are part Indian. From the paintings of Remington you see Indian traders of the mountain areas who were native traders. The cowboy figure has many of the characteristics of Native Americans—reverence for the land, sincerity and honesty, appreciation of the beauty of American wilderness, forthrightness and manliness. The great psychiatrist, Carl Jung, said that he could always detect the Indian part from the character of his American patients, even though they weren't of direct Indian blood. Rather he could detect the influence of Native American cultures upon the formation of the character of Americans. The Sioux, as much as any other Indian nation, have had this kind of influence upon our culture.

The Sioux revered the buffalo. In the 1840's Henry Chatillon, a Sioux guide of the white buffalo hunters, was disappointed in the hunters for reveling in shooting every buffalo possible, despite Chatillon's warning not to kill cows and calves. The principles of ecological preservation was strong among the Sioux. Most European and Anglo-American writers have not understood attitudes that Indian people have had toward animal life and flora and fauna. I do not pretend to be an authority on Sioux

84

religion. But my understanding is that they, like most other Indian peoples, think in terms of man as a part of this earth in the same sense as animals and plants and mountains and sacred lakes were a part of the earth. Almost everything in Indian society has religious overtones. Killing animals, hunting, has religious overtones.

The movements of nomadic tribes were regular and recognized by other tribes. While Sioux people moved from place to place covering large areas, their movements were in terms of traditional patterns recognized by other Native people. If there is indication of title in fee simple it seems to me, it's the designation of geographical landmarks and sacred places by Native people all over this country. If there is any indication of sovereignty and ownership of the land, it is in that, and is something that our legal system has never really recognized.

Europeans who came to this land had respect and understanding of Native geographical boundaries and controls to the extent that Native American people were able to resist the white advance, but where Indian people were not able to put up military resistance to white seizure of their land, these Native claims for their land were virtually ignored. In the history of the Six Nations Iroquois, they maintained a balance of power during much of the colonial period. During this period of territorial integrity, the Six Nations Iroquois were respected, but by 1768, the Iroquois were forced to sign the Treaty of Fort Stanwix and had to relinquish claims to a vast area of land.

It is now recognized by some of our leading writers in early American history that the confederation form of government which was adopted in 1781 by signing the Articles of Confederation was modeled in part on Indian confederacies, not only the Six Nations Iroquois, but also the Cherokee, Creek, Choctaw, Chickasaw and other great nations of Indian people. Benjamin Franklin was present at many treaty councils at which Iroquois members were represented. Beyond this, there is an interesting phenomena that most Anglo historians have overlooked. Jesuit missionaries, in their writings of contacts with the Six Nations Iroquois in the seventeenth century, wrote in great detail about Iroquois institutions of government. They described how Iroquois statesmen conducted themselves with the decorum of Roman senators. These *Jesuit Relations*, as they are called, were very popular reading in France in the seventeenth and early eighteenth centuries, and influenced some of the great French philosophers, such as Voltaire and Rousseau. The Indian ideals of democracy and self-government, the freedom of movement and confederation are found in the writings of these great French philosophers who in turn were read by the writers of the American constitution and those members of the Confederation Congress who drew up the Articles of Confederation. Direct contact with Indian people also influenced the formation of the confederation congress, when Indian leaders lectured colonial leaders on their weakness and their need for a confederated government to provide self-protection.

The Sioux, too, had a complete system of self-government, in terms of disciplinary action in case of criminal actions, in terms of distribution of food, in terms of the care of older people, in terms of the care of disabled people, in terms of negotiations with other Indian nations and with white people, in terms of providing for themselves over a period of years, in terms of maintaining their livelihood. Practically every segment of modern life today has a parallel in Sioux society—orphanages, old people's homes, social security, medical health and psychiatric health, and family structure. The social services that are provided in a complex society today have parallels in the Sioux tribal and confederation form of government.

American historians have tended to regard the Sioux as a nomadic people without the ownership of land, symbolized by the remarks of Theodore Roosevelt, that the

Sioux Territory was nothing but a big hunting preserve and that this should be made available to white people for settling.

Most of our presidents can be identified with policies or actions which were hostile to the American Indians. For example, George Washington's father was known by an Indian name which signified destroyer of Indian villages. And George inherited that Indian name among Indian people. Moreover, George justified having the name by his action in ordering the destruction of Iroquois towns and food supplies during the American Revolution. Thomas Jefferson, the great philosophical leader of American democracy, was an originator of the concept of Indian removal. Andrew Jackson, the father of the modern American Democratic Party, was the implementor of the removal plan. Abraham Lincoln ordered the execution of a large number of Indians at Mankato, Minnesota, as a result of a Sioux uprising. In studying American history we thus have a kind of upside down view of what happened to the Indians. Very often we must, in the search for the truth, approach history from the bottom up rather than from the top down. It is very hard for traditional Anglos to do this.

By studying hundreds of treaties and by studying reports and negotiations that resulted from those treaties we can summarize white objectives in dealing with Indians:
1. To acquire native lands.
2. To persuade Native American people to be friends and live in friendship with white colonies, or in many cases to be allies, or what might be called allied soldiers in the struggle against other European powers.
3. To supply furs to the trading companies.
4. In some areas, to enslave Indians or to impress them into a labor force. Around 1740, there were some 14,000 Indians who were slaves in the colony of South Carolina. Also, the Puritans had Native slaves, often called "servants." In New England it was a practice to ship Indians to new locations so they were far from their own people.

In short, the white man was concerned about the native person in terms of incorporating him into the labor force, to exploit him as a slave or field hand or worker, to exploit him as a gatherer of furs, to take his land, to have him as a peaceful ally, or to bring him into the orbit of the colonial armies that were fighting for imperialistic expansion into the interior.

The Indian Removal Act of 1830 was a long-term result of westward expansion of the Anglo-American frontier of settlement in which the Indian tribes of the interior came face to face with the agricultural cutting edge of settlement. The result was that white farmers cast eyes upon the superb land owned by Cherokee and other nations of the "five civilized tribes" of the southeast. The question of removing the tribes had been considered by some of our eminent writers and leaders for a number of years before the removal actually took place.

Most explorers who had been into the Plains area were convinced that it would never be settled by Anglo-American farmers, and such explorers as Zebulon Montgomery Pike brought back information that this was a great American desert. For years every map had this designation of the American Southwest and much of the Great Plains area. The government reasoned that the Indian people could be pushed out there and forever solve "the Indian problem." The proposition was first set forth by Thomas Jefferson. Echoing George Washington, Thomas Jefferson said that a boundary line should be set up to remove Indian people beyond, with trading posts on the edge, so that the Indians would trade and acquire an indebtedness and that the indebtedness could be used to acquire their lands without war. As Anglo population would increase and tiers of states and territories were added, the Indians would be overwhelmed. That is the proposition of Jefferson which was implemented by the legislation of 1830 in the presidency of Andrew Jackson.

Georgia settlers were the immediate cause of removal due to conflicts with the Cherokee Nation. At first the United States government resisted Georgia's proposal of removal as outrageous. The state of Georgia argued that the Cherokee had been changed into an agricultural people by the United States government, doing a disservice to the state of Georgia. Actually the Cherokee had been superb farmers from the days of pre-European history. Indeed the Cherokee and their allies gave the first settlers Indian maize and all the plants and garden products that sustained them.

During the removal, the Cherokee people were herded into compounds and forced to live under conditions of starvation and disease in order to sign articles of removal. When reading the details of these concentration camps, it reminds you of some of the recent horrors of German concentration camps.

The Delaware people, the great and peaceful allies of William Penn in 1680, were also removed to the far western frontier. In 1846, explorers described them as greedy scavengers of the Plains, dangerous because they were starving, roaming in small bands to keep alive in the hostile Great Plains area. Even today we can understand the plight of the Delaware who were among the great agriculturalists and a very religious people.

A series of Acts in the early nineteenth century called "Indian Trade and Intercourse Acts" established government trading posts or "factories." The stated objective was humanitarian, to help Indian people avoid being cheated by unscrupulous traders.

But in fact, if you read the records as I have in the National Archives, you will find that one of the chief items of trade at these government posts was liquor. It would almost seem that the official government policy at these factories was to drown the Indians in a Niagara of liquor.

There is no more heroic story than the saga of the struggle of the woodland Indian nations from 1607 to 1830 in holding off white armies, European and American. These woodland Indians stood off the best troops that the United States had in an effort to preserve their homeland. When Frederick Jackson Turner, the historian, wrote that these Indians were an obstacle to the westward movement of whites he was telling the truth. In a later period the Sioux Nation performed the same task in holding back the American occupation of the Louisiana Purchase area.

It is difficult for us to understand the apprehension Indian people had in coping with certain sadistic American military figures. The Sioux as well as other Plains Indians were aware of white cruelty in the early 1860's. They remembered the series of rash actions on the part of the Colorado militia which resulted in the massacre of Cheyennes at Sand Creek in 1864. Throughout the history of Indian-white relations Indian people were often forced to negotiate in an atmosphere of fear and apprehension.

During the treaty making by the U.S. Army in the 1860's the Sioux and other tribes had apprehensions that were very real about their security, the possibility that their food supply, the buffalo, might be exterminated, or the possibility that their land base might be curtailed. They feared the sea of white invaders supported by a powerful military establishment.

In one of the massacres soldiers actually skinned the bodies of native warriors and used the tanned skin for various personal objects. When we think of such incidents, it is less difficult for us to place ourselves in the posture of nineteenth century Indian people and understand their dilemma, to feel their fears and to see the obstacles they faced. They wanted peace; they were highly motivated in seeking peace. They wanted, above all, the kind of a treaty with the United States that would insure peace and security for their families and children.

Photo by Melinda Rorick

THIS CONCERNS US ALL

Testimony of William Bird, Cherokee Medicine Man, interpreted from Cherokee to English by Mr. Sam Dry Water:

Mr. Thorne: *Mr. Bird, how old are you?*

He will be 79 January the 1st.

And will you tell us what tribe you belong to, what Nation you belong to?

I am Cherokee.

And where do you live?

Chewey, Oklahoma.

Do you have a position in the Cherokee Nation?

I am a Medicine Man.

What is the position of a Medicine Man in the Cherokee Nation as compared to a spiritual leader in the Lakota Nation?

They are both together. . . .

Do you have an oral history about the Cherokee Nation?

He has oral history from his grandfather; he was on the Trail of Tears.

Can you tell us the oral history that you have about the Cherokee Nation you have learned from your grandfather?

Mr. Nelson: *I'm going to object to this on the ground of relevancy; it's irrelevant.*

The Court: *Overruled; I'll hear it. . . .*

My grandfather told me that when they left their reservation in Georgia, they had their homes there, and they had their own tribal chiefs, their own government, their own everything, and then they were told they had to leave. They didn't, they didn't want to, it was their home, they couldn't understand why, why they had to leave. . . . As we have said before we don't like to bring up this about the Trail of Tears too much.

Can you tell us any more oral history about the Trail of Tears and the resettlement of the Cherokee Nation in Oklahoma?

My grandfather told me, again I'll repeat, the hardships that they had on the Trail of Tears and about people dying. And when we arrived where they wanted us in Oklahoma they had been told that this is going to be your land, you can do what you want to. You can have your own, everything. You can have your own well, game, hunting and fishing. But later it didn't turn out that way.

Can you tell us two things: One, what happened to people on the Trail of Tears in terms of hardship and what happened when you were in Oklahoma so that it didn't turn out that way?

My grandfather told me of people he had seen, the old people, when they would give out on the Trail of Tears. You know, they were afoot. They would just leave them to die.

And what happened in Oklahoma in the land you were told would be yours?

They were told that when they were given this land, when they come to Oklahoma, that this is your land. You do what you want and nobody will interfere with you. His grandfather told him that for a while it was that way but the white man started coming. He remembers two families that come in later on and then they just kept coming. Then they were told that there is a law that has been passed by the white man, but his grandfather and the Cherokees understood this. The white man had not mentioned that would happen. They told them this would be their land. It wasn't the way they said it was.

In the Cherokee way of life, the Cherokee tradition, when a person gives an oath to tell the truth would they ever break that oath or break that promise?

Anytime they told one another that they would do something, they meant just exactly what they said. It was the truth. They would have no intention of breaking it. It would be the truth.

Do the Cherokee at the present time have an area of Mother Earth to use as their own as they did have in Georgia . . . Does the Cherokee Nation as a Nation have an area of land that is their land just as they had an area of land as a Nation when they were in Georgia . . .

We had about forty acres in Tahlequah, in the Cherokee Nation. That is the Cherokee Nation. That is the capital of the Cherokee Nation in Tahlequah, Oklahoma. We have forty acres, we have. This is about all.

I don't know if he would want to answer this and if he does not he certainly doesn't have to; but could you tell us how one becomes a Medicine Man in the Cherokee Nation, what the requirements are for becoming a Medicine Man and the responsibilities of a Medicine Man . . .

He would rather not reveal that. There is a long process of learning and other things. . . .

He may be excused, Your Honor . . .

He wanted to add one thing if you would permit it. We are here because of our Brothers, the Sioux, and somewhere down the line the old folks, the old timers knew that it was coming to this, so we are here now. These are our Brothers. This concerns all of us.

90

PART FOUR

The Sioux-United States Treaty of 1868

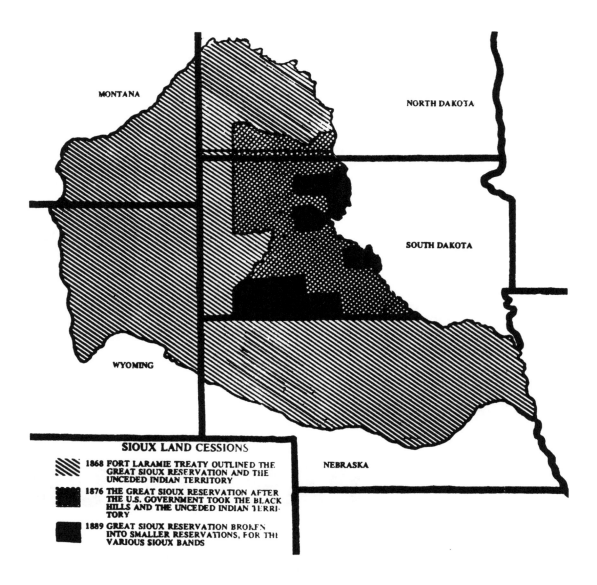

SIOUX LAND CESSIONS

1868 FORT LARAMIE TREATY OUTLINED THE GREAT SIOUX RESERVATION AND THE UNCEDED INDIAN TERRITORY

1876 THE GREAT SIOUX RESERVATION AFTER THE U.S. GOVERNMENT TOOK THE BLACK HILLS AND THE UNCEDED INDIAN TERRITORY

1889 GREAT SIOUX RESERVATION BROKEN INTO SMALLER RESERVATIONS, FOR THE VARIOUS SIOUX BANDS

PILES OF PAPERS IN THE TRUNK

                      And the understanding
which I understood at the time after my grandfather died,
August 12, 1912,
                at that age,
                   before that time
my grandmother, she didn't speak English
or no foreign language.
              She always keep track
of her husband's papers, and I was there with her,
learned a little touch of the foreign language.
When she have to look for papers, why it just come
in like the alphabet.
              So here's George Washington
and all
       down there.

                    Then you have her looking
anything
            come like from this foreign language,

                                        they call
                                        themselves
                                        the
                                        United States.

That time I understood that they were not united
here,
and they called them states.
                        And my country, which I learned
is my country,
            and they call the United States. And right
there,   how could I learn,
        how could they understand that these states
        be united in their language,
                            compared
to my physical
        and spiritual experiences.

At this time
my grandfather is talking
                    about like here
                    in court like this here.
The practice
in that short time in 1868 treaty-
that was a very short time,
and to this time I understand
there were piles and piles of paper
                        And that time
at that short period
my grandfather had that pile of papers
in the trunk
full. And my grandmother
                    always looking through
                    those papers,
and at that short time,
                    maybe it's a work of God
that take me to look into her trunk
and see what the papers were for.
                                —Henry Crow Dog

FORT LARAMIE TREATY OF 1868

April 29, 1868; Treaty between the United States of America and different tribes of Sioux Indians; Concluded April 29 et. seq., 1868; Ratification advised February 16, 1869; Proclaimed February 24, 1869.

Andrew Johnson, President of the United States of America, to all and singular to whom these presents shall come, Greetings:

Whereas a treaty was made and concluded at Fort Laramie, in the Territory of Dakota, on the twenty-ninth day of April, and afterwards, in the year of our Lord one thousand eight hundred and sixty-eight, by and between Nathaniel G. Taylor, William T. Sherman, William S. Harney, John B. Sanborn, S. F. Tappan, C. C. Augur, and Alfred H. Terry, commissioners, on the part of the United States, and Ma-za-poj-kaska, Tah-shun-ka-co-qui-pay, Heh-won-ge-chat, Mah-to-non-pay, Little Chief, Makh-pi-ah-lu-tah, Co-cam-i-ya-ya, Con-te-pe-ta, Ma-wa-tau-ni-hav-ska, Hena-pin-wa-ni-ca, Wah-pah-shaw, and other chiefs and headmen of different tribes of Sioux Indians, on the part of said Indians, and duly authorized there by them, which treaty is in the words and figures following, to wit:

Articles of a treaty made and concluded by and between Lieutenant-General William T. Sherman, General William S. Harney, General Alfred S. Terry, General C. C. Augur, J. B. Henderson, Nathaniel G. Taylor, John B. Sanborn, and Samuel F. Tappan, duly appointed commissioners on the part of the United States and the different bands of the Sioux Nation of Indians, by their chiefs and headmen, whose names are now hereto subscribed, they being duly authorized to act in the premises.

Article I: From this day forward all war between the parties to this agreement shall forever cease. The government of the United States desires peace, and its honor is hereby pledged to keep it. The Indians desire peace, and they now pledge their honor to keep it.

If the bad men among the whites, or among other people subject to the authority of the United States, shall commit any wrong upon the person or property of the Indians, the United States will, upon proof made to the agent and forwarded to the Commissioner of Indian Affairs at Washington city, proceed at once to cause the offender to be arrested and punished according to the laws of the United States, and also reimburse the injured person for the loss sustained.

If the bad men among the Indians shall commit a wrong or depredation upon the person or property of any one, white, black or Indian, subject to the authority of the United States, and at peace therewith, the Indians herein named solemnly agree that they will, upon proof made to their agent and notice by him, deliver up the wrongdoer to the United States, to be tried and punished according to its laws; and in case they willfully refuse to do so, the person injured shall be reimbursed for his loss from the annuities or other moneys due or to become due to them under this or other treaties made with the United States. And the President, on advising with the Commissioner of Indian Affairs, shall prescribe such rules and regulations for ascertaining damages under the provisions of this article as in his judgement may be proper. But no one sustaining loss while violating the provisions of this treaty or the laws of the United States shall be reimbursed.

Article II: The United States agrees that the following district of country, to wit, viz: Commencing on the east bank of the Missouri River where the forty-sixth parallel of north latitude crosses the same; thence along low-water mark down said east bank to a point opposite where the northern line of the State of Nebraska to the one hundred and fourth degree of longitude west from Greenwich, thence north on said meridian to a point where the forty-sixth parallel of north latitude intercepts the same, thence due east along said parallel to the place on the beginning; and in addition thereto, all existing reservations on the east bank of said river shall be, and the same is, set apart for the absolute and undisturbed use and occupation of the Indians herein named, and for such other friendly tribes or individual Indians as from time to time may be willing, with the consent of the United States, to admit amongst them; and the United States solemnly agrees that no persons except those herein designated and authorized so to do, and except such officers, agents and employees of the government as may be authorized to enter upon Indian reservations in discharge of duties enjoined by law, shall ever be permitted to pass over, settle upon, or reside in the territory described in this article, or in such territory that may be added to this reservation for the use of said Indians, and henceforth they will and do hereby relinquish all claims or right in and to any portion of the United States or Territories except such as is embraced within the limits aforesaid, and except as hereinafter provided.

Article III: If it should appear from actual survey or other satisfactory examination of said tract of land that it contains less than one hundred and sixty acres of tillable land for each person who, at the time, may be authorized to reside on it under the provisions of this treaty, and a very considerable number of such persons shall be disposed to commence cultivating the soil as farmers, the United States agrees to set apart, for the use of said Indians, as herein proved, such additional quantity of arable land, adjoining to said reservation, or as near to the same as it can be obtained as may be required to provide the necessary amount.

Article IV: The United States agrees, at its own proper expense, to construct at some place on the Missouri River, near the centre of said reservation, where timber and water may be convenient, the following buildings, to wit: a warehouse, a storeroom for the use of the agent in storing goods belonging to the Indians, to cost not less than twenty five hundred dollars; and an agency building for the residence of the agent to cost not exceeding three thousand dollars; a residence for the physician to cost not more than three thousand dollars; and five other buildings, for a carpenter, farmer, blacksmith, miller, and engineer, each to cost not exceeding two thousand dollars; also a schoolhouse or mission building so soon as a sufficient number of children can be induced by the agent to attend school, which shall not cost exceeding five thousand dollars.

The United States Agrees further to cause to be erected on said reservation, near the other buildings herein authorized, a good steam circular sawmill, with a grist-mill and shingle machine attached to the same, to cost not exceeding eight thousand dollars.

Article V: The United States agrees that the agent for said Indians shall in the future make his home at the agency building; that he shall reside among them, and keep an office open at all times for the purpose of prompt and diligent inquiry into such matters of complaint by and against the Indians as may be presented for investigation under the provisions of their treaty stipulations, as also for the faithful discharge of other duties enjoined him by law. In all cases of depredation on person or property he shall cause the evidence to be taken in writing and forwarded, together with his findings, to the Commissioner of Indian Affairs, whose decision subject to the revision of the Secretary of the Interior, shall be binding on the parties to this treaty.

Article VI: If any individuals belonging to said tribes of Indians, or legally incorporated with them, being the head of a family, shall desire to commence farming, he shall have the privilege to select, in the presence and with the assistance of the agent then in charge, a tract of land within said reservation, not exceeding three hundred and twenty acres in extent, which tract when so selected, certified, and recorded in the "land book," as herein directed, shall cease to be held in common, but the same may be occupied and held in the exclusive possession of the person selecting it, and of his family, so long as he or they may continue to cultivate it.

Any person over eighteen years of age, not being the head of the family, may in like manner select and cause to be certified to him or her, for purposes of cultivation a quantity of land not exceeding eighty acres in extent, and thereupon be entitled to the exclusive possession of the same as above directed.

For each tract of land so selected a certificate, containing a description thereof and the name of the person selecting it, with a certificate endorsed thereon that the same has been recorded, shall be delivered to the party entitled to it by the agent, after the same shall have been recorded by him in a book to be kept in his office, subject to inspection, which said book shall be known as the "Sioux Land Book."

The President may, at any time, order a survey of the reservation, and, when so surveyed, Congress shall provide for protecting the rights of said settlers in their improvements, and may fix the character of the title held by each. The United States may pass such laws on the subject of alienation and descent of property between Indians and their descendants as may be thought proper.

And it is further stipulated that any male Indians over eighteen years of age, of any band or tribe that is or shall hereafter become a party to this treaty, who now is or who shall hereafter become a resident or occupant of any reservation or territory not included in the tract of country designated and described in this treaty for the permanent home of the Indians, which is not mineral land, nor reserved by the United States for special purposes other than Indian occupation, and who shall have made improvements thereon of the value of two hundred dollars or more, and continuously occupied the same as a homestead for the term of three years, shall be entitled to receive from the United States a patent for one hundred and sixty acres of land including his said improvements, the same to be in the form of the legal subdivisions of the surveys of the public lands.

Upon application in writing, sustained by the proof of two disinterested witnesses, made to the register of the local land office when the land sought to be entered is within a land district and when the tract sought to be entered is not in any land district, then upon said application and proof being made to the commissioner of the general land office and the right of such Indian or Indians to enter such tract or tracts of land shall accrue and be perfect from the date of his first improvements thereon, and shall continue as long as he continues his residence and improvements, and no longer.

And any Indian or Indians receiving a patent for the land under the foregoing provisions, shall thereby and from thenceforth become and be a citizen of the United States, and be entitled to all the privileges and immunities of such citizens, and shall, at the same time, retain all his rights to benefits accruing to Indians under this treaty.

Article VII: In order to insure the civilization of the Indians entering into the treaty, the necessity of education is admitted, especially of such of them as are or may be settled on said agricultural reservations, and they therefore pledge themselves to compel their children, male and female, between the ages of six and sixteen years, to attend school; and it is hereby made the duty of the agent for said Indians to see that this stipulation is strictly complied with; and the United States agrees that for every thirty children between said ages who can be induced or compelled to attend school, a house shall be provided and a teacher competent to teach the elementary branches on an English education shall be furnished, who will reside among said Indians, and faithfully discharge his or her duties as a teacher. The provisions of this article to continue for not less than twenty years.

Article VIII: When the head of the family or lodge shall have selected lands and received his certificate as above directed and the agent shall be satisfied that he intends in good faith to commence cultivating the soil for living, he shall be entitled to receive seeds and agricultural implements for the first year, not exceeding in value one hundred dollars, and for each succeeding year he shall continue to farm, for a period of three years more, he shall be entitled to receive seeds and implements as aforesaid, not exceeding in value twenty-five dollars.

And it is further stipulated that such persons as commence farming shall receive instructions from the farmer herein provided for, and whenever more than one hundred persons shall enter upon the cultivation of soil, a second blacksmith shall be provided, with such iron, steel, and other material as may be needed.

Article IX: At any time after ten years from the making of this treaty, the United States shall have the privilege of withdrawing the physician, farmer, miller, blacksmith, carpenter and engineer herein provided for, but in the case of such withdrawal, an additional sum thereafter of ten thousand dollars per annum shall be devoted to the education of said Indians, and the commissioner of Indian Affairs shall, upon careful inquiry into their condition, make such rules and regulations for the expenditure of said sum as will best promote the educational and moral improvement of said tribes.

Article X: In lieu of all sums of money or other annuities provided to be paid to the Indians herein named, under any treaty or treaties heretofore made, the United States agrees to deliver at the agency house on the reservation herein named, on or before the first day of August of each year, for thirty years, the following articles, to wit:

For each male person over fourteen years of age, a suit of good substantial woolen clothing, consisting of coat, pantaloons, flannel shirt, hat, and a pair of woolen socks.

For each female over twelve years of age, a flannel shirt, or the goods necessary to make it, a pair of woolen hose, twelve yards of calico, and twelve yards of cotton domestics.

For the boys and girls under the age named, such flannel and cotton goods as may be needed to make each a suit as aforesaid, together with a pair of woolen hose for each.

And in order that the commissioner of Indian Affairs may be able to estimate properly for the articles herein named, it shall be the duty of the agent each year to forward to him a full and exact census on the Indians on which the estimate from year to year can be based.

And in addition to the clothing herein named, the sum of ten dollars for each person entitled to the beneficial effects of this treaty shall be annually appropriated for a period of thirty years, while such persons roam and hunt, and subject to the revision of the Secretary of the Interior, shall be binding on the parties of this treaty, twenty dollars for each person who engages in farming to be used by the Secretary of the

Interior in the purchase of such articles as from time to time the condition and necessities of the Indians may indicate to be proper.

And if within the thirty years, at any time, it shall appear that the amount of money needed for clothing under this article can be appropriated to better uses for the Indians herein named, Congress may, by law, change the appropriation to other purposes; but in no event shall the amount of this appropriation be withdrawn or discontinued for the period named.

And the President shall annually detail an officer of the Army to be present and attest the delivery of all the goods named to the Indians, and he shall inspect and report on the quantity and the quality of the goods and the manner of their delivery.

And it is hereby expressly stipulated that each Indian over the age of four years, who shall have removed to and settled permanently upon said reservation and complied with the stipulations of this treaty, shall be entitled to receive from the United States, for the period of four years after he shall have settled upon said reservation one pound of meat and one pound of flour per day, provided the Indians cannot furnish their own subsistence at an earlier date.

And it is further stipulated that the United States will furnish and deliver to each lodge of Indians or family or persons legally incorporated with them, who shall remove to the reservation herein described and commence farming, one good American cow, and one well-broken pair of American oxen within sixty days after such lodge or family shall have so settled upon said reservation.

Article XI: In consideration of the advantages and benefits conferred by this treaty and the many pledges of friendship by the United States, the tribes who are parties to this agreement hereby stipulate that they will relinquish all right to occupy permanently the territory outside their reservation as herein defined but yet reserve the right to hunt on any lands north of North Platte, and on the Republican Fork of the Smoky Hill River, so long as the buffalo may range thereon in such numbers as to justify the chase, and they, the said Indians, further expressly agree:

1st. That they will withdraw all opposition to the construction of the railroads now being built on the plains.

2nd. That they will permit the peaceful construction of any railroad not passing over their reservation as herein defined.

3rd. That they will not attack any persons at home, or travelling, nor molest or disturb any wagon trains, coaches, mules, or cattle belonging to the people of the United States, or to persons friendly therewith.

4th. That they will never capture, or carry off from the settlements, white women or children.

5th. They will never kill or scalp white men, nor attempt to do them harm.

6th. They will withdraw all pretence of opposition to the construction of the railroad now being built along the Platte River and westward to the Pacific Ocean, and they will not in the future object to the construction of railroads, wagon roads, mail stations or other works of utility or necessity, which may be ordered or permitted by the laws of the United States. But should such roads or other works be constructed on the land of their reservation, the government will pay the tribe whatever amount of damage may be assessed by three disinterested commissioners to be appointed by the President for that purpose, one said commissioner to be a chief or headman of the tribe.

7th. They agree to withdraw all opposition to the military posts or roads now established south of the North Platte River, or that may be established, not in violation of treaties heretofore made or hereafter to be made with any of the Indian tribes.

Article XII: No treaty for the cession of any portion or part of the reservation herein described which may be held in common shall be of any validation or force against the said Indians, unless executed and signed by at least three fourths of all the adult male Indians, occupying or interested in the same; and no cession by the tribe shall be understood or construed in such manner as to deprive, without his consent, any individual member of the tribe his rights to any tract of land selected by him, as provided in Article VI of this treaty.

Article XIII: The United States hereby agrees to furnish annually to the Indians the physician, teachers, carpenter, miller, engineer, farmer, and blacksmith as herein contemplated, and that such appropriations shall be made from time to time, on estimates of the Secretary of the Interior, as will be sufficient to employ such persons.

Article XIV: It is agreed that the sum of five hundred dollars annually, for three years from date, shall be expended in presents to the ten persons of said tribe who in the judgement of the agent may grow the most valuable crops for the respective year.

Article XV: The Indians named herein agree that when the agency house and other buildings shall be constructed on the reservation named, they will regard said reservation their permanent home, and they will make no permanent settlement elsewhere; but they shall have the right, subject to the conditions and modifications of this treaty, to hunt, as stipulated in Article XI hereof.

Article XVI: The United States hereby agrees and stipulates that the country north of the North Platte River and east of the summits of the Big Horn Mountains shall be held and considered to be unceded Indian territory, and also stipulates and agrees that no white person or persons shall be permitted to settle upon or occupy any portion of the same; or without the consent of the Indians first had and obtained, to pass through the same; and it is further agreed by the United States that within ninety days after the conclusion of peace with all the bands of the Sioux nation, the military posts now established in the territory in this article named shall be abandoned and that the road leading to them and by them to the settlement in the Territory of Montana shall be closed.

Article XVII: It is hereby expressly understood and agreed by and between the respective parties to this treaty that the execution of this treaty and its ratification by the United States Senate shall have the effect, and shall be construed as abrogating and annulling all treaties and agreements heretofore entered into between the respective parties heretofore, so far as such treaties and agreements obligate the United States to furnish and provide money, clothing or other articles or property to such Indians and bands of Indians as become parties to this treaty, but no further.

In testimony of all which, we, the said commissioners, and we, the chiefs and headmen of the Brule band of the Sioux Nation, have hereunto set our hands and seals at Fort Laramie, Dakota Territory, this twenty-ninth day of April, in the year one thousand eight hundred and sixty-eight.

ORAL HISTORY AND WRITTEN HISTORY
From the expert witness testimony of Professor Roxanne Dunbar Ortiz.

I think there is a lack of respect for a perfectly legitimate method of learning and passing on knowledge through the oral tradition of a people. The European and American imperialists have claimed that what is written is superior to what is spoken. What I am saying to you right now would be considered irrelevant if the reporter was not recording it. I could tell someone everything that has been said here in this courtroom. I could tell the essence of what happened. I could give all the facts that are essential. But that would not be respected.

The Indian way is to pass such knowledge on by telling the stories, repeating them over and over. The European, having lost the oral tradition, or at least among its educated classes who rule their countries, they have to write things down and refer to them, or they use tape recorders. People who pass knowledge orally develop the skill of remembering and telling.

For the European or the American, the oral tradition is weak. They do not pass on information very accurately, so they believe this is true of everyone. Now, though, oral history is becoming more respected among historians, as minority historians are emerging. At the last American Historical Convention, one of the primary subjects of discussion was the use of oral history.

For my own study I was required to talk with people in the villages of northern New Mexico. In reality, written history is questionably valid, I have found. Generally what has been written are chronicles of events that support whatever regime happens to exist. When you study Russian history, for example, what is written down was written by the Czar's chroniclers who would have been executed had they written anything negative about the czar or his policies. Whole aspects of a people's history is ignored in the history books.

In my studies of United States history I have found less extreme but similar distortion. The very origins of the United States was based on colonialism. Yet United States historians call colonialism "manifest destiny." When they write of the 1880's when Cuba and the Philippines and Hawaii were taken by conquest, they call this "The Age of Imperialism" in United States history. But what happened with the Indian people, with the taking of half of Mexico?

What does "manifest destiny" mean to small school children or to the historians themselves? It means that what happened was an inevitable process, a natural occurrence, ordained from on high. For some liberals it means a natural, though unfortunate disaster. But it was not. The taking of Indian land, the colonization of Indian people was a conscious policy and it is called colonialism. One cannot expect the general public to go out and read twenty or thirty thousand books and research archives to get an undistorted view of United States history, as some of us have done.

For written history, you must document. You cannot state an opinion or fact or observation or theory you may have developed. You have to document what someone else has said or use an "original" document. That is why historians have so much trouble developing historical studies of certain areas of the world or even of their working class, women and national minorities. Generally, even with the new respect and need for oral history, what is written is considered valid whereas the oral tradition is considered legend with certain poetic or cultural value.

The basis of my knowledge is stories that were told to me as a child. I had a store of information, and yet when I entered high school and then went into college, I felt inferior and uneducated because my knowledge was not considered valid. Later as I did research, I would find facts in written documents that would tell things I had first heard when I was five or six years old. I began having more confidence that I did in fact have knowledge. Most of the people, though, do not have the opportunity to continue in American education and are continually made to feel that they are ignorant and lack knowledge of their own people, their own history.

What was written when Europeans first came here was written by the colonial agents, settlers, and missionaries. They reported on the cultures and behavior of Indian people. Their reports tended to substantiate their motives—to take the land. By definition such reporting is subjective, not objective. There is a vested interest in addition to the cultural chauvinism of the colonialists whose purpose it was to degrade the Native people. What objective history really means is considering all the facts, what really happened.

The source of knowledge regarding United States history is the oral tradition of Indian peoples themselves. Dee Brown's *Bury My Heart At Wounded Knee* is an example of objective historical writing. Academic historians say it is a one-sided, emotional view because it is presenting the Indian view and it presents the human tragedy and suffering involved in the events. That is an erroneous criticism. The study is not a history of the Sioux nor does it chronicle the oral tradition of the Sioux or other people. It is an history of the military conquests by the United States in the second half of the nineteenth century.

As a professional historian, I view Brown's book as objective. Had he followed simply official military accounts, government records or previous histories, his work would have been distorted. He studied those accounts and used them, but he also considered the actual events, the massacres, the assault of the United States on the Plains Nations. He described all events. He was not one-sided, nor was he writing only from the Indian viewpoint. He was objective in his account.

The fact is that there was military assault and conquest, there was deception and diplomatic manipulation, there were massacres. The United States did and does break treaties. These are facts, not just the Indian point of view. It happened. No historian would accept accounts of Nazi officials as to what happened in Nazi Germany because those accounts were written to justify that regime. Yet American historians are still subjective about their own history with a few exceptions. They try to justify and rationalize what happened, give excuses, or lay blame on a few exceptionally cruel generals or wild frontiersmen. There were too many massacres for them to be accidental. There were too many buffalo for them to become extinct in a period of five years. Genocide is colonial policy, not accident.

In interpreting the Sioux Treaty of 1868, you have to preface an evaluation with the basic concept of the relationship of the Sioux to the land. You do not have to have proof that the relationship existed in the minds of those who signed because that was the only way an Indian at that time could possibly think about the land. After allotment, in the late nineteenth century, you might find a few individual Indian families who had come to accept the private property concept, but not in 1868.

The Sioux relationship with the United States was the only relationship the Sioux could have understood, that of two independent nations. That was based upon their relationships with other Indian Nations. Those relationships were not ones of conquest or submission, of submerging other cultures, annihilating other peoples, forcing language or religion upon them. Conflict existed and agreements were made between Indian Nations. Sometimes diplomacy ended in war. But the mode of dealing or of interchange was one of mutual respect and agreements were binding, sacred, and could not be broken.

The Sioux would have to be deceived quite a lot and for a long period of time to come to mistrust another nation. The land base, the boundaries which were agreed to, were regarded by the Sioux as the base over which they had total control, and they believed that this would be respected even if the United States had greater military power, because of the agreement. As the United States began to encroach on the Sioux and break the treaty agreements, the Sioux resisted. They were under attack. Unless they regarded themselves a nation, why would they resist? Would they not just have accepted the superior authority if they recognized the United States as such? They did not. They resisted. They knew the treaty had been broken by the United States.

The Sioux had no intention to change their basic culture and social organization. They gave up some land and agreed to certain specific things with the United States, but they did not give up self-government. To them, the treaty did not imply anything about United States jurisdiction or self-determination or form of government or ceremonies. Such things could not be touched through intertribal or international agreements. The Sioux were to retain their customary practices in relation to what the Americans would call criminal justice or criminal law. When agreement was made in terms of settlers being in contact with the Sioux, and there was possibility of trouble, they were perfectly willing to make an agreement that would be acceptable to both parties for the sake of peace.

I cannot conceive nor have I ever heard that agreement regarding border conflict would mean that the United States had jurisdiction over Sioux people or that it meant that the Sioux recognized the higher authority of the United States government.

Article I of the Treaty which deals with bad men among whites and bad men among Indians deals with just that, the relationship of the two, conflicts in the area which might occur. It would not imply loss of sovereignty or giving over to the United States authority to govern the Sioux. In the case of an Indian wrongdoer and white wrongdoers, the Article states that they are to be turned over to the United States, but if the Indian is not turned over by the Sioux, compensation or restitution was to be made from United States annuity payments. Of course this refers to Sioux wrongdoing to a white settler. The agreement fits perfectly with Sioux legal tradition because the practice was either to hand over the wrongdoer or compensate for damages.

Sioux legal tradition is not recognized by the United States. Anthropologists and historians have defined civilization in such a way as to exclude Native people. Degree of civilization is, from the Anglo-American point of view, based on several factors. One factor is written language. Another factor is a sedentary existence with permanent structures and permanent towns or cities. Another factor is the division of labor in terms of classes and the development of hierarchy. In those terms, the more highly civilized the people, the more likely they would have a class that would not work, but who would rule and control most of the wealth. Another factor is the concept of property, private property. By these terms, except for the factor of permanent settlements, Indians are not "civilized."

Often writers distort Indian societies or observe them after they have been colonized. Native American societies developed the major foods which now feed the world. They were the most highly developed agriculturalists among human societies. For most, hunting was supplemental to farming until the Europeans arrived and forced many peoples into a hunting economy to survive.

In the Sioux tradition if there was some trouble between families, clans, bands, or with other nations, and there was a person who was responsible, it was in the interest of the people from whom he came to punish him because that wrongdoer could cause trouble for all. The collective was, in such a case, more important than the individual. Indian peoples think in terms of the people, of maintaining peace, of flourishing, of being wealthy. Being wealthy, in Sioux or Indian terms does not mean what it does in capitalist terms, but rather it means harmony, to be able to have leisure time for ceremonial and cultural practices and development.

Oral history, as the academics are now using it, can be distorted because they are going out as interviewers and they interpret what they hear. That is not the same as a tribal person receiving the oral history through the elders within the cultural context. When information or knowledge is passed from Sioux to Sioux in the traditional way, certain things are easily comprehended. But for the academic, trained in the educational system and from another culture, the oral knowledge might not be meaningful or might be distorted in interpretation.

The purpose of Indians in passing knowledge to each other is to learn and to be able to act properly every day and in the future, to pass knowledge on, and to bring about change. The purpose of the scholar, on the other hand, is to write a specific book about a subject that interests him intellectually, or to become famous, or make money, or develop programs to further control Indians. The motive and method is important. Usually the academic person is choosing informants, as they are called, choosing them for particular purposes, and they are paid.

In this courtroom, the traditional Sioux people are choosing to testify themselves and are choosing who will speak for the whole of the people, rather than their being hand picked as individuals and paid to answer certain questions. Here it is possible to have a true representation of the oral tradition where I have doubts about the academic endeavor. Though some scholars are sincere, it is not clear how they can understand Indian tradition fully, or transmit it correctly, except for rare exceptions. Some, like the scholars who have testified here, are examples of sensitive academic persons who are objective in their approach, have no vested interest in distortion, and who realize their own limitations.

An example of distortion of Sioux tradition is the distortion made by the United States attorney when he inquired about the punishment of a Sioux by killing his horse. He stated that such killing was inconsistent with Sioux reverence for life. I felt the prosecutor was trying to show that the Sioux are indeed savages. For the Sioux, nothing would be killed without valid reason with ceremonial surroundings. Wanton killing was never practiced, but death was not seen as abhorrent or evil.

Judge Urbom: *Was the horse considered guilty? Is there in the Indian culture a guilty horse?*

Professor Ortiz: No, the horse as a hunting animal belonged to the person and would be part of that person.

Judge Urbom: *And if the person was guilty of wrongdoing, the killing of a horse would mean you were killing a part of the person? Is that any different from saying the horse is guilty?*

103

Professor Ortiz: Killing the horse would have nothing to do with acts of the horse. I do not believe you can say that it had to do with the horse except to the extent that the horse was a part of that person and was sacrificed to make a moral point to the wrongdoer, which was judged more important than the life of the horse.

Judge Urbom: *All right, but then is the killing of a horse a manner of punishment to the person, or something different?*

Professor Ortiz: It would be punishment.

Judge Urbom: *The purpose of the killing would be to punish the person. I take it not with the view of taking something away from him but something else?*

Professor Ortiz: It would not be like taking property from him, but rather that he would have a relationship with the horse, the exact opposite of the horse being a mere object or valuable commodity.

THE SACRED TREATY
Father Peter John Powell

There are many parallels, your Honor, between the Lakota sacred ways and the sacred ways of Christianity, parallels which the Church has abysmally and heartbreakingly disregarded in the past. Here are a people who, long before any contact with white people, knew that there was a Supreme Power Who ordered the relationships of men and women to each other, and Who ordered the relationships of men and women to creation as a whole.

In 1941, as a young man, I was studying anthropology; and at the same time I was very much interested in Plains Indian history. At that time I began recording Lakota and Dakota oral tradition, first among the people on Crow Creek and Lower Brule Reservations, and, later on, in the 1940's, on Rosebud and Pine Ridge Reservations. In the intervening years I have returned, on many occasions, to talk with the older people concerning Lakota historical concepts and the oral traditions of the Lakota people; not only as these concepts and traditions relate to their (the Lakotas') relationship with the government or with the treaties made with the government, but also as they relate to Lakota relationships with the whites in other areas of life.

A number of Lakota elders still living in the 1940's recalled very vividly the Treaty of 1868. Among them were Sitting Bull's two nephews, White Bull and One Bull. My field work among the Cheyennes also has involved recording Cheyenne recollections and Cheyenne oral traditions concerning Cheyenne concepts of what was said in the (1868) Treaty. John Stands in Timber, whose book has been published by Yale University Press, was my Cheyenne father. I have in my possession all his documents, recording testimony taken from Cheyennes who were active at that point, (i.e., the 1860's and 1870's), who still were living in the 1920's and 1930's. These documents I have studied in my own present research concerning the Cheyenne Chiefs and military societies.

The Lakota believed that the (1868) Treaty had set aside, in perpetuity, the lands west of the Missouri River, which comprised the greater Sioux Territory, for the use and possession of the Sioux nation. As regards the matter of law enforcement upon the Sioux lands: that law enforcement would be carried out in the traditional way, as it always had been done. Thus law enforcement would be left to the Council Chiefs and to the members of the *Akicita* societies. They would be the law enforcers. They would be the ones who would carry out the legal action taken against anybody who had broken any of the terms of the Treaty. That the Lakota reserved to themselves the right to take judicial discipline (against their own people) is perfectly clear. And, if the Lakota did not choose to discipline their own people, they left open to the United States the right to take funds from the Treaty payments as reimbursement for the lawbreaker's wrongdoing. But the carrying out of the discipline itself was reserved by the Lakotas themselves, to be administered by the Chiefs, or delegated by the Chiefs to the warrior society members.

According to the oral history that I have received, the Lakota always have regarded themselves as a holy nation, a nation set apart by Wakan Tanka, the Great Mysterious, a nation to whom special revelation has been made through the seven sacred ceremonies. They are a nation whose mother is the Earth. Time and time again the old people said to me, "We cannot sell our Mother, the Earth." Time and time again the old people repeated the fact that, perhaps, under the terms of the (1868) Treaty, the tribe might grant temporary occupation of the Lakota lands to someone else by special invitation. However, such a special invitation involved only use of the lands—never possession. For the Earth, the Mother of the People, could not be sold.

The Lakota people, then, consider themselves to be the custodians of Mother Earth. The Lakota at all times kept to themselves not only the right to continued occupancy of their tribal land; but they also kept to themselves the spiritual right to live upon their land. They were, and are, the guardians of their Mother the Earth.

I think that whites rarely, if ever, have understood the sacredness of the context in which treaties were concluded by Lakota people. Every treaty was sealed with the smoking of the pipe. "The pipe never fails," my people, the Cheyennes, say. For the pipe is the great sacramental, the great sacred means that provides unity between the Creator and the people. Any treaty that was signed was a sacred agreement because it was sealed by the smoking of the pipe. It was not signed by the Chiefs and headmen before the pipe had been passed. Then the smoking of the pipe sealed the treaty, making the agreement holy and binding.

Thus, for the Lakotas, the obligations sealed with the smoking of the pipe were sacred obligations. Inherent in those sacred obligations were the continued occupancy of that land, which, in Lakota tradition, at least as I have heard it, has belonged to the Lakota people since they moved out upon the high plains. At no time have I heard any oral tradition, nor have I seen written in documents, any sign that the Lakota people were passing jurisdiction over their lands or people on to the United States. Their intention clearly is that they will continue to be an independent nation. The land was theirs by sacred right; and they continue to keep ownership—I should say occupancy, rather than ownership—of that land. At no time did they think in terms of dissolving the Lakota nation as a sacred nation. This is Lakota oral tradition as I have received it.

The Lakota retained for themselves their older forms of tribal government. These forms of government are paramount in their lives. The Lakota people retained for themselves self-government upon a land that was theirs by sacred right. From listening to the Lakota, I have received no concept whatsoever that they have given up their right to self determination. They have retained the rights to continued use of their lands. They recognize that they themselves, and they themselves only, are the custodians of their land. They are, to use an Anglo term, the rulers of those lands. The United States visits those lands by invitation, and by invitation only. For these lands belong to the Lakota in perpetuity.

For the Lakota life is a sacred circle, the holy circle that shares in the eternity of Wakan Tanka. For, as is true of the life of Wakan Tanka himself, the sacred circle has no beginning and no end. The Lakotas were, and are, a people whose entire way of life is rooted in the supernatural. Their lives are lived within the context of the sacred circle, the circle formed by the pipe everytime the pipe is passed around to the seated Chiefs and headmen in council. So the sacred circle and the sacred pipe are manifestations of the eternity of Wakan Tanka Himself. A vow sealed with the sacred pipe cannot be broken. If it is, death or harm comes to the people. Thus those treaties made with the United States on the sacred pipe, were, indeed, sacred agreements, blessed and ratified in the Presence of the Great Mysterious Himself.

Let me develop this holy concept a bit further. Wakan Tanka, the Great

106

Mysterious, is the Creator, the source of all creation. It was Wakan Tanka who sent Wohpe, the Beautiful one, daughter of Wi, the Sun, and Hanwi, the Moon, to bring the Sacred Pipe to the Lakota People. With the Sacred Pipe Wohpe, who also is called the White Buffalo Maiden, taught the Lakotas the seven sacred ceremonies. Of these, the greatest is the Sun Dance. At the heart of the Sun Dance theology is the belief that through the sacrifice of one man's body in this holy ceremony, blessing and new life are brought to the people and to all creation. This knowledge that it is through one man's sacrifice that blessing and re-birth are brought to mankind and to creation was known by the Lakotas long before Christian missionaries arrived in any number. Yet here is a Lakota theological concept that is strikingly similar to the sacrifice of Christ, and the pleading of that Holy Sacrifice in the Mass. Again, the Lakota knew this sacred way of life long before the white men arrived on their lands.

Fred Zephier, Yankton Sioux, American Indian Movement leader, holding "Treaties and Agreements." Photo by Michelle Vignes

I have spoken of the holiness of the Earth, the Mother of mankind and all living things. From the Earth comes life for the people. Thus, just as it is unthinkable to give away the life of our human mothers, so the Lakotas cannot give away the life of their Holy Mother the Earth. Thus, title to Mother Earth can never be transferred to the United States. All that can be transferred is the temporary use of the land. This is not ownership—only use. Thus it was only temporary use of certain parts of their vast land that the Lakotas granted to the United States in the Fort Laramie Treaty of 1868.

Throughout the twenty-one years of my priesthood, I have not known any traditional Lakota people ever to break an oath made to Wakan Tanka and sealed with the pipe. After generations of white attempts to destroy this sacred way of life that is the Lakota way, the Lakota people and their way of life still continues.

For generations Lakota history has been preserved in oral form. This oral history has preserved the Lakota interpretation of the meaning of the Treaty of 1868. For generations there have been men who not only have been recognized as being holy men, but also as men whose excellent memories set them apart from other people. By virtue of their holiness and by virtue of their good memories, they became the custodians of the tribal tradition. Thus the handing down of history orally is a sacred part of tradition, not just a happenstance kind of thing. History is the living of sacred events. Thus oral tradition is much more important among both the Lakotas and Cheyennes than it is among the whites.

Oral tradition is the very heart of the matter, your Honor; the very heart of the relationship that the Lakotas have with everything living. I have noted an amazing consistency in the oral tradition recalled by the older people, especially as this tradition relates to the tribes and their treaties. Though I have sometimes noted minor variations in oral tradition, I have never known the central core of that oral tradition to vary in the memories of those persons recalling it.

In tribal oral tradition, as it was and is recalled by the older people, the 1868 Treaty is referred to as "a peace and friendship treaty." These older people, both Lakota and Cheyenne, constantly use the term "peace and friendship treaties." What they mean basically is that these were treaties in which the people agreed to continue to live in peace and friendship with the United States; while, at the same time, they retained the use and occupancy of the lands which were theirs by divine right.

There is nothing in the oral tradition that I have heard which refers to the United States as being the protector of the Lakota people. The Lakota people always assumed that they were perfectly able to protect themselves. In the pre-1868 treaties the government was granted the right to establish certain forts along emigrant trails through Indian country, and to station white soldiers in these forts. However, the Lakota consensus here is that the purpose of those white soldiers was to assure the fact that no misdeeds against the Lakota people would be committed by the emigrants. Those soldiers were there to keep peace between the whites and the Lakotas. Actually, those soldiers were the very first ones to bloody the ground by their killing of Lakotas and later Cheyennes.

The role of soldiers in the Lakota tradition was the role maintained by the *Akicita*, the warrior societies. The *Akicita* kept law and order among the Lakota people. As far as the Lakotas were concerned, the job of the white soldiers was to keep law and order among the whites as they passed through the Lakota tribal lands.

When the Lakota Chiefs and headmen signed the treaties, they envisioned the same vision of authority they always had known. They believed that their *Akicita* would keep law and order among the Lakotas; while the white soldiers would keep law and order among the whites. Neither would interfere with the other; but both would do their respective jobs among their respective people. There was a division of power there; but it was a division of power where the Lakotas and the whites kept the right to exercise authority and discipline over their own people, and over their own people alone. In Lakota belief, the white soldiers had no right to punish wrong-doers among the whites.

However, the United States did not accept this Lakota interpretation of the keeping of law and order. The United States claimed law and order jurisdiction over the Lakota, and, in carrying that out, forced its soldiers upon the Lakota people, without the Lakotas ever accepting this outside interference. The Lakotas still believe that this soldier interference was a violation of their right to police themselves, using their own Chiefs and *Akicita* to do so.

There is also the matter of United States citizenship. Here the concept among the Lakota people is much the same concept existing among Indian people as a whole.

Your first and primary identification is as a member of your tribe. Secondly: your identification is as an Indian, a Native American. Thirdly, in the case of some non-traditional Native Americans, there is the identification as a citizen of the United States. However, your primary citizenship, if I may use a white term, is with your people. These are your own people; these are your tribe. Your first and most important relationship is with them.

Some Lakotas vote in state and federal elections and some do not. The position of many traditionalists is that there is no sense in voting in white elections because white elections, per se, violate Indian self-determination; and secondly that nothing will be wrought for Indians by participation in elections. However, increasingly, Lakotas are becoming aware that they possess the potential to become a political power in the Dakotas.

On the other hand, I do not think that citizenship in the United States is an important factor in the lives of the Lakota people. What is important is that they are Lakota. The importance of the Treaty of 1868, as the Lakotas envision it, is that the treaty recognized Lakota sovereignty. Thus, in traditionalist terms, there is no reason why the Lakotas should become citizens of the United States. Under the terms of the Treaty there would be peace and friendship between the Lakotas and the United States. However, the Lakota reserved sovereignty for themselves. And, as far as the traditionalists are concerned, the Lakotas still possess that sovereignty.

Indians were granted citizenship in 1924. However, I believe that the older people I knew viewed that citizenship as a gift from the government that no Lakota really needed or wanted. The Lakota citizenship that really mattered was in the Lakota nation. If the government wished to make the people citizens of the United States, I think that the older people assumed that this was perfectly all right. However, it was of no real relevance to the people themselves because they still were Lakota.

A traditionalist among the Lakota is one who holds fast to the Lakota sacred ways, to the Lakota sacred concepts, and to the Lakota position that the Lakotas themselves have right to and occupancy of the land designated by the Treaty of 1868 as comprising the Great Sioux Reservation. As regards the mixed-blood families among the Lakotas: some have taken the white position; however, some have strongly accepted the traditionalist position. Thus, the amount of blood really has nothing to do with your identity as a traditionalist Indian.

The Lakota concept of land was that the Lakota people could preserve their land from encroachment by any other tribe. Any other tribe who attempted to trespass upon the lands without Lakota permission could be driven out. Some conflicts occurred over encroachment. However, I know of no oral tradition that says the Lakotas obtained their land west of the Missouri by conquest from other tribes.

The Lakota feel that it is barbaric to imprison a man, to take away his freedom, and especially to shackle him. Soldiers with manacles, locking up a man in a guardhouse, represented genuine inhumanity to the Lakotas. Among the Lakotas a murderer might be forced into exile. However, to deprive a man of his liberty by forcing him into a small room, and keeping him in chains, was a concept both strange and repugnant.

Freedom was the great birthright of any Lakota.

TREATIES ARE MADE BETWEEN NATIONS

From the testimony of expert witness, Raymond J. DeMallie, Jr., Assistant Professor of Anthropology, Indiana University.

My major studies have been of the Sioux Nation with particular emphasis on the nineteenth century. I have gained an understanding of the Sioux people concerning the terms of the treaties as understood by those Lakota who signed the treaties with the United States during the nineteenth century.

Studies verify the accuracy that the Lakota have of the various terms of those treaties via their oral history. The Sioux would not anticipate abrogating a treaty unilaterally nor would they anticipate an abrogation of a treaty by the United States. Once entered into, the treaty would be considered an inviolable agreement between the parties. Unilateral abrogation would not be a part of the thinking of the Lakota about a treaty agreement. It is an agreement that encompasses the whole world, the sacred and secular, a promise they are bound to keep, made on the Pipe.

The Sioux dealt with criminal offenders in a certain manner. They viewed negatively the methods used by the United States for dealing with criminal offenders. The Lakota method emphasizes harmony and restoring the unity of the group, so you get restitution as a very important mechanism and you get reciprocity as the very basis of the system for punishing an offender. The goal was to reintegrate the wrongdoer into the group. What shocked them most about the United States was that they would take not only the Indians, but their own, and put them into guard houses and lock them up, which did no good for anyone. This was abhorrent to the Indians.

The Sioux most definitely would not surrender the right to deal with Indian persons who were accused of committing crimes in Indian territory. This opinion is based on the documents particularly surrounding the negotiations of every treaty, the treaty council proceedings, which are available in the National Archives and in the Congressional Serial Set. There is ample discussion of exactly this kind of issue. There are also specific historical examples of the United States attempting to punish a Lakota and of the resulting lack of cooperation on the part of the Sioux, because they did not feel that it was the right of the United States to punish one of their own people. This is manifest in historical records. The Sioux felt themselves to be a single coherent people and that their way of life was superior to any other way of life, and that they would certainly not surrender their own autonomy.

The Sioux understood provisions of the nineteenth century Sioux-United States treaties which dealt with this subject of criminal jurisdiction over acts committed on Indian lands in terms of self-government. In the first place whether the treaty was proclaimed or not it was solemnly made by the Sioux and signed by them in good faith.

Article 1 of the 1868 Treaty would, in my understanding of it and considering the relationship between the Sioux and the United States during this period, be a treaty of friendship between the two nations that would allow the United States to come up into Sioux country and take a portion of land to build military posts. The Sioux at this time did not have a concept of owning land, so I do not believe that they could have had a concept of giving it away or selling it. My understanding would be that the Sioux would have felt themselves to be giving the whites the right to locate themselves here, to use the land.

In the treaties of 1815 at page two and pages three, four, and five (*Treaties and Agreements ... of the Sioux Nation*, a publication of the Institute for the Development of Indian Law) Article Three reads, "The Undersigned Chiefs and Warriors, for themselves and their said tribe, do hereby acknowledge themselves and their aforesaid tribe to be under the protection of the United States of America, and of no other nation, power, or sovereign, whatsoever." The Preamble reads, "The parties being desirous of reestablishing peace and friendship between the United States and the said tribe, and of being placed in all things and in every respect the same footing upon which they stood before the late war between the United States and Great Britain, have agreed to the following articles."

Historical documentation for the period shows that the United States was concerned that the Indians living in the western part of the country and the Louisiana Purchase area also understood that the territory was in some sense no longer controlled by Great Britain nor controlled by the Spanish or the French. The purpose of this treaty essentially was to announce to the Teton that the U.S. was in control and that the Sioux were and no longer had a reason to deal with the British in Canada. It was an announcement that a war had been fought between the United States and Great Britain and that the United States had won. It was a promise on the part of the United States government that they would protect the Teton and the other nations in the area from any incursions by Great Britain. Certainly implicit in this would be that traders would also be sent to the area and the relationship between the United States and the Indians would continue as it had been before. There is definitely nothing in regard to the question of whether the Sioux were or were not turning any Indians over for criminal prosecution by the United States.

There were treaties between the United States and the Sioux in 1805, 1815, 1816, 1825, 1851, 1858, 1865, and 1868. In none of these treaties did the Lakota agree to turn over criminal jurisdiction to the United States. The purpose of most of these treaties was to insure a relationship of friendship and mutual cooperation between two equal parties.

The 1865 treaties do not represent valid treaties with all the warring Sioux bands. I have searched out every bit of information in the National Archives in terms of manuscript material and have been working on this material for nearly ten years. Look at the treaty council proceedings and look at the names of the Indians who signed the treaties and you will find that for the warring bands, like the Hunkpapa or the Oglala, there is not one single name of an important chief who led in the fighting at that time. These treaties were not made with the most important leaders of the Sioux, so I would not consider them to be legitimate treaties inasmuch as they did not have the approval of the most important Sioux leaders. As an ethnohistorian attempting to look at the cultural perspectives of an historical event I would conclude that the Sioux would not have felt these to be binding treaties because the chiefs did not sign.

In the Treaty of 1868, I find nothing that indicates that the Lakota, the Sioux Nation, understood that it was turning over to the United States any jurisdiction with regard to criminal matters for alleged crimes committed within the jurisdiction of the Sioux, within the Lakota territory. The Treaty does not surrender that right. The Sioux have a traditional way of life, a traditional way of dealing with offenders and transgressors against other persons and property. Even today under the United States-imposed Tribal Council there is a method of dealing with criminal offenders. There are written tribal codes and tribal police forces.

Regarding the Treaty of 1868, the historical documentation shows very clearly in my opinion that the major purpose from the perspective of the Sioux for signing this treaty was to end the state of hostility that existed between them and the United States. This was symbolized by the removal of Fort Phil Kearney, the most important fort. After that fort was destroyed, Red Cloud came down to Fort Laramie in November of 1868 and actually signed the Treaty. Most importantly it was the cessation of war. I believe we can conclude that from the historical documents. For example, if you look at the very good synthesis produced by Professor James C. Olson in his book, *Red Cloud and The Sioux Problem* (University of Nebraska Press, 1965), you will find a very good discussion based again on documents in the National Archives that the further feeling of the Sioux at this time was that they would live in the territory that they were then living in and that they would trade at Fort Laramie. The aspect of trade and aspect of peace were the two essential ones of this treaty as I understand it.

Part of the 1868 Treaty reveals that the Sioux were defining their own homeland where they would maintain their own way of life also by the Treaty. In 1868 it appeared to the Sioux that they were dealing with the United States from a position of strength because they had just gotten what they demanded, namely the removal of those military posts.

The 1816 Treaty, page six, reads, "The undersigned chiefs and warriors as aforesaid for themselves and their said tribes do hereby acknowledge themselves to be under the protection of the United States, and of no other nation, power, or sovereign, whatsoever." This does not indicate abrogation of sovereignty. Sioux culture is based very firmly on their system of kinship. The kinship system provides all the moral context of the society and when one deals with another Sioux one always deals in terms of kinship. When Sioux dealt with other people who were not Sioux, they felt the necessity of establishing a kinship relationship so they would know how to deal. These are patterns of behavior, models for behavior.

When dealing with Commissioners, in this case it would be William Clark, the Sioux used kinship terminology much as the government officials also had to relate themselves to the Commissioners. They would call the Commissioners by the term "Father" or "Grandfather" and the commissioners would have called them in return most likely, "Sons, children." That does not mean that to the Sioux they established themselves as children in effect as compared with the "Father," the United States. The point I am trying to make is that the Sioux used the kinship metaphor, kinship terminology, to establish a context for the family and for peaceful, harmonious relationship.

When the United States used the term, "children," referring to the Indians, they were attempting to put them into a subordinate position, a position in which the Indians were presumed not to be able to act for themselves. The Indians, on the other hand, understood "under the protection of the United States" to be the same kind of kinship metaphor which they used in any kind of interaction between human beings, whereas the United States was using it as a cliche, you might say. They used it in a most off handed manner and did not really mean anything by it, not implying the moral relationship between parent and son or grandparent and grandson that would be implied in the relationship as the Sioux understood it.

The two parties were using terms that happened to translate into English the same way, but their understandings of these terms were totally different. The relationship terms as used by the Sioux imposed on any social interaction a context of harmoniousness, getting-along-togetherness, peacefulness. The inferior/superior positions of the two parties are implied in the English translation of these terms, but not in the way the Sioux used them. Between Sioux and other tribes, terms were used which showed respect because you don't act in a disrespectful manner to someone and then attempt to make peace with them.

The concept of protection would have been very poorly explained by interpreters, in my opinion. The understanding of the Sioux would simply be that they had a friendly relationship with a people who are materially wealthier, and perhaps if there is an inequality in the relationship it is to be looked at on the level of material goods because the whites had metal objects, guns, copper, brass kettles. The intent was to establish a peaceful relationship and a trade relationship.

The 1825 Treaty states, "It is admitted by the Sioune and Ogallala bands of Sioux Indians, that they reside within the territorial limits of the United States, acknowledge their supremacy, and claim their protection." It is my opinion that the interpreters speaking with the various Sioux in 1825 would not have made this concept understood to the Sioux inasmuch as they felt that the land belonged to the people who lived on it, the people who used it were the people who had the land, and that the land and the people were one and the same. To suddenly ask them to understand that the land they were living on belonged to the United States would have been a senseless concept in their terms.

In 1825, the Sioux people regarded themselves as a sovereign independent nation equal to the United States and regarded themselves as capable in all respects. The treaty situation was one introduced to them from the outside and it was totally new to them. To say that they felt themselves to be able to handle themselves as well as any other group seems meaningless to me. Written formal treaties did not exist before the Europeans came into the area. In that respect the two equal parties were not equal. My own understanding of these treaties with the Indians, the councils that were held on the Mississippi and on the Plains up to the 1850's, is that it was a case in which citizens of the United States, usually military men, came out with a large supply of various kinds of material goods. If we can believe the historical documents, and there are certainly enough of them, they came primarily to make peace, simply to insure that these Indians would not pledge their allegiance to Canada, to the British. The intention of these commissioners was merely to secure their friendship and allegiance. To accomplish this end, quantities of goods were given out, very large quantities in some cases. And as I understand it, it is likely the case that many of the people, perhaps even the leaders who signed some of these documents, did not understand the articles that they were signing. They simply felt that they were agreeing to be friends and receiving these material items.

In the 1865 Treaty, Article 1 states, "The O'Gallala band of Dakota or Sioux Indians, represented in council, hereby acknowledge themselves to be subject to the exclusive jurisdiction and authority of the United States." There is a problem of translating from one language to another. Translating between radically different cultures is well nigh impossible for very difficult concepts. You would have great difficulty in understanding Lakota religious concepts when they are interpreted into English because they are extremely complex. The treaty concepts are based upon western European tradition and though you might be able to translate these words into Lakota and have them mean something, unless they have some basis in reality (as perceived by the Sioux), the Indians would be totally unprepared to understand what was meant.

The 1867 Treaty, Article 10, indicates that the chiefs and headmen, have the right to establish certain rules and regulations. They are authorized to adopt such rules, regulations or laws for the security of life and property, the advancement of civilization, and the agricultural prosperity of the members of said bands upon the respective reservations, and shall have authority, under the direction of the agent, and without expense to the Government, to organize a force sufficient to carry out all such rules, regulations, or laws, and that all rules and regulations for the government of said Indians, as may be prescribed by the Interior Department: *Provided*, That all rules, regulations, or laws adopted or amended by the chiefs or headmen on either reservation shall receive the sanction of the agent.

The Interior Department would have probably been interpreted to mean "men who worked for the President." The Sioux were not doing anything other than affirming those customs which they have always followed, namely, they make their own rules, and then there is something about the agent and the Interior Department which would be totally incomprehensible. It is not just the language. It has to do with concepts that they did not use in their own lives, with a foreign body, a group of people as mysterious as the government of the United States would have been to the Sioux.

The Treaty of 1868, Article 1, concerns the delivery of bad men or criminal offenders who do wrongs, commit crimes in Indian country. The third paragraph specifically says that they will deliver up the wrong doer to be tried and punished and in case they willfully refuse so to do the person injured shall be reimbursed from the annuities. This specifically gives to the Sioux a choice. The part about reimbursement from annuities for wrongdoing makes perfect sense to the Sioux. This is the traditional concept of restitution in the sense that if there is a wrong done it is usually righted by making some sort of a restitution. In this case rather than have the Indian offender taken to Fort Laramie and put in jail as had been done in the past, the treaty says compensation may be made from material goods.

Spotted Tail and some other Brule Sioux had been taken to Fort Leavenworth one winter and kept there in custody of the War Department. At the time of the 1868 Treaty the Indians were aware of the practice of the United States government, acting through its War Department of taking offenders in Indian country, including Indians. It is my understanding that this is why this particular article is in the Treaty, because this was so contrary to Indian custom and to the Indians' desire. They preferred to have other means written into their treaty. The Treaty concerns the Sioux as a group, as a social and political group, not as individuals.

Though the Article states that wrongdoers among Indians be turned over to the United States, it also states the alternative of restitution from the annuities. Given the historical context of the troubles that the Sioux had at Fort Laramie with various arrests and attempts of arrest of Indians during the 1850's, it is my belief that this particular section is inserted so that the Sioux have the ability to deal with Indian wrong doers themselves. If the government is going to insist on making an issue of it, then they can do so by taking away some of the annuity monies.

Traditionally, chiefs or the entire tribe could make restitution if an individual Indian committed a wrong on another Indian of another band or tribe. The amount of restitution would depend to some extent on the resources of the offender. As much as could be given would be given back in the traditional form, in the form of horses or other goods.

Article 1 makes provision for the payment of compensation from annuities due to the Sioux. The Commissioner of Indian Affairs was to prescribe such rules and regulations for ascertaining damages under the provisions of this Article as in his judgment would be proper. For the Sioux the significant aspect was that it would be a civilian as opposed to the military who would decide how much would be required to make up a certain wrong. At an earlier time, in 1854, there was an occasion in which the Chief of the Sioux who was appointed under the Treaty of 1851 went to Fort Laramie and offered to pay to the commandant of the Fort a certain number of animals in restitution for a cow that had been killed. The cow belonged to a Mormon settler. The military commander at the Fort refused to accept the animals and instead sent out Lt. Grattan together with thirty men to arrest the offender. This ended up in a bloody massacre. The point is that by negotiating for the 1868 treaty, the Sioux were able to secure for themselves the assurance that such problems in the future would be handled by the direct representative of the President rather than by the military authorities. I believe this was one distinction that was quite clear in their minds—the President as opposed to the military.

The confusion surrounding the Treaty of 1868 was what caused Red Cloud and a number of other Sioux leaders to go to Washington in 1870. We have pretty complete transcripts of all that was said at that time. Red Cloud and the other Oglala chiefs specifically denied any knowledge of Article 6 in the Treaty. They said that it was never explained to them. After that time, after 1870, in discussing the Sioux, commissioners continually slipped in for the record statements regarding the future inevitability of the Sioux taking up farming. In the actual discussions during the treaty councils, this is never phrased in such a way that the Sioux would understand that they were expected within the next five years to take up agriculture. This being the case, and in light of the historical evidence, Red Cloud was correct and true in what he said. At the treaty councils in 1868 there was very, very little said about agriculture. The record exists. We could document the number of lines that deal with agriculture as opposed to war or other items.

What the Sioux did understand and we know was interpreted correctly is that war would cease. This was the major thrust of the Treaty. As far as Red Cloud was concerned, this was extremely important. Peace was reestablished. Red Cloud and other Sioux understood that they would once again have free privileges of trading with the whites. By this time they had become dependent on many types of European manufactured goods, particularly rifles and blankets. Red Cloud assumed that he would be able to trade at Fort Laramie as he had been doing many years before the Treaty. Fort Laramie was not within Dakota, but rather in Wyoming, and the government was attempting to preserve all that land for white settlers.

The established boundaries of Sioux land were never fully explained to Red Cloud and the other Chiefs. The government hedged on this issue because on the one hand they set aside a tract of land for the sole and exclusive use of the Sioux, while on the other hand, in a vague sort of way, they refer to the lands which lie to the south and northwest of the reservation, and say that the Sioux may also hunt there as long as there is sufficient buffalo there to support the chase. To the Sioux, this did not appear to be a cession because that is what they had always done—hunted wherever there were buffalo. It is my belief, based on the historical records, that the Sioux couldn't, just simply didn't understand this as giving away of land, selling of land. This is what led to the wars of the 1870's and eventually to the Custer battle. The War Department suddenly decided that all the Sioux should be within the permanent boundaries of the reservation. The Sioux did not even know what the United States meant by those boundaries.

There is nothing in supporting documents to evidence that this aspect of the 1868 Treaty was clearly interpreted to the Sioux. It is my understanding that the Lakota right down to the present have maintained autonomy and along with it sovereignty over their land.

115

THE SIOUX NATION AND THE TREATY
Wilbur Jacobs

I regard the Sioux people as a Nation. I would say that today Sioux people are a Nation of Native American people, and that there are many justifications for taking this viewpoint. The Sioux Treaty of 1868 shows that the American government regarded the Sioux as a Nation. Later, with white advance, the Treaty was violated and conditions were imposed on the Sioux that three-fourths of the male population did not sign, as was stipulated in the Treaty:

> No treaty for the cession of any portion or part of the reservation herein described which may be held in common shall be of any validity or force as against the said Indians, unless executed and signed by at least three-fourths of all the adult male Indians, occupying or interested in the same; and no cession of the tribe shall be understood or construed in such manner as to deprive.

Violations were made of that provision. The Sioux Treaty was, in many respects, a treaty between equals, and the fact that a period of negotiation took place between them of over three years before the terms were finally agreed upon, in my judgment makes it almost a constitution of self-government with defined territorial integrity for the Sioux Nation.

There were consistent series of violations, blatant violations of the Treaty, one of the first being when gold was discovered in the Black Hills. Changes in the 1868 Treaty reduced the land area of the Sioux to a fraction of its original size.

Violations continue up to recent times. It seems to me that the government was guilty of misconduct in the Wounded Knee, 1973, episode, resulting in this hearing and the trials in St. Paul. The bringing of federal marshalls and armaments, the intrusion of certain federal police officers violated the terms of the Sioux Treaty of 1868.

I believe the Sioux Nation exists today as a political and as a religious and as a social and cultural entity, and that it has many of the attributes of what we call a nation-state, in terms of linguistic and cultural identity, in terms of self-reliance, self government, in terms of religion, and in terms of a small land base that remains. I am speaking of a nation-state in terms of sovereignty.

In looking back on the 1868 Treaty, my opinion would be that if there is a dispute in modern times as to some of the terminology I would lean toward the oral history version. If you study treaty terms that were negotiated with Indian people you find that they went through a very secret route of negotiation, of committee alteration, of revisionism and argumentation, and then committee reports on the floor of Congress, and then final approval by the Senate.

In my knowledge of Native American history, the elders of most tribes that I have encountered have developed a system of memory or a recollection that surpasses the beliefs of modern Americans. It is nevertheless true that these histories are passed on from generation to generation by elder people in the various tribes. The details are passed on and tribal continuity and cultural identity is maintained with the past. From

116

my conversations with elders of the Lakota people, they, like other Indian people, have developed a long memory of events of the past. Some of this information is secret.

Persons who do not have a written language are more apt to develop a keen sense of memory. There is little question but that this is true. Among Native American people the cultivation of a memory for the history and oral tradition is highly developed. Moreover, native languages are, in some respects, more precise, actually more exacting and descriptive than the English language. This may be surprising, but it is true. Because Indian languages are not written languages we tend to think of them as crude and lacking in essential qualities of preciseness.

The language of protection in Sioux-United States treaties is one found in British treaties as well. The meaning of the word "protection" to the Sioux was an agreement to live in peace and friendship with the United States within an area claimed by the United States government. It did not mean that the United States government owned that territory or that they were literally under United States protection. The term "protection" is one that is paternalistic and is analagous to other terms that are used in relationship with Indian people in modern times. It was a term that was used throughout the British empire. Protectors were supervisors or agents, and it is very misleading. My judgment is that the Sioux people never thought literally of being under the protection of the United States. Who did they need to be protected from? The outlook of the Lakota people up to the present is that they are a sovereign people entitled to govern themselves within their land.

It was customary in treaties with Indians for the United States' negotiators to insert certain provisions with the view of getting them on the record. In my judgment there are such provisions that may not have been fully discussed and agreed to by Indian people at the time of negotiation. One example is the turning over of their own people to some unknown authority to punish. Who among the Sioux had any conception of what the United States machinery of justice was? It was alien to the life style, religion and method of governing of the Sioux people.

There are also treaty terms that were undoubtedly fully discussed. The language of Article 1 of the 1868 Treaty reflects, I think, hard bargaining between negotiators. This shows the insistence on the part of Sioux negotiators that they have the option of dealing with the offender in their traditional way. The traditional method of dealing with crime was by compensation. For instance, a Lakota who murders another Lakota might have the obligation of providing for the murdered man's family for the rest of his life. Banishment from the tribe was an extreme punishment, the worst punishment of all, to be separated from your family, tribe, homeland, and religion.

Sioux leadership was in the hands of those who by personality and by generosity, by physical strength, wisdom, and other attributes, actually provided the leadership. This leadership was often passed on from generation to generation in distinguished families among the Sioux. Two types of leaders, then, existed. One, a younger man, who by virtue of his distinguishing himself as a war leader and a hunter might be tantamount to a military leader or war chief. Another would be the civilian chiefs or counsellors who were the elder statesmen of the Nation. Among the Sioux there were various societies that white people call "Indian police." For infractors of the law, offenders could be brought to trial, and their offenses could be determined. The Sioux were governed in a very democratic fashion with freedom of movement, freedom of self-expression. That is not to say that there were no constraints. There were severe constraints, and violators of those constraints were subject to discipline.

There is another important question concerning Sioux sovereignty. The connection between the Louisiana Purchase and the sovereignty of the Sioux Nation is

117

a very important one. Even at the time of this "purchase" many people felt that the United States was in an illegal position in making such a bargain. The boundaries of it were ill defined and the diplomatic language between the American negotiators and the French negotiator, Talleyrand, were such that the American negotiators asked this very question of the boundaries. Talleyrand is reported to have said, "You have made your purchase, make the most of it." There was also another cloud on the American title, the suspicion that the United States had bought the territory which was claimed by another nation, Spain, and that Napoleon just sold it as a matter of expedience.

Given that situation to begin with, we come back to the question of ownership and the Sioux Nation, since the Sioux were the aboriginal people who lived in this area, and since these lands are claimed by right of discovery of the first explorers in occupance. We can say that the Sioux people were the ones who occupied the vast area and from the view of the Doctrine of Discovery, which the European lawyers were fond of arguing, the Sioux Nation had a good title in fee simple by European terms.

It seems to me that this area of the Louisiana Purchase might rightfully belong to the Sioux Nation. As far as Napoleon was concerned in selling the territory, the rights of Native people were never considered. In this sale or purchase this was the pattern that was followed. Europeans, for centuries, had been prepared to occupy and to take lands occupied by tribal peoples. The pattern was later followed in the partition of Africa. It was imitated in certain parts of the Orient and followed by America in its attempts to take over Pacific islands. In the Louisiana Purchase there was an arrogant disregard for the rights of Native peoples, and the United States, in making the purchase, made no qualms about taking title.

PART FIVE

Lakota Oral History
of The Treaty

EVERYTHING THAT BELONGS TO THE TREATY

And Now
to this time
I understand,
I understand about the Bible and the
                    dictionary.
                    It says,
the white folks always make believe,
and they always forget—
                    that's why the Great Spirit
gave the white folk that Bible and the dictionary,
so that they
              would never forget.

To this time
          why the treaty,
                    none of us,
                    none of us,
your Honor, Judge,
              none of us here
                          are older than I am.
So I have to give my expressions
              or expressions in actual conversations.
I have to give you
with my face
and everything,
          that belongs to the Treaty.
You will know we should tell nothing wrong
besides.
          I thank the honor
              of the judge
              and the prosecutors
and the witness here
          in this here.
                    —Henry Crow Dog

120

ORAL HISTORY
Beatrice Medicine

Beatrice Medicine testified as to the traditions of her family. Ms. Medicine is from the Standing Rock Sioux Reservation. She has been a Visiting Professor at Dartmouth College, New Hampshire, and Visiting Professor at Stanford University. She is a professional anthropologist.

I grew up as a Lakota speaker and feel that all the oral history I know I learned through my father and his grandfather who is a signer of the 1868 Treaty.

In my training as a professional I have concentrated on Lakota culture as it has continued to the present. The very nature of the discipline, anthropology, relies on the oral statements of what we call informants.

I have become very aware of the oral traditions and the oral history of my people. The Lakota way of life is a life style that has allowed my people to maintain their integrity and their way of living as a distinct culture despite various efforts to change us.

We have what we call four cardinal virtues. For men they are bravery, honesty, generosity and fortitude. For women they are chastity, hospitality, industriousness, and generosity. The role of women is highly regarded in this male-oriented warrior society.

My information is based upon the statements of the older people who were telling us about these treaties and the Lakota life style. They say that all the treaties of the Lakota Nation were made with the utmost honesty and with the utmost faith that the Lakota people would keep those treaties. I think this is tied very strongly to the nature of the leadership and the fact that they represented the expression of the four cardinal virtues.

The Lakota had a very definite law way system in which there were a series of tests and a series of treatment for those people who transgressed from the four cardinal virtues. There was a definite system of leadership, called *naca*, which means the ultimate leaders. We had to go through the route of two leaderships and through various *Akicita* or soldier societies. It was these people who had definite control of various transgressions. For instance, if in a buffalo hunt, one hunter went out before the entire group went, this jeopardized the welfare of the whole people. The ultimate leader would send certain of the soldier societies, and they would whip the transgressor. In a dire case, such as murder, there is a statement of how it can be treated. The decision makers, the *Naca*, would apprehend the person who transgressed. All the *Tiospaya*, or extended family, of both groups would meet and the person who transgressed would then go through a ritual in which he would put his hand on the person, or kiss the person which means that he would assume the responsibility for the family of the deceased. People were not locked up. Sitting Bull said that he would never be taken and bound, *yu ska pi.*

Jails were foreign because we do not believe in isolating people from us nor making them feel guilty. The whole element of shame and guilt was foreign. The Lakota is brought up with the idea that you don't transgress and go against the four cardinal virtues, because you are going to bring shame upon your *Tiospaya*, extended family. The notion of justice is extremely different between the way I was brought up and the way I have had to learn to live in the white man society.

121

Based upon my studies and oral knowledge, I do not believe the Lakota Nation would give the United States the right to deal with Indian persons who were accused of committing crime in Indian territory. We have our own way of dealing with transgressors within our own society and we still have much of this in terms of social control which is operative at the present time.

Treaties between the Lakota and the United States from 1805 to 1868 were made between two sovereign nations. The "protection" terminology was interpreted by the people to mean an alliance, protection between two sovereign nations during the War of 1812. Formerly the Lakota had been allies of Great Britain.

As a child growing up, whenever the older people got together, they talked about the history that had gone before us. This is very typical of societies that do not have a written language, the bringing into the consciousness of children and adults the oral traditions that are important to us. As a child I was taught not only oral history but folklore. Every night when my grandmother or my grandfather would tell us these stories in our language we would have to remember precisely when we were asked about them. I have great faith in the oral history of my people and the transmitters of this oral history.

The Lakota were aware that there were other powers in the world besides the United States. They have words for the French and English. They viewed treaty agreements and the language of protection as a statement of external relations with other nations, and themselves as a unique national group. The law ways of our society operated so that if any transgressions occurred it was within the power of the chief and the *Akicita* to take care of it. However, if a white person came and transgressed then it was the duty of the *Akicita* to deliver him to the foreign authorities as the Treaty states.

The idea of autonomy, both as a nation, as a people representing the Lakota Nation, is implicit in the way the Sioux have viewed treaties and still do. Certainly there is no implication that the Sioux would hand over the handling of their internal affairs. There is a strong value in Lakota life which is the ideal of reciprocity and restitution for any kind of wrongdoing or transgression. Agreements on the part of the Sioux to make restitution must be seen within the traditional Sioux context.

Prior to 1868, the United States began trying to create Chiefs in order to enact treaties. Agents representing the United States would go out and entice various members of some of the bands to come to an agreement. We call these people who succumbed to the pressures, *Maka Utacipi*, or Earth Eaters. Some of these signed away lands or rights when they were unauthorized to do so. The 1865 treaties were signed by such unauthorized individuals.

Under the 1868 Treaty, Article 1, transgressors among the Sioux could either be dealt with by the Sioux or turned over to the United States.

Even in the present day, our traditional people, the elders in our tribe state that we have never violated a treaty we have made as the Lakota Nation. The 1877 Treaty which deals with the cession of the Black Hills is called the *Paha Sapa* Treaty, Black Hills Treaty, by our people. The people feel that the treaty was one designed to take away the sacred Black Hills. Those who signed it were and are regarded as traitors by my people. The signers were people who were not part of the older *naca*, those leaders designated authority. Also the three-fourths of Lakota males who were required to sign a treaty were not represented in the 1877 agreement. This is the history I grew up with.

There is some confusion about who had authority to sign treaties. It has been asked here why Sitting Bull did not sign the 1868 Treaty. Sitting Bull was a medicine man, not one of the *naca* leaders of his band. He was a medicine man and a prophet, someone who was able to predict events, a seer in English. He was also a political leader at one time in his life when he took the band of Hunkpapa and Sihasapa into Canada after the Custer battle. Whether or not Sitting Bull accepted and recognized the 1868 Treaty as being binding and valid is not very significant in terms of Lakota social organization. He was a medicine man and was not one of the leaders who had authority.

During this period, however, there was change in some of the social control mechanisms. There were dissidents among the Sioux who were regarded as traitors. Other dissidents who did not have authority, like Crazyhorse and Sitting Bull, are regarded with esteem and respect by the Lakota people. Sioux society operates by a consensus of agreement and consensus of opinion. There is a flexible organization. *Tiospaya*, extended kin groups, had the freedom to splinter off if they did not agree with the consensus. But these *tiospaya* do not represent the band or the whole people.

Lakota Society is a warrior society. This does not mean warring to kill people, but the prestige of counting coup, to touch an adversary and leave him alive. This was not seen as an act of hostility but as an act of prestige gain. White historians tend to emphasize that a designated chief could not control his warriors. My oral history says that one of the strengths of Lakota people is a personal autonomy in decision making. If someone felt they were willing to go on an expedition, not to kill someone, but to touch them and count coup and come back with enhanced prestige they could do so. Our definition of war is quite different from the American definition of war.

Irma Bear Stops

The traditional Lakota way of life means our sacred way of living.

We are to respect one another and honor each other. Everything that we talk about, that we pass from generation to generation must be regarded in this manner so that people can have respect for one another and live in unity among each other and to help one another and to guide others.

We look upon the Earth as our Mother. You have a mother and she takes care of you since you were born. She provides for you and she sees that you are grown up in the way that you are supposed to. We are taught to respect the elders and to watch out for the older people.

The Sacred Pipe was given to us from the Great Spirit. Whatever promises are made through the Sacred Pipe are to be honored and respected. Using the Pipe to live by is really hard for people. You cannot fool the Great Spirit. The Pipe always comes in first with everything. The promises that you make are included—such as with the Treaty.

The 1868 Treaty meant that the land rightfully belongs to Mother Earth and the Great Spirit. We are supposed to live on it and take care of it so that it can provide all the things. No white man shall come into the reservation. We are supposed to govern ourselves. We are supposed to take care of our own.

We did not ask the government to come and make the Treaty with us. They asked the people, our grandfathers. They came to them and asked to make the Treaty with them. The Indians didn't sit around and wait for the government to come to them.

Oral history is the way I understand the past. It has been handed down from our grandfathers to our fathers and mothers, and it has been taught to us. We are to pass it to the younger generations so they, too, can know about our way of life.

The Treaty was made with the Sacred Pipe. Lakota people honor that Treaty. The 1868 Treaty is taught to us since we were young and the older people talk about it because that is the way of our history. In the future, when people read the writing of the 1868 Treaty, they will understand that there is a lot of difference. The government did not understand what the Indians were trying to tell the government, and it assumed that is what they wanted.

Severt Young Bear

Mr. Young Bear testified on three occasions: Official Transcripts, pp. 548-567; 573-589; 1375-1378. After being examined by the Defense Attorney, John Thorne, there followed a number of cross-examinations by the Federal attorney, Mr. Nelson, and questions by Judge Urbom.

Mr. Young Bear also served as the principal Sioux interpreter in the proceedings.

Mr. Thorne (Defense Attorney): *What kind of Native American Indian are you, Mr. Young Bear?*

Oglala Sioux.

How long have you lived at Porcupine, South Dakota?

All my life.

And how old are you?

Forty.

You understand we have been using the term, "traditional Indian." What does that term mean?

It means the people that retained a traditional way of life, our culture, our songs, our religion, anything that has to do with our way of life; that is my understanding.

Live by the Sioux way of life, in other words?

Yes.

And in the course of living in the Sioux way of life, is there a tradition of oral history?

Yes, there is.

Are there also songs that are part of the traditional way of life?

Yes.

Are the songs themselves involved in oral history?

Yes.

Can you tell us how songs are involved?

There are different types of songs that the Sioux people have. We call them traditional songs. Now in our modern times, we have a different kind of a song; we call them pow-wow songs.

But traditional songs tell a story when you sing. For instance, the Warrior Society have their different types of songs. The Fox Society that was mentioned here, has different types of songs, and the Elk Clan or Elk Society, they have different types.

And even with the traditional way, the Indian people respect that each other's nations or tribes are different. They're different.

Their songs we respect; there are certain songs that when we go visit another tribe at their Indian pow-wow or gathering, they sing their songs, and we don't sing those because that's their songs, and Sioux have many songs like that.

In these traditional songs, do they at times tell stories about past history?

Yes, with the Warrior or the Fox Society, and there are some songs that tell the story about a warrior going on a raiding party, or the warrior that knocked his enemy off the horse while he was galloping the other way. There is some strong meaning in those songs. A lot of warriors sing them to themselves or early in the morning they get up and they sing those songs.

I can recall when my grandfather's singing, they would call him *Pokhala*, that means the Fox Society songs.

And they more or less stayed within the warrior, himself because if he started singing those songs, and if he sang it in a gathering like this, one of them might be a different tribe, and that song will hurt his feelings. There might be trouble.

Were any of your ancestors involved in the signing of the 1868 Treaty?

Not that I can recall.

Do you have any oral history concerning the 1868 Treaty?

Yes.

From whom have you obtained that oral history?

From my father and my grandfather and from various meetings that I attended with the traditional people. Ever since I was in my younger days, I always attended traditional meetings. Sometimes I sat there for six hours and I was probably the only young person that was within that meeting because they was mostly all old traditional people at that meeting, and it took patience to sit there listening to that oral history.

Now when you took the oath before testifying here just now, you took the oath upon the Pipe?

Yes.

The Pipe has meaning in traditional Sioux life. Is that correct?

Yes.

What is the meaning of the Pipe, and taking of the oath of the Pipe?

It means, it puts a bond on the person, like myself. If I put my hand on that Pipe or if I prayed with that Pipe, whatever I say in those prayers is a bond on me that I have to live up to those words. A lot of times there's a meeting where they prayed with a Peace Pipe, there's never a minutes or a contract signed, but the word of mouth and shaking of hand that seals that as a document of a treaty or of a meeting.

It means you live up to your word and you tell the truth and live honestly?

Yes.

As you have heard, the oral history of the treaty, have you also studied the 1868 Treaty?

Yes, I have.

You are familiar with the Treaty itself?

Yes.

And you have heard the oral history about the Treaty?

Yes.

Can you tell me what the oral history is that you have been taught concerning the understanding that the signers of the Treaty had; the Indians who signed the Treaty, how did they interpret that Treaty with regard to the land—the Indian land that was set forth in the Treaty?

That is not really what was taught to me, but what I learned from my elders.

From the oral history?

Yes, that this Treaty was made with a Nation, the United States Government and the Sioux Nation, and from the oral history—from the people, like where I live, they talked that the Sioux Nation never sat there with their hands out and said we want peace and friendship; it was the government that came to us and asked for peace and friendship.

You mean the United States Government?

Yes, the United States Government, and they made this Treaty with the government, but from the oral history that I learned, is that the Sioux people never gave up anything as far as their land, their sovereignty, or as a people, or even our culture, because what we have as Indian people in our culture, songs, and our traditional way, it's still present even though with all the tradition we have to live through, up to the present time.

Now, according to that oral history, and as I ask this question, you understand that I'm asking you of the oral history as to how the Indians who signed the 1868 Treaty interpreted that treaty, and all my questions will be based upon that, and I want your answer based upon the oral history. Do you understand that?

Yes.

What does that history tell you with regard to the rights of any outsiders, in other words, people who are not Sioux, in terms of their right to come on the land?

That this land was our sovereign Nation, that any outside people, that any outside people we're talking about, the white men, there were some agreements made between the government and the Sioux Nation, and they were supposed to keep their people out, and we maintain our way of life within this.

When you say they were supposed to keep their people out, the United States was to keep its people out of your land; is that correct?

Yes.

Now, in the Treaty there is language that speaks of, "If bad men among the whites," now under the Treaty in your oral history, was it understood that white people could come on to the Indian land if you allowed them? If the Indian people allowed them to come?

Yes.

Now, let's assume a white person or a citizen of the United States was allowed on, and again these questions are all directed based upon the oral history as the signers understood the treaty. Assume that that white person does a bad thing to an Indian or someone on Indian country. What does your oral history tell you the Sioux agreed in that treaty to do at that time?

From the oral history that I understand, was that the government people was supposed to control these people within—even though they were authorized by the United States Government to come in and be accepted by our people, like the agents, fur traders. When they committed a crime or harm against a tribal member, it was the government's responsibility to punish him.

You would turn that person over to the United States Government?

Yes.

That was what was understood; is that correct?

Yes.

Now the Treaty also speaks in the same article about "If bad men among the Indians," meaning if there was a member of the Sioux who harmed somebody, who was on the reservation with permission, or who harmed somebody, it speaks of the Sioux agreeing that they would turn that person over to the United States Government, the Indian, and if they refused, then the person harmed was going to get some money, and that money would be deducted from the money the government was to pay the Sioux. What does your oral history tell you about the meaning of that language in the treaty, if it tells you anything at all?

From my understanding of the oral history on this part, is that if there's any harm done by an Indian, it was up to our chiefs, or the band itself, to give up that warrior to the United States Government.

But one thing we've got to understand is we are different bands, we have different chiefs, different warriors, and if one of the brave warrior commits a crime and it's up to the chief to give him up, and if he doesn't want to do it then the rest of the chiefs cannot make him give up that individual because maybe that's one of his brave warriors, outstanding fighter, or brave, within the band.

That's why my understanding is that damages could be paid by money.

Then if I understand you, you're saying it was the decision to be made by the Indians to either give up the Indian to the United States, or they didn't have to, they could keep him; is that correct?

Yes, they didn't have to. . . .

At the time the 1868 Treaty was signed, there was or was not a written language that the Sioux people had? In other words, did you have a written language then?

No.

There was no copy of the Treaty written in Lakota?

Not that I know of.

It was written in English; is that correct?

Yes.

Now, this treaty reads, after describing the boundaries, "And the same is set apart for the absolute and undisturbed use and occupation of the Indians herein named, and for such other friendly tribes or individual Indians as from time to time they may be willing, with the consent of the United States, to admit amongst them; and the United States now solemnly agrees that no persons except those herein designated and authorized so to do, and except such officers, agents, and employees of the Government as may be authorized to enter upon Indian reservations in discharge of duties enjoined by law, shall ever be permitted to pass over, settle upon, or reside in the territory described in this article." In that section it talks about people being authorized to come on to Indian land. What does your oral history tell you about who gives that authorization?

The Sioux Nation.

The Sioux Nation?

Yes.

In other words, it is the requirement of an authorization by the Sioux?

Yes.

And then with regard to friendly Indian tribes, it speaks of also the consent of the United States being required. What does your oral history tell you about that? Does it need just the consent of the United States, or the consent of the Sioux and the United States, or what?

The consent of the Sioux Nation first, and if the Government was willing to go along with it, well it was my understanding that any decision made within this Indian land or Sioux Nation was really up to the Sioux Nation. . . .

There is a final section I would like to ask you about. That is the section in Article 12, and it says, "No treaty for the cession of any portion or part of the reservation herein described which may be held in common shall be of any validity or force as against the said Indians, unless executed and signed by at least three-fourths of all the adult male Indians, occupying or interested in the same." What does your oral history tell you about that section of the treaty?

My understanding on that is that the land within the designated area mentioned in treaties belongs to the Sioux Nation. It belongs to us as Sioux Nation. That they can't force anything on us, or change any part of the treaty, or make another treaty unless they have the three-fourths vote of the male adults of the Sioux Nation.

This article in the English language speaks of a treaty for the cession of land. As you have just related it, in the oral history understanding, it required a three-fourths vote of all adult male Indians to do any changes under the Treaty. Is that correct?

Yes.

In other words, the understanding at the time was that it wasn't just three-fourths for the cession of land, but was three-fourths for anything?

Anything, yes.

Mr. Nelson, for the United States, Cross Examination: *Mr. Youngbear, I will also read a portion from the 1868 Treaty, as follows: "It is hereby expressly understood and agreed by and between the respective parties to this treaty that the execution of this treaty and its ratification by the United States Senate shall have the effect, and shall be construed as abrogating and annulling all treaties and agreements heretofore entered into between the respective parties hereto, so far as such treaties and agreements obligate the United States to furnish and provide money, clothing, or other articles of property to such Indians and bands of Indians as become parties to this treaty, but no further." Would you please relate what your understanding from the oral history is of the meaning and significance of that language, and particularly the past part which says, "But no further?"*

To my understanding it means that we can make any changes with the United States Government as a Nation if we want to make any changes as far as rations, clothing, and then as far as the land and our way of life within that land, it belongs to us. It requires a three-quarters vote to make any changes.

What's your understanding of the oral history insofar as whether or not this language I have just read to you keeps in effect prior treaties between the Sioux and the United States?

My understanding was that from the oral history I received from the traditional people in every meeting that I went to, everything was the final treaty, and the only treaty that the Sioux people recognize was the 1868.

So that language that says it annuls prior treaties insofar as they concern provisions for money, clothing, and other articles of property, but no further, has no meaning or significance at all?

Sure it does as far as our way of life and the land. It means that any changes within that Treaty and any further negotiations with the Sioux Nation requires a three-fourths vote of the People, and as far as the clothing and other things, people never did talk about that. Very few people said they were not living up to part of it because we were getting stale bacon and rotten beans. What their main concern was, the land and our way of life within that land.

From my understanding, the oral history is that the Treaty that they signed, that the Sioux Nation acted as a sovereign Nation. And that the land was ours, everything within the land was our way of life and this land, this is the biggest issue. The only topic that I heard people say was "our land." They never did mention that they owned it jointly with somebody else.

Later on some of the elderly talked about what happened to the Black Hills, that they were taken without the three-fourths vote.

Was there any reference in the oral history that you are familiar with, to treaties between the Sioux and the United States prior to 1868? Do you know any oral history concerning treaties in 1865?

There is one instance where I heard from the oral history, that they mention the 1865 treaty. The government signed the treaty with some chiefs. The bands met with them on the river somewhere around Fort Pierre. They had a meeting there and they didn't have enough representatives of the Sioux bands. They made some agreements on this and they went back to Washington, revised it, the treaty, and they came back again to the same point, and they sent out to bring in the chiefs here.

When they came back, the chiefs they expected were not there at that meeting, so the government got sore and appointed some chiefs, "Hey, Chief, come here, you look like you make a good chief," so they signed some documents and according to my oral history they were politically appointed chiefs.

Later on, after they were appointed as chiefs, whether they signed or not, they met again during the springtime on the southwest side of the Black Hills. Some of these appointed political chiefs went to that meeting, and the chiefs of the Sioux said, "Well, who are you?"

And they said, "We are chiefs because we were appointed chiefs by the United States Government."

So one of the chiefs that earned to be called a chief, stood up and said, "How do you earn to be a chief? Did you go on a raiding party and steal a horse, or did you touch enemy by hand? This kind of appointment you earn by bravery in battle of facing the enemy or touching the enemy or killing the enemy." This broke up that meeting, and that is what I pick up in oral history. . . . (Recess)

Mr. Thorne, Defense, Redirect Examination: *Mr. Young Bear, in the testimony we had yesterday, and in line with some of the questions that you answered, I want to raise the question of the term, "fight to death." Is that term related to the Crow-Sioux relationship?*

My understanding of oral history is that fighting to death is not really an idea of wiping out a whole tribe. Usually a warrior that pledges that he will go on a certain war party or raiding party to prove that they are trained as an independent warrior into manhood as early an age as 6 or 8 years old. When he pledges that he will go and do certain things, and he makes that vow. He will say "I will go and face the enemy and touch him or get into a fight with him," and whoever wins will win.

What they mean by fight to death is that when you make a pledge you will face the enemy, whether he takes your life or whether you take his life, that you will not run from him. When this is done they tie a rawhide around his waist with a stake which is usually about 10 or 12 feet. With that, once you face the enemy, the warrior drives that stake into the ground, and that prevents him from running. That is what we call in our traditional way, the fight until death.

And do I understand you to say that doesn't necessarily mean a person will be killed? It is a way of describing a particular act of proof of one's bravery, and it doesn't necessarily mean that someone will be killed? Is that right?

Yes.

Mr. Nelson, Federal Attorney, Recross Examination: *I believe Mr. Thorne mentioned the dealings between the Sioux and the Crow. What is your understanding of the oral history as to whether or not there were wars or battles between the Sioux and the Crow?*

Yes, there were some . . .

Mr. Thorne, Defense, Redirect Examination: *In this regard, Mr. Young Bear, I know when you use the word war you are using a word common to the white people, but if you can translate that into the same kind of understanding as the Sioux understands the word war. Were these battles or wars between tribes wars of conquest or were they a more man-to-man relationship?*

Man-to-man, a battle.

It's a man-to-man battle, is that it?

Or a small band against another, a war party against another war party.

Let me ask you this: You have talked about touching the enemy, does the act of one man touching the enemy have any special meaning?

Yes, that is one of the biggest acts of bravery—riding up or running up and touching the enemy. . . .

Judge Urbom: *Why is touching the enemy considered an act of bravery?*

Because when you go into battle with another tribe on a man-to-man basis you either take his knife or he takes yours, or he will knock you off your horse or it's an idea of proving how brave a person may be.

Was there, as you understand it, a general purpose in those confrontations of meeting the enemy either individually or as small groups, or band would meet the enemy. Was there the general idea that there would be a killing of the enemy or at least an overcoming of the enemy physically, either involving death or in injury or physically subduing? Is that always involved or generally involved?

Not all the time. Sometimes there is a kind of a stand-off, and finally two or three or four days they get worn out.

But was touching the enemy then a matter of bravery essentially because it was anticipated that if one tried to touch another there would at least be danger of death. Is that true?

Yes.

Who was considered, if you can make any description of it, an enemy?

It really means like there are two parties going and they will meet each other and something might happen and then they start fighting each other over territory or herd of buffalo.

It could be a condition which existed before the two parties saw each other or it could be something which occurred when the two parties saw each other, is that true?

Yes.

And were these encounters characterized by the use of some kind of particular weapon or were the kinds of weapons varied?

It varied like some warrior society you accomplish so many acts of bravery and then your final test they will give you a staff. It is something like a long cane, what you call a shepherd's cane. It means that this is more or less like a final act of bravery. They give you the staff to meet a greeting party. In order to prove that you are brave enough to do that, no matter what kind of weapon that your opponent has, you knock him over or push him off the horse with this staff. There is no way to harm that person.

Was the Warrior Society or portion of the Sioux society called the Warriors a particular group of people who had met these basic qualifications or were they people who were in the process of meeting the qualifications?

No, they were already some people.

Do I gather then that beginning at an early age there was a training period that all of the young men went through?

All of them.

And was the goal for all young men to enter into this warrior group, and from there to move into other positions of leadership, or were there some that were not expected to go into the warrior group at all?

There are some that never meet the qualifications and they are those who are not brave enough to go on raiding parties or travel with other groups, then they were used around the camp areas.

Once a person had met the qualifications and became a member of the Warrior group, what were his duties other than going on a raiding party?

Hunting to provide food for his family plus the rest of the people that live together in that band.

Was that the group also that could be called the equivalent of police force?

No, there is a different society for that, and this pertains with the village itself.

You mean there was another group that protected the village itself?

Yes, they may be part of the Warrior Society but as far as the discipline or the control of the village, they were under the elderly, which is a more or less advisory type of elderly and a chief. They were enforcing the laws of the band.

An internal security group?

Yes.

131

That is they were enforcing the rules and laws of the Indian society as to the Indians in that particular village?

Yes.

By whom were the chiefs selected?

Usually by an elderly person, people of that same organization.

Well, was there a vote of some kind?

Inherited.

By inherited, do you mean by that, when a chief would die one of his sons automatically would become chief, or do you mean that he selected someone before his death?

It usually is that he appoints or selects one of his sons, usually the oldest, or else it will be someone in the family.

Is it correct then that typically the chief would select his successor usually from his family?

Yes.

And would there be some group or persons who would either confirm that or disagree with it, or was there some other group that had something to say about whether this other person would become the chief?

Usually, it would be the elderly of the village where they themselves were the raiding parties, and they might be in some ceremonies or rituals, and they would give advice to the chief if his son could qualify.

Mr. Thorne, Defense, Further Reredirect Examination: *You have indicated in answering some of his Honor's questions that this battle that might come, using that term in applying the meaning of what battle means to the Sioux, this confrontation could be over territory or an incident between people. Were there areas that were defined as the area of the Sioux Nation and the area of the Crow, and when one encroached on the other there would be a dispute over territory? In other words, if the Crow came into Sioux country would the Sioux try to move them out?*

My understanding of oral history is that the Sioux guarded the Black Hills at all cost.

At all cost?

That land is sacred. Any other tribe, you mention Crow, if they try to come in and hunt or camp within the Black Hills area, they were pushed out . . .

You talked also about the touching of the enemy where you physically touched a person, was that an act that required great skill?

Yes. You have to be a brave and skillful as a warrior.

I may not be pronouncing this correctly, but was there a society, or is there a society in traditional Sioux ways of government known as the Akicita Society?

Yes. That is the one I mentioned to the Judge. They are the enforcer of the law of the village or the band, and they have internal control of the village or of the band. . . .

Would this Akicita Society, the ones that police the village, be like a police department in white man's terms—taking care of a city?

Not really. They only act when the order is given by the elders, the council of Elders, or the Chief. . . .

132

Were there attempts on the part of Indian Nations to turn members of other tribes into their own tribes, thus a Sioux trying to turn a Crow into a Sioux, to get the Crow person to join the Sioux?

There was one time when during a forced march of the Cheyenne to Oklahoma, a few hundred came back. They were weak and they were hungry and they were on their way back so the Sioux took them in. That's how our relationship with the Cheyennes started. The Arapahos the same way.

Mr. Nelson, Federal Attorney, Rerecross Examination: *With regard to other tribes, were they ever captured? Was there any practice of capturing of such people and using them as servants or slaves?*

No. There is no traditional ways. Either the enemy goes back to the tribes or he fights to death in a man-to-man battle.

As you understand it then there is no history of instances of taking such persons and holding them in a slave-like situation?

No. We have no such traditions.

Now with regard to the Akicita, isn't it true that society's basic function was to police the hunt or when the band or village was on the move? Is that a correct understanding of their role?

Yes. They were the protectors. That is what it means—*Akicita*, the Warrior Society.

Now with regard to relations with other tribes, and possible assimilation I guess would be the word, of people from one tribe to another tribe—is it not true that there was a practice of taking women and children from other tribes and making them Sioux?

Once there is a battle, like sometimes where a pledge is made where the whole family will go and avenge the woman's brother's death—sometimes the whole family is involved. But in our traditional ways if there is a woman involved they will respect her and they didn't take the women and children. Sometimes they were brought back and became part of the village . . .

If there were surviving women and children after the battle from another tribe would they be taken and adopted as part of the Sioux people?

Yes.

John Thorne, Defense, Reredirect Examination: *Mr. Young Bear, do you know whether or not the Sioux attempted to convert other members of other Indian tribes to the Sioux way of life?*

No, because we respect each other's traditional ways. There was never a time in my oral history where there was ever an attempt to convert anybody to the Sioux because it was up to the individual himself; and in oral history a lot of times they respected each other.

Did the Sioux have, and here we are using a white term, missionaries? In other words, persons that would go in among other tribes not for battle, but would go into other tribes and try to explain the Sioux way of life to them and to many other kinds of persons? Did they have people that did that kind of thing, or do you know?

No. I heard some history on missionaries but they were there to convert the Indians from savage—they wanted to civilize them.

All right. But did it work the other way? Did the Sioux at times have people that would go talk to others and try to explain the Sioux way of life?

No. . . .

Mr. Thorne, Direct Examination: *Will you give us your oral history as you have had it, as you have told us before, in terms of the understanding of the Lakota people concerning both the Department of Interior and the War Department as these departments dealt with the Lakota people?*

My understanding of the oral history from my father and from my grandfather is that there's a distinction between the War Department and Interior. At that time they didn't recognize the Interior Department.

You mean at that time, back in the early 1800s and through the 1860s?

Yes. *"Tankacilapi* and his helpers" is how they called the Interior Department or President of the United States, and they recognized the War Department as a soldier with long knife.

That came from the carrying of the swords, is that right?

Yes. The advice that my elders gave me was that there is always a war plan and a peace plan, that kind of rolls over the Sioux people. When they sent in delegations representing the Father and his helpers, they are talking about peace. They are talking about peace in the Interior and at the same time the War Department's in the back door trying to create a fight or disturbance with the Indian people. That is what my grandfolks told me—that there are a lot of rich white men or politicians involved where there was gold in the Black Hills, our sacred Black Hills. That is why they pushed the War Department into creating a disturbance or fight with the Sioux people.

As Matthew King mentioned, if you review the written history and also our oral history of the Sioux people, there is always a peace plan, a peace plan and a war plan.

Both being used by the government at the same time?

Yes.

Alex Chasing Hawk
Testimony in Lakota and interpreted by Severt Young Bear.

I am sixty-five years old. I grew up hearing my grandfather talk about the 1868 Treaty. My understanding is that when the Treaty was made between the Sioux Nation and the United States, both nations would lay down their arms. My understanding concerning the Sioux Nation is that what we know as Sioux territory now is that any ceding of land required three-fourths of the male adult vote.

My understanding of the history is that under the Treaty the people will govern themselves under the leadership of our Chiefs. Our law and order will be maintained by the Sioux people. I understand that during and after the signing of the 1868 Treaty the Sioux people have honored their promises that were made in the Treaty but that the United States government many times violated their own promises and have even made war against the Sioux Nation. General Custer was wiped out by the Sioux people when he attacked, so in revenge of this the United States government massacred Indian people at Wounded Knee in 1890.

My understanding of the oral history is after the signing of the Treaty that the land mentioned in our Treaty belonged to the Sioux Nation as undisturbed use of the Sioux people. But after the 1868 Treaty, the United States government had forced some Acts on the people such as opening our land and invasion of white people.

Regarding ownership of individual tracts of land by Indian people for agriculture, there was a promise on behalf of the United States government that the family or the head of the family was supposed to be allotted 320 acres which he will farm and whatever he grows on that land will be used for the family. Another promise is that some form of implements such as plows, horses, oxes, were promised to the families.

Evelyn Gabe
Mrs. Gabe works for the Indian Public Health Service. She has also taught for the past two years at Standing Rock Community College in Indian Studies, developing curriculum for the Standing Rock Reservation.

Pazetho John Grass was one of the signers of the 1868 Treaty and was my great-uncle. I have learned history from my father, Francis Bull Head. He was a councilman for many years. I learned from my uncle, Eugene Young Hawk, who was a tribal council member for twenty-seven terms and was Tribal Chairman for the Standing Rock Sioux for two terms. I have also learned from my brother, Xavier Bull Head, who is very well educated in our Indian way of knowing these treaties and anything else that pertains to our welfare.

The oral history of the Treaty of 1868 as I have learned from my elders and from my relatives all pertains to a beautiful word in our language, *Wohlakota*, which means peace, peace between the two nations, two sovereign nations, *Milahanskan*, which means the United States and the sovereign Sioux Nation of our Lakota people.

I come from four bands, though I grew up in the Hunkpapa country where I was born and raised. According to our oral history as it has been told to me by my parents, grandparents, and by the holy men and wise men that I have talked to, our origin from the beginning of time goes way back thousands of years.

In our beginning, our seven men were created and came from the constellations in the skies, the seven stars of the dipper. Seven women were created from *Minnewiconi*, the water of life. Where our history is concerned we refer to it with a deep meaning, like the water of life, and the blessing cup which is the Big Dipper and the seven stars that shine.

My father and holy men that I have talked to have often told me to remember this oral history because it is very sacred to us. It assured our future and our way of life would continue in years to come. For this reason, in the major treaties that have been made, they referred to the beginning of time. The treaties that have been made, we believe, were made from the beginning of time to the end. That is how sacred they held their treaties, and our people have lived up to them.

We feel that certain articles of these treaties have been violated. We were never to take up arms again and our boys were forced to. No more lands were to be taken away from our people, yet treaty after treaty and Act after Act after the 1868 Treaty has violated the Treaty because later ones never were endorsed by the three-fourths male members of our Sioux Nation.

We have a tribal system of government as one nation to another equally level with the long knife soldiers' form of government. According to the 1868 Treaty our people have never taken a white man to court in our system of government because we respect and honor our Treaty. Likewise, I think that the United States government should honor their Treaty and not take our boys to their courts. Our tribal system of government, our leaders, Chiefs, and our headmen are to govern.

Our way of life is to enjoy our system of government that we have had from the beginning of time. We have Chiefs and headmen. They were elected in the most simple way. When it came time to choose these people, our leaders, it took 100% vote of the band they represented. We enjoy always a 100% form of democracy and our Indian system of government throughout North America must have looked good, because Benjamin Franklin copied this type of government from the American Indian.

Our holy Pipe is our most sacred religious ceremony. Shortly after the creation of man in this country, it has been told to us that a virgin lady brought the peace Pipe to our people to use. This Pipe is used at the beginning of all ceremonies, treaties, or anything that is held sacred. When we take this oath on the Pipe we have a good heart and a free conscience to guide us in everything we do.

We never had Sundays or denominations, but our Indian religions is everyday, every second of our life. It starts before sunrise when families get out and give thanks to the sun and its gift of energy and life. Mother Earth belonged to all, or Indian people and they are to live on this earth without any hindrances. It hurts for us elders to think that we have to be in controversy over this territorial disagreement.

The Lakota people have always had sovereignty over our land from the beginning of time. I do not know how the United States got it from Spain or how Spain got it to begin with.

The United States government has its own way and method of interpreting the Treaty and we have our sacred and traditional way. When we refer to our Indian country as sovereign Indian country we have that sacred right to try our boys in our own country. You must remember the thousands and thousands of years before anyone ever thought of coming from Europe to North America, our system of government, our system of education, our entire life was based upon verbal and oral history.

We were pressured by the military. I don't like to remember that history because so much of it is so sad. But we were under such pressure that at that time our people were even afraid to talk. When you think of the past, especially around 1864 and 1865 under the presidency of Lincoln, the "savior of his country," 368 of our warriors were hung in one day and that is the biggest execution in history.

Blokahankate, Francis He Crow

My great grandfather and grandmother were at Fort Laramie in 1868 when the Treaty was signed. After the signing of the 1868 Treaty my grandfather was at Custer's battle where Custer was trespassing on Indian territory. My grandfather was born back in 1878 and when he was twelve years old in 1890 there was the Wounded Knee massacre. My great grandfather was killed with his three daughters and my grandmother was wounded. My grandfather escaped. My grandmother lost a lot of blood and was taken back to Pine Ridge to an Episcopal church and they stayed there for awhile and then they moved them to another place and that is where they stayed until she got married to Weasel Bear.

My grandfather used to talk about the 1868 Treaty. Before they signed this Treaty, the Sioux Nation refused to sign because the United States government and the Sioux Nation signed treaties before, several of them, and the United States never kept them. They didn't sign the Treaty right away but had a counsel with the government leaders. They had counsel with other bands and they talked about this treaty. The chiefs and head men say thay are going to sign it but the members refused because they cannot trust the United States. They were talking about it and the members asked the chiefs and the head men if the United States guarantees the treaty and if the promises are made that will be kept, then they would sign. The United States guaranteed it and

136

this treaty will last until the end of the world. This Treaty will last until the river stops flowing, and the green grass and the stars stop shining, this is how they guaranteed it.

The Sioux Nation accepted but Red Cloud still refused to sign it even though the rest all signed. Red Cloud moved out of Fort Laramie and later that year they sent out scouts and interpreters to him. He said he understood it and if the United States would move all their forts from Indian territory and withdraw all the military he would sign. So the United States did and Red Cloud signed the 1868 Treaty sometime in November. Right after that they violated the Treaty by Custer entering Indian territory.

The Treaty was between two nations, the Sioux Nation and the United States. Before the Sioux signed it they used the Pipe and talked to the gods through this Pipe and peace was to be forever. They asked the United States and when they made that promise the United States told about their Bible. So there were two nations making an agreement and it was to be forever.

Back before signing this 1868 Treaty, the Indian believed they were a sovereign nation and after this is the way they believe. When they made this treaty of 1868 the traditional way, the Indian power is three-fourths of the adult males. Without that there is no power to change the Treaty.

My grandfather told me that the seven council fires each take census. They cut the willow and put it there and do ceremony and prayers. When they make an agreement, if any member does not agree, they withdraw their stick and they count. This comes from law back thousands of years. This is the Sioux Nation power. The chief cannot sign any agreement without the members. The seven stars is the set of their laws, so when they make it law, it is just like a star and it is going to be forever.

The United States violated the 1868 Treaty. We made a promise, but the first article was violated. The United States government misinterpreted Article 6. The treaty does not specifically recognize intermarriage with white, and so-called squawmen and half breeds who were living with the Sioux people when the 1868 Treaty was made. The United States used the squawmen and half-breeds to sign agreements. Sioux full bloods refused to sign. They tried to force them but never had the three-fourths, so they were in violation.

The United States government and the Sioux Nation both say if they agree to something they must have three-fourths of the Sioux and the United States government Congress Act, and President proclaim. The Lakota people were to govern themselves. In Indian territory if a white man does something and they have proof they turn him over to whites. If the Indians do anything it is up to the Sioux Nation. If they violate any law and it is serious, the Sioux Nation condemned them from the reservation. This is the way my grandfather used to tell me. Same between Indian Nations. My grandfather was telling me about the Cheyenne and the Sioux. The Cheyenne had their land and the Sioux theirs. If the Cheyenne catch any Sioux on that side, they hold them and he has to pay for it. If any Cheyenne violated he is the one that has to pay for it.

Robert Yellow Bird, Pine Ridge

I work as a community organizer to help Indian people receive the services and benefits that are available to them through social services, employment and to inform them of their rights as guaranteed by the Constitution and by the Tribal Government under our treaties. I am the state coordinator for the American Indian Movement for Nebraska. I am also the regional coordinator for the Committee to Reclaim Fort Robinson for the Sioux Nation. We contend that Fort Robinson, located in western

Nebraska, was illegally constructed and erected on sacred Sioux land in violation of the 1851 and 1868 treaties. We are presently involved with the Nebraska State Legislature that would introduce a bill that would return the Fort to the Sioux Nation and restore our rights as guaranteed by both these treaties.

Oral history is the social customs, the spiritual aspects and practices, and the economic values, moral values, that have been handed down from generation to generation, passed from grandfather to grandson, from father to son, from mother to daughter. I have received oral history from some of my direct relatives and others of the elders of the Sioux Nation.

The immediate history and the history that I am mainly involved in regarding the treaties is that the United States government came and approached the Sioux Nation and the Plains Indians, as they were called, to sign a peace treaty and to guarantee them certain rights. Along with the Sioux, the Cheyenne, Arapaho, Blackfeet, the Crow, the Mandans, Arikaras. In 1849 when the California gold rush was in its height, many immigrants and gold seekers and travelers were passing through Indian country committing depredations among our people. The United States, in order to provide safe passage and to answer the call for protection for these immigrants, approached the Sioux, the dominant Nation of the Plains, and asked them to sign a treaty that would give these immigrants safe passage through their country. The agreement would also allow the United States to erect temporary forts to insure the protection of these people and to insure the protection of the Sioux from the whites. The treaty was signed solely for that.

For the people, the Treaty meant that the Indian people would govern themselves, that our land would encompass all land north of the North Platte River to the Big Horn Mountains, that we would be a sovereign nation, that we would not have to abide by the laws of the United States so long as we stayed within our country. I have been told that when we signed this treaty, when our grandfather signed this treaty, that we were guaranteed to live the way we wanted as long as we stayed within our territory, and that our territory was defined as what our grandfathers who signed this treaty stated it would be.

I have been taught that when you use the Pipe, it is very sacred and you do not back out of your pledge. The Lakota understood those promises would mean freedom to run their own lives of their own people, and that the United States would not interfere in any way.

Most of my direct forefathers, my uncle, my grandfather in the Lakota way, were murdered at Wounded Knee in 1890.

Gordon Spotted Horse, Standing Rock

I have learned our history from my dad, as he did from his father before him and I will be passing on information to my children and other young people.

The 1868 Treaty described a boundary which the United States was not to enter under any circumstances. The Lakota people would continue their traditional way of life and be a self governing people like any other country.

Though we have chiefs and headmen today they are not in charge of the process of the government because the treaties have been broken. The Lakota continue to honor and respect the Treaty of 1868. The treaties made with the United States before 1868 were all broken by the United States, so this 1868 Treaty was to be an everlasting Treaty.

The 1868 Treaty stands out in discussion by Lakota people over and over. It is considered to be the final Treaty of the Lakota people.

WE LAKOTA HONOR THE TREATY

The following testimonies of traditional Lakota people were given in Lakota and interpreted by Severt Young Bear.

JOHN LOOKING CLOUD: I am fifty-four years old. My understanding of the oral history is that the Pipe was used in making of the treaty. The land belongs to the Sioux people and when they signed the Treaty they touched the pen and at that time the people represented each other. What they mention in the Treaty was that this land belongs to the Sioux people only and that no white man will come within our Indian land. After 1868, I understand that the Black Hills were leased, not ceded.

ALEX ONE STAR: My understanding of the oral history is that the Indian people and the Indian nation and the white man and the United States government will now after the signing of the Treaty have peace between them.

When anybody other than Sioux people going to our country would have to be authorized by the Sioux Nation. The Sioux people would be the only ones to live on our land to make use of it. That it is our land.

My understanding is that the Sioux people and their leaders will govern themselves. After the signing of the 1868 Treaty, from then on, only three-fourths vote of the Sioux Nation could bring change. After the 1870's there were many agreements that were made between Sioux and the United States where the United States attempted to get our people drunk to make agreements but none of them had succeeded.

Whenever any promise is made with the Pipe our people honor this to the day they die.

EUGENE WHITE HAWK: My understanding of the oral history from my mother's father is that there were some agreements made in the Treaty and these were interpreted through the interpreters that they used at that time. The Sioux Nation touched a pen and these agreements were made.

My understanding of the oral history is that when this Treaty was made there was going to be peace between the Sioux Nation and the United States government. My understanding of the whole history from my grandfather is that when this Treaty was made the land designated within our boundary lines would be the Sioux Nation and the people, the Sioux people, would live as a Nation.

Any white man that is going to come in will have to have the permission from the Sioux Nation and only authorized people sent by the United States government will be accepted in. My understanding of the oral history is that the land that was set aside for the Sioux Nation, the Sioux people live within that area and that they will govern themselves under the leadership of their chiefs and headmen.

DAVID SPOTTED HORSE, Standing Rock: I am sixty-four years old. There are seven council fires of the Sioux people. I am from one of the seven council fires, known as

139

the Hunkpapa. The Sioux people, seven men, came to the Black Hills and settled, and from them came the seven council fires.

From my understanding of the oral history of the 1868 Treaty the land belongs to the Sioux people and our way of life within that land belongs to the Sioux people. It is the supreme law of our Nation that only the President of the United States can set foot in our Indian land. And that is what I heard.

ELLIS HEAD, Rosebud: My ancestor, Spotted Tail, signed the 1868 Treaty. My grandfather told me about it. From my understanding there were several meetings with the people and that after the meetings, after the several meetings, the Treaty was signed. My grandfather and Spotted Tail were cousins. From my grandfathers talking I know that the land mentioned in the Treaty belongs to the Sioux people and the Sioux people will govern themselves on that land.

WINNIE RED SHIRT, Pine Ridge: From my grandmother I know that there were two nations and they wanted peace, and that there would be no war between those two nations. That is how this Treaty was made.

JACKSON TAIL, Pine Ridge: I am seventy-six years old. I know history from my grandfather. My understanding of the history of our Treaty is that when the Treaty was signed their main concern was land. During negotiations of the Treaty there were few white men and there were few Sioux people so they talked Nation to Nation and during the talking they would make peace.

My understanding is that the land designated in the Treaty, that land belongs to the Sioux people only, and any white man that comes upon our land has to be authorized by the Sioux people first. The land that belongs to the Sioux Nation will be governed by the Sioux people themselves under their leadership of their leaders and the chiefs. The reason they want to govern themselves clearly states they didn't want the United States to govern over them and that is why they never once mentioned the word "white men."

When a Lakota makes a promise with the Treaty sacred to him and whatever he asks through the Pipe will be honored because of the bond that he is tied with to the Pipe.

My understanding of the history of the Treaty is that whenever bad white men commit crimes in the Indian country they will be turned over to the United States and that the Indian people will handle their own people. Any crimes committed in Indian country the white people will take care of their own people and the Indians will take care of their own people.

FRANK KILLS ENEMY, Pine Ridge: I was born in 1894. I am a traditional Lakota. We live in our own way of life.

The Treaty was signed by the Lakota Nation to stop the war. And the land within the Sioux Nation belongs to the Sioux and no white man will come into our land. The Sioux Nation will govern itself. The people will live under the Pipe.

THE UNITED STATES HAS NO JURISDICTION
IN SIOUX TERRITORY
Vine Deloria, Jr.
From the expert witness testimony of Vine Deloria, Jr.

I did a two year study on ratified and unratified treaties and agreements of all tribes with the white man. This study included not only the Sioux treaties but also the treaties of other tribes and some colonial treaties between the individual colonies and the eastern tribes prior to the establishment of the United States. In doing this research you have to deal quite frequently with the proceedings of the negotiations, the report of the Commission which did the bargaining with the tribe, or the agency report which attempted to explain how the Indians understood the treaty in addition to the text of the treaty itself. Whatever written documents exist, in fact any documents that would tell how people conceived of the treaty and its effect on them, whether those are scholarly interpretations or simply diaries, are useful in this task. Quite often you can discover unratified treaties that had disappeared from people's notice in the casual remarks that are contained in these documents. So a treaty study is not simply looking at the texts of treaties and the case law and attempting to find a suitable legal interpretation. Much of the work must be an historical analysis of what happened.

I think the oral tradition comes into this process when you start comparing the substance of the treaty proceedings with the information you gather in talking to people on a reservation, at an Indian conference or in a discussion with traditional Indians who are concerned about the treaties. The central issues that were prominent during the time when the treaty was being discussed are still the important issues for Indians today. These issues have always been important, each generation of Indians has been concerned about them, and while the language has changed somewhat and become more technical, people still preserve the original point of view regarding the treaty articles and issues and remember the interpretation which the government originally gave them.

Negotiations for the 1868 treaty went on from late August of 1867 to November 1868 when Red Cloud finally signed and agreed to give the United States peace. At that point the United States stopped trying to get more concessions from the Sioux and, since Red Cloud was the major holdout among the Sioux chiefs, stopped trying to get more Sioux to sign the document. The process of getting the consent of all the influential Sioux leaders is recorded in the documents of the Peace Commission and their attitudes are also recorded. On the whole the Sioux, even when you consider the broad spectrum of opinion that was represented by the tribal leaders, were telling the United States, "If you don't get out, we are going to push you out." The Sioux people not only considered themselves a nation but they were prepared, some were even eager, to fight to the death against the United States. They definitely considered themselves a distinct and separate sovereignty which had to receive the respect of other nations, particularly the United States. They had a military fighting force that, while small, was still the most potent single force the United States would meet on the field of battle until they encountered Geronimo's band of Apaches nearly twenty years later.

While the treaty speaks in technical language, the oral tradition describes the treaty promises in much more blunt language. The people were promised "free and undisturbed use of the land." The Sioux interpreted this literally and the United States commissioners at the negotiating sessions interpreted it the same way. Free meant free. The United States could not and cannot come in and police the people without their consent. The United States cannot levy any tax against the Sioux. The boundaries of the Sioux nation were to be respected. In other words, the Sioux were given a guarantee by this treaty that they would be free and protected. This fact, this attitude, can be documented many, many times in the official records. Today it forms a basic attitude of the traditional people insofar as they interpret any move by the United States to coerce them in any direction.

Following the 1868 Treaty the United States made several legal attempts to purchase the Sioux lands before they finally went ahead, in violation of the treaty, and took them in a most peculiar manner. There is no question but that the taking of the Black Hills was illegal, that the Sioux had title to these lands that had been confirmed by the United States when it ratified the treaty, and that the loss of the Black Hills was a theft from the Sioux, not a legal confiscation in any way. The United States avoids any inquiry into the manner in which this land was stolen from the Sioux. The Indian Claims Commission has said that the United States illegally took the land but even then they had to literally rewrite the historical facts to arrive at this conclusion since there is not a shred of evidence that the taking of the land had any legality whatsoever. The White House recently sent a letter to the traditional chiefs saying that they recognize the 1868 treaty as a valid and binding legal document. I can only assume that the White House is with us while the Indian Claims Commission has its own version of history.

The pressures on the government to open the Black Hills area increased in the 1870s and finally in 1875, the Allison Commission was sent out to the west to get the Sioux to agree to a cession of that area. Miners were pouring into the Black Hills and while the government was trying to keep them out, it was not very successful. Even when the government did prosecute people for violating the treaty, courts would not uphold the treaty. A case in Nebraska in the federal court can be cited to verify this fact. Anyway, the commission failed miserably in its efforts to get the Sioux to cede the Black Hills. It was an entirely wasted effort. None of the influential chiefs would even discuss it. So in November 1876 President Grant simply pulled the army out of the Black Hills and allowed the miners to flood into the area, establish mining camps and file claims. The United States simply stepped aside and refused to enforce the treaty.

In January of that year the Sioux camps that were away from the agencies were declared hostile and the Army was sent to fight them. The Custer war followed that summer when the different columns of soldiers began to converge on the Sioux in the Powder River country. After the Custer fight Congress passed a statute denying all further appropriations and annuities to the Sioux until they ceded the Black Hills. Another commission was sent out to get signatures. Many of the people were starving because the summer's fighting had destroyed all their supplies, yet they would not sign. The treaty required the consent of three-fourths of the adult males for any valid cession of lands. The commission knew it couldn't get the required number so it had some chiefs sign and claimed that since these chiefs sometimes represented their bands politically that they in fact "represented" three-quarters of the adult males. When this so-called agreement was sent to Congress, a preamble was attached to it and the

Congress approved it on the last day of February, claiming it to be a valid agreement with the Sioux. The United States has claimed ever since that this statute was legal but courts and most historians regard it as a fraud. Even the Indian Claims Commission and Court of Claims have stepped gingerly when asked to rule on its legality.

There are, of course, many additional facts that should be included in any attempt to interpret the 1868 treaty but I think a number of things can be shown to be beyond contention. First. I don't think the Sioux thought that they had surrendered any land or any political rights in signing this treaty. Red Cloud refused to sign until the forts on the Bozeman Trail were abandoned. When the Army left, his men burned the forts and then he came to Fort Laramie and touched the pen. The United States officers pretended that he was not important and that the treaty had already been approved without his consent, and the government records show this attitude. But the historical reality was that there was no peace of any kind until Red Cloud agreed to the terms and the forts were abandoned. So the question of the United States having some kind of civil and criminal jurisdiction over the Sioux as of 1868 is simply ridiculous and absurd. The records certainly do not bear out this contention. There is not any mention of prosecuting any Sioux for anything in a court of law and this threat would most certainly have been made if the United States had thought it had any control over the Sioux at that time.

There is no acknowledgment that I can find, other than a few speeches made at forts along the river by very tame headmen who had long since accommodated themselves to the government and wished to reaffirm their support for the government, that the signing of this treaty would do any more than guarantee that there would be peace between the Sioux and the United States, that there would be no more whites allowed within the boundaries of the Sioux nation, and that the Sioux had the right to choose their own agents and traders. It was not until 1870 when Red Cloud went to Washington and had the actual text of the treaty read to him that he learned for the first time that he would have to accept an agency near Fort Robinson and could not have his agency near Fort Laramie. So you see if there was any fraud or misconceptions about the treaty, it was because the government had changed the terms of the treaty in the period after the signing or had deliberately misinterpreted the treaty at the time of negotiations. But in no case did it assume any kind of jurisdiction over the Sioux in 1868.

The oral history reflects the attitude of the Sioux quite accurately and the records bear out the contentions of the tradition. The Sioux not only didn't think they were surrendering any rights, a number of them were quite arrogant about even signing a peace treaty. A good percentage felt that they had beaten the United States and that the United States was suing for peace. This was true in many respects; the Lakota were definitely negotiating from a position of strength. The Northern Sioux, in fact, wanted to prohibit any steamboat travel on the Upper Missouri and were quite insistent on this point. To pretend today that the United States was all-powerful during the years when this treaty was being negotiated is simply to read present conditions back into the past and rewrite, falsely, American history.

What practical comments can we make on the text of the treaty as it survives today, especially with regard to those articles and phrases which would seem to give total civil and criminal jurisdiction to the Sioux, excluding the United States? In the first place, the United States Senate did not often simply accept the terms of an Indian treaty. It could refuse to ratify an Indian treaty if it did not like the terms. It often did so. It could pass an amended version and then send another negotiating commission to the field and get the consent of the tribe concerned to the amendments. When this situation occurred it was often the Indian agent, the local captain of cavalry, or some government flunky who wandered into the wilderness and got a few signatures on a piece of paper to make it look as if the United States had indeed gotten the consent of the tribe to the amdendments.

This particular situation actually happened with the Horse Creek treaty at Fort Laramie in 1851. The original agreement called for the United States to pay annuities to the tribes for fifty years. The Senate reduced that period to ten years and then a few chiefs agreed to that amendment after the fact. In 1868 when the actual chiefs arrived at Laramie the first topic of discussion was the failure of the United States to provide annuities for fifty years as promised in 1851. They had not even then been informed of the change by the United States nor had they agreed to it. So their intent, for the most part, was to reaffirm the provisions of the old treaty rather than to cede new rights and privileges to the United States under a new agreement.

Everytime I have examined a document dealing with a treaty, not simply a Sioux treaty, but those of the Pacific Northwest tribes, the Navajo, Apache, Southern Plains, and even unratified treaties, I find that if the United States had not wanted to agree to the terms contained in the document, the Senate would have changed the terms of the treaty prior to ratification. That the Senate failed to change the text of the treaty, plus the fact that the oral tradition is always most concerned with the enforcement of precisely those provisions which are in contention and which the Indians accuse the United States of failing to keep, indicates to me that the Indians in fact had these particular rights, that the United States orally assured them that they had these rights, that a particular section of the treaty guaranteed these rights, and that the United States, and often its courts, will attempt to blur the issue so that the rights are neglected, forfeited, abandoned, or deliberately sidestepped whenever Indians ask that they be enforced.

Often one hears of a particular aspect of the treaty through the oral tradition long before one can discover the provisions in treaty negotiations or accompanying documents. That is why many of us feel that the oral tradition is, in a real sense, more accurate in preserving the spirit and meaning of the negotiations than the written record or any attempt by a state or federal court to interpret the treaty. Before I even began to read documents on Medicine Creek treaty in the Pacific Northwest, traditional Indians were telling me about Articles 6 and 12 of those treaties that concerned fishing rights and trading privileges. When I finally found the proper documents they verified everything the traditional people had told me about them. In the same way the concern of the Sioux people for the protection of the land base and the non-interference of the United States in Sioux affairs almost dominated any discussions of treaty rights. The first time I ever heard the figure of $70 million regarding the Black Hills was from a full-blood Oglala who was speaking on it. He reminded us that Red Cloud's final proposal to sell the Black Hills was that the Sioux would be fed, housed and clothed for seven generations. Years later I ran across Red Cloud's speech and the speeches of other Sioux chiefs and these very figures. So the government records and the oral traditions of the tribes are describing the very same thing, they intertwine to an amazing degree and I would say that the written record verifies the oral tradition while the oral tradition illuminates the written word. It is difficult, after all these years, to really say when I first learned certain things about the treaties and whether it was first in a written government report or from a traditional Indian telling me to look for certain things in the text of a treaty.

Some treaties do indeed contain phrases which speak of the supremacy of the United States, but such assumptions were not relevant to the Sioux or to other tribes, and they certainly didn't conceive of this supremacy in a political sense, economic perhaps, but not political. These were people who did not speak English, who did not have elaborate political structures, and who had no technical language which would describe such things as sovereignty, divine kingship, social contracts, or other abstract concepts that make up the intellectual tradition of western peoples. Jurisdiction, for example, was a practical matter. If any particular Indian did anything that aroused the ire of the whites, the tribe knew it would have to punish him, hand him over, or make some reparations. It might have to fight the Army or surrender the offender. But saying that the Sioux acknowledged federal jurisdiction is different. In some cases if the offender was a close relative of an important chief the United States would just overlook his crimes because it was politically smart to do so. Just as, perhaps, today, the United States overlooks crimes committed by politically influential people.

The Sioux knew they had a peculiar relationship with the United States and they tried to protect that relationship. They ably governed themselves until 1883 when there was a big hue and cry because Crow Dog was not hanged for killing Spotted Tail. When national publicity emphasized the fact that under Sioux law Crow Dog need not be executed but might make reparations, and that the tradition demanded that this alternative be offered Crow Dog, the whites became outraged and demanded that the United States assume jurisdiction over the Sioux. This was not a case of conflict of laws so much as a case of misunderstanding of cultures and the effort by whites to impose their cultural values in a uniform manner on the Sioux. Before that case you have a fifteen year period when everything ran smoothly under traditional Sioux law and the government made no effort whatsoever to interfere with the manner in which the Sioux handled murder and manslaughter. So it is not possible to say that the Sioux knew they were giving up their own jurisdiction in the 1868 treaty or even that they felt obliged to follow federal law in the operation of their own code of law.

If you read the Commissioner of Indian Affairs reports year after year, during those years between the signing of the treaty and the Seven Major Crimes Act, you will discover no effort whatsoever to impose or enforce United States law on the Indians. You will find constant manipulation of treaty annuities, continual efforts to discredit and undermine traditional chiefs, tribal laws and customs, and the Indian way of life. Red Cloud and Sitting Bull are generally slandered in these reports because the agents were dependent upon them for enforcement of peace on the reservations and the agents resented it. So we discover no concern about the criminal jurisdiction over the Sioux, even into the 1890s. Rather we find continual petty bickering and childish attitudes of the Indian agents toward the Indians and devious suggestions on how to avoid fulfilling promises made under the treaties.

After the Crow Dog case, the United States Congress passed the Seven Major Crimes Act, asserting United States jurisdiction over Indians on reservations for certain crimes. No agreement was made with any tribe in passing this act. It was not mentioned that the act was to supplant existing treaty provisions. No effort was made to amend treaties which forbid such an assumption of jurisdiction. But the most independent tribes were ringed with units of cavalry and so I guess the United States figured that might made right and didn't bother to question whether its action was legal. If it had checked the treaties, if the United States intended to act legally, it would have had to check the language in Article I of the 1868 treaty and come to grips with the provisions contained there. There is qualifying language there to the effect that the Sioux nation had the right to either turn the wrongdoer over to the United States or to allow the United States to take compensation from the annuities due them for his wrongdoing. I can think of nothing from studies I have done nor from Sioux oral history that would suggest that the Sioux Nation ever gave, or ever intended to give, civil and criminal jurisdiction to the United States.

There was a common, unarticulated tradition among most of the tribes and the United States regarding these matters. Generally the wrongs committed by either side were not regarded as important unless they became a cause celebre among either the Indians or the whites. If an incident aroused the fighting spirit on either side then some form of compensation or retribution would have to be made publicly to pacify the injured parties. Otherwise people did not bother very much about killings on either side. These things were very informal. I can give an example from my own family history. In the 1860's my great-grandfather was picked to surrender the bodies of two Santees (which meant he had to kill them) to the Army to show that the Yanktons had not been involved in the Minnesota fight. General Sully, who had originally requested that the Yanktons do this, then demanded that the Yanktons make a further demonstration of their loyalty to the United States by giving up any Santees who might be living with the Yanktons. My great grandfather refused, saying that the Yanktons had complied with Sully's original request, and that if he wanted more dead Santees he would have to fight the Yanktons. At that point both sides cocked their guns and when confronted with the show of force, the United States forces promptly waived the jurisdictional question. That was the way the frontier was, and you can't imply that the Sioux in signing any treaty, ever thought that they were submitting to a process whereby they would someday be in a federal court with endless appeals leading up to the United States Supreme Court. Insofar as the United States has never legally and specifically changed this understanding with the consent and understanding of the Sioux, and insofar as the United States cannot point to a specific treaty proceeding, hearing, or other form of consent in which the Indians understand that they will now be involved in the United States court system, we cannot say that the United States has ever legally taken jurisdiction over the Sioux Nation of Indians.

PART SIX

The Sioux Colony

The young people are the future. Photo by Melinda Rorick

AND I CAN'T UNDERSTAND THE STATUE OF LIBERTY

And I can't understand the Statue of Liberty.
They should have that statue of liberty in California
facing east.

The history,
the history of the Revolutionary War
and the Civil War
and the rest of them
all of them there,
        is just like two masters
        fighting
over this piece of land.

One language
                Language is going to ruin
                the whole world
If people behave, they will behave

So I want to say
                any loyalty and loyalness
                and faith and charity.
                                So-
I don't know what is charity.
I know what is loyal
and loyalty.
                But the people talk about
                that spoon of food
                which I get is very real.
It used to be a trainload from Washington,
When I get over there,
                        I don't know the ounces,
but just a little bit I get.
                I'm still—
I stand the starvation
The Indians are the only ones
could stand the starvation.
                I'm starving
for my own way of life
which I have to do
because all my buffalo were gone.
                They said
they are carrying diseases
because they have no brand.
                So now
the white folks
they bring their buffalo,
white and black and all that,
                        and
                        they have a brand.
And the different brand
from Nebraska and Illinois,
                and like this,
Why I'm trying to be a white man,
                        but
I couldn't get in there.
I couldn't be digested because
                all my
in place of that, I have diabetes.
                        —Henry Crow Dog

THE GREAT WHITE FATHER
Wilbur Jacobs

Very often government policy was confusing because it was based upon white altruism and acquisitiveness. What could be better than to have government trading posts under the supervision of government agents to insure fair treatment of Indians? Yet government policy in such cases, as Jefferson predicted, tended to put Indians in debt. Indian indebtedness could be used to purchase Indian land.

When we look at the Dawes Allotment Act of 1887, we can discern a policy of white justice and forbearance for Indian people. The Dawes Act of 1887 governed United States land policy toward Indians until the Franklin D. Roosevelt administration, when the Indian Reorganization Act was passed which encouraged expansion of the Native American land base. What is better policy than to lead Indians into a path of progress? Why not turn them into white Protestant American small farmers practicing our system of private ownership of property? Why not do this? Why not take the big communal reservation and divide it up, giving each male Indian 160 acres, and eventually give those individuals citizenship to bring them into the orbit of American society? What higher objectives could we have than that?

Yet when we examine the details of what actually happened, we see a process of dispossession and loss of tribal sovereignty among many Plains Indians, as Indian reservations, that had been negotiated by treaty.

An extension of this allotment scheme surfaced in the 1950's when certain Congressmen and Senators came to the conclusion that some Indian people were on the threshold of being good Christian farmers. These Congressional leaders decided that whole reservations could therefore be terminated and they enacted House Concurrent Resolution 108 (83rd Congress, 1st Session, which passed August 1, 1953). During the Eisenhower administration, the plan of termination was put into effect, and some Indian people lost their tribal land base largely as a result of the handiwork of Congressional leaders who were seemingly convinced that they were helping Indians to achieve a better life.

Yet such dispossession, that is the loss of a tribal land base, was a contributing cause for disillusionment and despair. Some tribes have had religious protest movements coming out of their extreme hardships. The Ghost Dance was one of these. Segments of almost every Native American tribe, groups of tribes, went through this cycle in some degree. Study of the Sioux people gives one an appreciation of their historic hardships as well as their cultural vigor and strength. It is amazing in this year of 1974 to see the Sioux maintaining their cultural integrity with their past despite the almost steamroller white occupation that has taken place in a period of a hundred or more years.

THEY GOT OUR WARRIORS DRUNK

Claudia Iron Hawk

My grandfather's uncle, Sitting Bull, Tatanka Yotanka, never signed the 1868 Treaty.
He was a medicine man and a leader of the people.

My grandfather, Iron Hawk,
is a nephew of Sitting Bull.
My grandfather told me the history
of the 1868 Treaty.
When I was a child and my mother died
and my grandfolks were raising me,
I used to go around with them.
I travelled all over with them.

In 1868, when they signed that Treaty,
my grandfather was a warrior.
This treaty was signed by the chiefs.
The government promised
to lay down its arms
and there would be peace.
The government promised
the Indians it would support them,
educate them and feed them
until the last Indian survived—
     and not even their animals which they left
     in their homesteads were still alive . . .
     until the rest of them . . .
                  Until the end
of the world would come
That is what they told me.

They said the agreement was made
so that this side of the Missouri River
clear up to the Big Horn
would be occupied by the Lakota,
the Sioux Nation.
The whites were not supposed to come
on the land unless they had permission
by the chief and head men,
the wise men and leaders of the Sioux Nation.
The Lakota people were to be governed
by the wise men of the bands.

In 1876, the whites broke that Treaty
by coming into the Black Hills.
General Custer came and they had a white flag
and they came in and killed
a lot of our children.
They broke the Treaty and came
inside with weapons.

My grandfather told us that at one time
there were some men with liquor
and they got our warriors drunk
and had them sign agreements or treaties.

I was brought up with medicine men.
I was raised by the Pipe and respect the Pipe.
I never lie when I put my hand on the Pipe.
That is our sacred belief.

RATIONS NOT FIT FOR HUMAN CONSUMPTION
Matthew King, Oglala elder from Pine Ridge

Mr. King is a Lakota historian and spokesman. He serves as Chief Fools Crow's interpreter on official occasions.

I speak and write about Indian affairs. I used to lecture in different schools all over the country—universities, high schools, organizations, television, and radio. Recently I helped Chief Fools Crow in trying to negotiate a peace between the United States government and our Indian people. I was the official interpreter on that occasion. I am now writing the history of the Sioux people, our life and beliefs.

The Sioux are a Nation. We believe in nature, natural laws, the great spirit. We are not materialistic. Sioux history goes back thirty or forty thousand years.

The Sioux have exercised their religion longer than the Pipe. The Pipe was presented to us only recently, maybe four hundred years ago. If we are in trouble and need help we must use the Pipe to pray. The mysterious person who presented the Pipe said that prayers must be answered. We have been using the Pipe ever since. There cannot be a ceremony without the Pipe. There is no other way. The Pipe is a power which was given to us and we must use it according to the instructions.

The Pipe was used in many of the negotiations between the United States government representatives and the Sioux Chiefs. But the white man doesn't believe in the Pipe and broke every treaty that was made with Indian Nations—371 of them. The Indian never broke a single treaty.

Songs and dances play an important role in the life of the people. Creation, no matter what it is, is anything that has life. The universe is the tabernacle of the Great Spirit and we must study it. We must study the moon, the stars, everything that contains our world. We must understand, we must respect. It took the Sioux thirty thousand years to observe those laws of nature. The white man has a long way to go.

All people have the same relationship with the land. Mother Earth produces sustenance to all human life and animal life. Everything we get from the Earth, we must pray to the Great Spirit that made it possible for us. Even our herbs that we use for medicine, we don't take without due consideration of whoever created the Earth, the power that is on the face of the Earth. White people look upon the land differently.

We are sorry that the white man does not think about the destruction of Mother Earth. Recently they have started strip mining on some of the most beautiful country in the world, in Montana. The Cheyenne are crying about it because they would rather keep it as it is because it is their religion. They do not want to hurt Mother Earth.

I do not hate white people. I feel sorry for them. We only take what we need from the Earth. Same way with the buffalo. They just killed what was needed. They don't destroy. We believe the Great Spirit has provided for all the people and we don't sell the things. We would give something away.

I was brought up in a period of time when some of the Chiefs were still living

153

back in 1908—the ones who signed the 1868 Treaty. I was old enough to understand. I heard Red Cloud and other chiefs talk. I was always an attentive listener and what they say, all of them, has been handed down. That is the law of nature, because you cannot lie. You have to tell the truth, and remember. They advocated peace among the people. They lived by that law because the world is a peaceful place to live in. They knew that the Great Spirit wanted everybody to live in peace in creation. They did not know what violence was until it was inflicted on them. Then they had to fight for their lives.

I remember the rations the United States government sent. Those rations were not fit for human consumption. They had white bacon which turned yellow, and kept it in warehouses for I don't know how long. The rice and beans had mice droppings in them. I saw it.

The Treaty of 1868 was signed in good faith by our chiefs and by General Sanborn and Henderson, two civilians and five generals. They drew up the 1868 Treaty and it was signed. Eight months later, the same people who drew up the Treaty drew up a resolution and presented it to the President that there would be no more treaties and that the Indian department should be turned over to the War Department to use stronger methods against Indians, to put us in concentration camps.

That is where we are. Those concentration camps are still in existence.

Then they tried to make them sign new agreements. They threatened to take rations away, to exterminate the people. They said, "We will rub you off the face of the earth and we will take you to the south to the hot country." Our Chief said to go ahead and kill us for we won't be worse off, and they never signed. Three-fourths majority were to sign any changes.

We had no written language. We used the sign language when we talked to the other tribes. From 1860 we had some Indian missionaries, religious people. When the white man religion was introduced, many of the Indians became ministers in the Episcopal Church, the Catholic Church, the Presbyterian Church. I have a father and two uncles who are ordained Christian ministers. I went to a seminary myself, but I did not become a minister.

Between 1851 and 1877, the United States made eight peace treaties, and eight war plans abrogating the treaty just made. The ones who drew up the Treaty of 1868 never meant to keep it, because eight months later here are the same ones that made the changes that the Indians will be in a concentration camp. All those treaties were made by the white man. He drew them up, approached us.

We ceded nearly two billion acres to the United States and the government said they would give back half, and also pay. But we never gave up the Black Hills because that is sacred ground and we have many people buried in the Black Hills. The whole area is a religious law of nature. It cannot be sold.

The 1868 Treaty is one important thing in Sioux life. What the white people brought was problems, and the people discuss that. They said they didn't understand the white people and they didn't understand what manner of men these white people are that make promises and then change them. They don't believe in that.

The interpreters for the treaties were not very good in making interpretations. For instance, some things were never recorded in these treaties but have been handed down orally. The Union Pacific Railroad was to belong to Indian people where it ran through Indian country. That meant, too, that they would have free passage. This was never recorded. Also, the mineral rights were only ceded for two feet of the surface. Wild game was never settled. Damages for the slaughter of buffalo, twenty or thirty million, was never taken into consideration. Many of the things in the Treaty do not explain all that happened to Indian people. That is what we are trying to correct.

154

The Sioux Nation is a sovereign Nation longer than the white people's government. We have thirty-one leaders, or headmen. The Chief's job is different from the President of the United States because every Indian thinks he is responsible for the actions of the Chief. The Chief is closely watched. If he makes a mistake he is out. There is no trial. He is out and that is all. They do not have to go through court spending thousands of dollars. Chief Fools Crow has to be acknowledged because he is the only senior Chief we have among the Oglala Sioux.

Chief Fools Crow and Chief Red Cloud, traditional Lakota Chiefs at negotiations with United States representatives at Wounded Knee, 1973. Photo by Melinda Rorick

In form, the United States Government is established under the Indian way of governments—chiefs, subchiefs, and head men. All of these have been copied from the Indian.

When the United States Government wanted to exercise sovereignty, the Indian people, who were already sovereign Nations, gave permission to the United States so they could negotiate with Indian people. We recognized their sovereignty by negotiating with them. None of those agreements signed after 1868 are recognized because the three-fourths clause of the 1868 Treaty was never used. The Indians say they are illegal.

The 1868 Treaty clearly states that law breakers will be handled either by the United States government or the Sioux government. We have one case where Two Sticks killed some white ranchers and the Chief arrested Two Sticks and presented him to the proper United States authority and they hanged him.

155

We have never known the white man to keep peace. There are a lot of white people who killed Indians that were never apprehended or even brought to trial. We kept our Treaty but the United States never did.

The United States promised to give half of the original land base back to the Sioux Nation. Now recently the United States offered the Sioux 105 million dollars. Where did they get that money?

The government of the United States is a foreign government as far as the Sioux are concerned. Indian people are supporting that government with our resources, our land, gold, minerals, everything in this country.

They just took the Black Hills. They got 408 people to sign it over, when it legally, by the Treaty, had to be 7,800 people sign.

Always the United States government representatives say that the 1868 Treaty is either void or not in force. I think we can do the same thing. We never broke a treaty but I think we could void all of our treaties legally. It would be the same thing because we are sovereign nations. We made the Treaty with the United States Government as a nation. We want to get the land back.

They have an organization which they call a "tribal council." The Bureau of Indian Affairs drew up the constitution and by-laws of this organization with the Indian Reorganization Act in 1934. This was the introduction of home rule. Mostly younger people are on it. The traditional people still hang on to their Treaty. They are a sovereign Nation. We have our own government. We have no written laws. The law of nature is our law. We have Chiefs—principal Chiefs and Chiefs. And we have Sub-Chiefs, Headmen, Warriors. We have different societies—Fox Society, White Horse Society, Badger Society, and others.

We had wars with other tribes under the influence of the United States. They furnished guns. They wanted certain territory and they got other tribes to war against the Sioux Nation, like the Pawnee. With a little concession of new guns and power there was war. That was for territory. The United States wanted certain land. They want Indians to fight each other and get rid of the people who occupied certain territory.

I will tell you an incident that happened between the Pawnees and the Sioux when my grandfather was wounded. They used to get along with the Pawnees. They used to trade and give. Before guns, they used tomahawks and bow and arrow. They used to have sham battle, friendly battle when they met. Once my grandfather with thirty-eight others went on a hunting trip and there were some Pawnees who came over the hill. They were warriors. The Sioux recognized them, so they didn't do anything. When the Pawnee came close they suddenly started shooting at the Sioux and killed all but three. My grandfather was wounded, but managed to get back to his people.

The Sioux asked the Pawnee for an apology, but they did not come. So the Sioux went against them. This was a result of what the United States did to influence the Pawnee. Probably they gave them money or tobacco to fight the Sioux. My grandfather used to tell me that.

The United States had their own scouts going to Indian countries. Some of them married Indian women, and they reported back to their own government what was possible. That was the trouble we had in the beginning. They used gifts inducing some tribe to fight another for certain territories. The United States wanted the land and wanted to get rid of the occupants.

The Bureau of Indian Affairs has more influence in the operation of the tribal council. They are operating under a policy that is against the traditional people.

WE HAD NO CHOICE
Marvin Thin Elk

I practically grew up with the 1868 Treaty. The Treaty was made during a time when the Red Nation, the Sioux Nation, was together. The Treaty was done with the Pipe so it is highly honored.

The United States did not live up to the Treaty. There were numerous occasions and numerous incidents that happened after the Treaty was signed with the Pipe when the United States violated it. The Treaty said that the Red Man would lay down his arms and not be hostile anymore. But in World War I, the Indian was given a rifle and sent across the ocean to fight. There were many other violations.

I have heard from my relatives of the numbers of attempts that were made to get headmen and chiefs to sign treaties concerning the Black Hills. The commissioners could not get these men to sign. So just plain warriors were given watered whiskey to get them half-drunk and then they dragged them over there and tried to make them sign. Some of them could not even make it to the table where the paper was.

The Treaty said that the Great Sioux Nation will govern itself and will govern its people. We have leaders and head men. The Rosebud Reservation, where I am from, is in the body of the Great Sioux Territory. The Great Sioux Nation never did become a part of the United States.

My belief is that the whole United States, so-claimed, is the Red Man's country. But today, since the 1868 Treaty made the boundaries of Indian Territory, I gather that the Indian Territory exists and the United States exists.

I have served in the military forces of the United States. We use the United States Post Office. But we have no choice.

THEY DON'T LISTEN
Nellie Red Owl
Mrs. Red Owl's testimony was given in Lakota and interpreted by Gladys Bissonette.

I was born in 1907. I was taught by my grandparents, my grandfather to live the traditional Oglala life for all my life. I hope to raise my grandchildren in the same way, in the traditional way.

I know a lot of our ways. I still remember those teachings that my grandfather had given to me to this day. My grandfather and my grandmother told me that in everything the Great Spirit comes first. We do not have these courts and these jails in our traditional life. I do not believe in these courts.

My grandfather told me that this land was ours and that the Great Spirit has given us this land. I believe that no one is allowed to take it away from us. I am Indian so that is the way I believe. I have the Sun Dance and I have gone to the Sweat Lodge. The Pipe is sacred and through the Pipe we Indians, we Lakota know this. The Pipe is sacred and through the Pipe we made the Treaty.

When the treaties were signed, the United States did not keep its promises. When

Nellie Red Owl on the courthouse steps at Lincoln. Photo by Harald Dreimanis, Journal-Star Printing Co., Lincoln, Neb.

they signed those treaties—when the Indians signed those treaties, those treaties belonged to us. When they signed the treaties there was agreement that no white man was supposed to enter into Indian territory. The chiefs and head men were supposed to govern the territory.

Today the Chiefs and Headmen take care of us but when they go to Washington D.C. to negotiate with the Interior Department, they don't listen to our leaders.

158

Reginald W. Bird Horse

Mr. Bird Horse is called Tako Eyanke (Running Antelope) in Lakota. He is from the Standing Rock Sioux Reservation.

We are Lakota which is the Sioux Nation, now known. My grandparents told me of the 1868 Treaty. From what was told to me, the Lakota Nation was and is a Nation. The Treaty was between the United States and our Lakota Nation. In the beginning, the land that the Treaty was talking about belonged to the Lakota Nation, belonged to the people. It was given to us by the Great Spirit and ever since then we have never sold any.

I have been told by my grandparents, this land is not for sale. The Treaty says that this land shall be ever for the Lakota People. Through our Chiefs, we are supposed to run our own government, not the United States government. Since the United States government had come over and wanted to make a treaty with the Lakota Nation, we agreed that if any crime was committed by the white man within our Nation, that there would be some agents to report him to. The Indians were to turn this white man over to his United States Government. If an Indian committed a crime, whether against the whites or against another Indian, the Indian would be dealt with by our own people. We could turn him over if we wanted to. But here are two nations, saying that we will deal with our own and you deal with yours.

My great, great grandfather was a Hunkpapa Chief who signed the 1868 Treaty. The English version of the Treaty is confusing. In there it says the Indian could be taken by the United States Government. I find in what I have been told and from what I understand, the wording in the English version is to the United States' advantage. The United States should honor the Treaty.

We are not going to change. We are Indians. We cannot live and believe like white people because we are Indians. I am Indian. I live the traditional way. The other way I have tried. We have families. We have to go out and earn a living, so I drive a bus. Whenever a meeting is called with the Episcopal Church, I attend. Other than that, I am an Indian traditionally. I attend dances, ceremonies. I fast. I pray to the Holy Spirit.

My grandfather said that they have never agreed to the Citizenship Act of 1924. It was forced upon us. Another one, the Indian Reorganization Act, was also forced. We did not agree. They did not ask the Lakotas. Another is the Allotment Act.

THEY ARE THIEVES
Paul High Bear

Mr. High Bear testified in his native Lakota which was interpreted by Beatrice Medicine, whom he requested because he knew Ms. Medicine's father, Sitting Crow (Martin Medicine), who knew the treaties well. Mr. High Bear is an Elder of the Standing Rock Sioux people.

Mr. Thorne, Defense Attorney: ... *Do you have an oral history about the 1868 Treaty?*

Yes.

From whom did you get this oral history?

Various of my grandfathers told me this.

What did your grandfathers tell you about the 1868 Treaty?

The first thing that was done was to take away the horses, and they took everything else, and they starved us.

Does your oral history tell you what the chiefs understood the agreement to mean with regard to the land?

The papers that were presented to them they understood would be continuing. They would be continuing in the Lakota way.

Who was to live on the land the treaty reserved for the Lakota people?

The Lakota people will live there because it belongs to them.

Who was to govern the Lakota people on the land, according to the chiefs who signed the agreement?

The chiefs and the head men who signed with truth were the ones who were supposed to govern the people; this is what the agreement ...

Mr. Nelson, Cross-Examination: *Did your grandfathers tell you anything as to what the United States would do with regard to the Sioux people after the 1868 Treaty?*

The understanding is that they would see them as another group of people and treat them as such.

Do you have any oral history of knowledge gained from your grandparents concerning treaties other than the 1868 Treaty?

The difficulty, it is difficult to translate. He said that the life style of the Lakota would continue and it would be done thoughtfully and gracefully and this is what they had agreed upon.

George Gap

Mr. Gap is Oglala from Pine Ridge Reservation. He testified in Lakota and the testimony was interpreted by Severt Young Bear.

I am 74 years old. My grandmother told me history. I remember about the 1868 Treaty.

From my understanding after the signing of the 1868 Treaty one of the promises that was made was that the Union Pacific Railroad was to have only one side of the track right of way. The other side belongs to the Sioux people. The north side of the track, and the north side of the North Platte River will belong to the Sioux people. From my understanding the tract of that land where the track was on was leased out, but I don't know how long, or to whom. That is what I remember.

Only the Sioux, the Lakota were to live in our territory under the Treaty. They will govern themselves within the Sioux Nation. Chiefs will lead the people such as Red Cloud and Spotted Tail.

The Pipe was used in making the Treaty. When using the Pipe, as an Indian Nation there are some laws, sacred laws that contain the usage of the Pipe. Whenever we use the Pipe, the agreement is sacred.

DISPOSSESSION
Roxanne Dunbar Ortiz

In the case of New Mexico, another case of violation of Treaty rights may be seen, showing United States bad faith. Article VIII of the *Treaty of Guadalupe Hidalgo* between the United States and the Republic of Mexico, guaranteed the property rights of the people within the ceded territory. The United States agreed to protect those property rights.

Half of Mexico was ceded to the United States after the United States Army defeated Mexico. The area that is now California, Colorado, New Mexico, Arizona was taken. Texas had been taken earlier by the Anglo slave owners.

Article VIII of that Treaty included language that was used to dispossess the Native people of their land base. The Treaty guaranteed property rights insofar as laws under which property had been held did not conflict with property laws of the United States. The United States used that wording to disclaim the community land grants which had been made and recognized under both Spanish and Mexican laws. This was contradictory because when Florida and Missouri were taken from the Spanish, the community land grants were recognized by the courts. Claiming a conflict between United States law and Spanish/Mexican laws was simply an excuse for taking the land.

Another issue regarding that Treaty emerged in the late nineteenth century, when land settlements were taking place. The courts required written documents of ownership. Many of the titles to those lands were passed down from generation to generation. In many cases, grant papers were lost. Yet no matter how many witnesses were brought to testify that certain people had always used and occupied the land, grants were denied if documents could not be produced. The oral tradition was considered invalid. This, too, contradicts Anglo-American common laws of property which recognize long and continued usage, from time immemorial, as claim to ownership.

The United States says it does not recognize Sioux sovereignty and that the Treaty of 1868 is invalid. What about Mexico? The United States still recognizes that country's sovereignty, but also broke its Treaty with Mexico.

Another means by which land was taken in New Mexico, like other areas, was through the work of individual entrepreneurs. They would send their agents, often lawyers, to individuals and buy share of a community grant, until they had bought up all the shares. This practice was illegal under Spanish and Mexican laws. The villagers who sold shares of land did not speak English, and given their tradition of common land holding, did not understand that they were giving up their rights to use the land.

Just as for the Sioux and other Native people, selling land was incomprehensible. Yet the United States and States introduced the money economy and money taxes. Subsistence farmers and tribal people did not have money, so they would sell to con men for practically nothing, still not understanding that they were doing anything more than selling use rights.

Another means for dispossessing Native people was accumulation of debts at various trading posts. People would have to cede land to pay the debts, since they had no money, and usually land was demanded. The people would be asked to sign a document which they could not read, receive a small amount of money or cancellation of debts. Then perhaps a year later, a stockman would come in, post eviction notices, and drive the people off the land. To this day Native people do not accept the concept of private ownership of land.

I believe that the United States knew what it was doing. The conflicts did not result from mere lack of communication between peoples of two different cultures. Clashes of culture can be positive, produce something new. Cultural contact produces cultural growth. But the United States was practicing colonialism. They wanted certain things, and the means did not matter. Early colonialist leaders like Thomas Jefferson realized that Native people of this continent would never submit to United States authority unless they gave up their collective concepts of the land and their cultures and their social systems. That was the basis of the General Allotment Act. Senator Dawes, who authored the Act, stated very clearly that the Native people would remain resistant to United States authority until they gave up the notion of the collective control of the land. The Dawes Act sought to divide up the land, reservation land, into separate family plots which could be sold, introducing private ownership. The method has not worked to change the concept of owning land, but it did work to dispossess the people of millions of acres of land. As Senator Dawes, author of the bill, said in 1885:

> I feel just this; that every dollar of money, and every hour of effort that can be applied to each individual Indian, day and night, in season and out of season, with patience and perseverance, with kindness and with charity, is not only due him in atonement for what we have inflicted upon him in the past, but is our own obligation towards him in order that we may not have him a vagabond and a pauper, without home or occupation among us in this land.
>
> The head chief told us that there was not a family in that whole Nation (Cherokee) that had not a home of its own. There was not a pauper in that Nation, and the Nation did not owe a dollar. It built its own capital . . . and it built its schools and its hospitals. Yet the defect of the system was apparent. They have got as far as they can go, because they own their land in common. It is Henry George's system, and under that there is no enterprise to make your home any better than that of your neighbors. There is no selfishness, which is at the bottom of civilization. Till this people will consent to give up their lands, and divide them among their citizens so that each can own the land he cultivates, they will not make much more progress.

The carvings in the Black Hills, sacred Sioux territory under the 1868 Treaty. Agnes LaMonte speaking July 4, 1975. Photo by Melinda Rorick

PART SEVEN

From Victim To Victor

SO THAT THEY WILL GO, YOUR HONOR, JUDGE

Now,
I speak the foreign language
to make my interpretation
                of what this law looks like,
                if it has to be looked like.

So to that time
none of us, our white relatives,
would understand my language if I speak
my own language.
                It would take you quite a time.

I'm truant.
I'm truant from my home,
from my life.
I'm truant
                into the spiritual life.

Now I have to—
                the government said
                is going to take care of me.

I need a cook,
I need a doctor,
I need a professor of law.
                On that part,
                on the other side is

I am the law myself.
I am born loyal.
                Loyalty
                and charity
                and salvation.
                On that part,
                I don't spend one cent.

I don't know what—
I don't want nobody to spend one cent
on me
to take care of me.

And Christ is that way.
Christ, we should save Christ.
                We should save John F. Kennedy
                and Martin Luther King.

We have to, your Honor,
            Judge,
                        we have to save you
                        and save him.
We will do it
in calling to serve
                        no two masters.

Democracy or Republican
I have got the democracy color.
                        But the people
want to explain
the democracy word.
                        And the Great Spirit,
                        hear me,
                                    Lakota,
                                    Wohlakota.
He agreed with me
and I agree with him.

In my words,   I would agree
                        to shake hands with you,
but for no mistake.
And the trademark they had
in Black Hills,
                        they had carved George Washington,
                        them others
there.
            Them people didn't own that piece of land,
            but they make some carving over there.
Anybody could realize
                        you have to go to Washington
                        Europe
and carve my face over there.

So let's have a good treaty
at this starting moment.
                        So that they will go,
                        your Honor,
                        Judge.
                                    —*Henry Crow Dog*

NATIONHOOD OR GENOCIDE
Roxanne Dunbar Ortiz

An aspect of sovereignty is recognition by other sovereignties. Native Nations recognized each others' sovereignty traditionally. I doubt that the United States will admit that it ever recognized the sovereignty of Indian nations, or that it will once again.

There is a matter or profits. There are important and valuable resources on Native land. Presently, under the puppet tribal governments that the United States Government has imposed, the United States can use Indian land or allow corporations to exploit the resources. If Native Nations were recognized as sovereign nations, then the people themselves would determine how their resources would be used.

There is also a political question. The United States does not want to set a precedent by recognizing the sovereignty of any "internal" colony. Many people could not understand why the United States fought in Vietnam, a small country of peasants with little modern technology. While there were resources there that were sought, the main issue was political. The victory of the Vietnamese people, the defeat of the technological giants with their vast armies and machinery, gives a lot of inspiration to colonized peoples all over the world.

This technological giant that seems to control everything can only continue to control by murdering the people, if the people decide the United States will no longer control them.

The existence of an Indian Nation, like the Sioux Nation, is even worse politically for the United States than the defeat at the hands of the Vietnamese. To a great extent, the Sioux Nation's fight for liberation is analogous to Vietnam. The United States Government and the people who control it, moneyed interests, cannot afford an independent Native Nation, because of the example it would set for other Native Nations, for Puerto Rico, and for other small nations under United States control, direct and indirect.

I do not believe that the American people, the majority of the people in the United States, would be threatened in any way by Indian independence or the end of United States imperialism. Mostly they are ignorant of United States policy and the Indian situation, and the world situation. And they are also controlled and oppressed by the United States Government and the corporations.

SOVEREIGNTY
Vern Long

Vern Long, from Pine Ridge Reservation, testified in Lakota, and the testimony was interpreted by Severt Young Bear.

In April 1973 Chief Fools Crow and I went as representatives to the United States President concerning the 1868 Treaty. We met with the President's representatives at the boundary line of Pine Ridge. A message was sent down from the White House, but the messenger was not allowed to come onto our present Reservation, so he delivered the message to the boundary line and we met him.

The Oglala Sioux tribe prevented the representative from crossing that boundary line. The message clearly stated that white people did not have any jurisdiction within Indian country unless we approved.

Francis Boots, Mohawk Nation

Mr. Thorne, Direct Examination: *Do you hold a position with your nation?*

Yes, in the traditional council of my people, I am a head warrior.

And when you speak of traditional council, what do you mean?

Traditional council is the council that our people have always had. Where I come from, we belong to the Iroquois Confederacy; this is the Confederacy that our people have always followed and Mohawk is part of this Six Nations which is the Iroquois Confederacy. So this is the traditional, ancient Council of our people.

Have you traveled about the United States and met with members of other Indian Nations?

Yes, I have. I have traveled quite a bit and met with a lot of traditional people for quite a lot.

When you have met with these other traditional people, have you learned from them their oral history as they understood various treaties that they entered into with the United States Government? That takes a yes or no answer as to whether or not you have discussed this.

Yes, we have.

Now in the course of discussing their oral history, have you specifically talked with them concerning their understanding through their oral history of what the signers of those treaties between the various Indian Nations and the United States, understood concerning their rights of self-government, their rights of sovereignty, their rights of leading their own lives in such lands as they reserved for themselves under those treaties? Have you discussed those things with them?

Yes, but mostly from a spiritual or sacred way.

Will you tell us what you mean when you say "in a spiritual and sacred way?"

There are certain teachings or a certain way of our people, as was expressed in this courtroom earlier, that for example when our people would take oaths on things or make a promise or say something, that it is a sacred way. That is something our people have been handed down to respect when you promise, when you put your approval, that is sacred understanding, for example.

In other words, when you give your word, you intend to live to that word?

Yes, that is considered a very spiritual thing.

In other words, it is a sacred part of your life, a spiritual part of your life, to live up to those things you say you will do: is that correct?

Yes.

And you have then, as I understand it, discussed in this spiritual way the understanding that has come through the oral history, that has been given to the various members of the Indian Nations you have talked to, the interpretation the signers placed on these treaties regarding self-government and their sovereign right and their independent rights of sovereign nations. Is that correct?

Yes.

Mr. Boots, in regard to your discussions with these people, will you give us your opinion as to the understanding the Native Americans had via their oral history of what the signers of the various treaties between the United States and the various Indian Nations, understood those treaties to mean with regard to their own right of self-government, their own sovereign rights, their right to govern themselves?

In talking or speaking with other Native Americans about their understanding of oral history in dealings with treaties, the headmen or people who represent the Nation are always concerned about the people's well-being the people as a Nation, with the understanding it had a land base, that it has a definite identity as a group of Indian people.

I think in speaking with many Native Americans and their understanding of oral history, they all, in my mind, my understanding, feel the same way that they have dealings with the United States, but they were specific dealings. They were in no way giving up what was given to them, in our way of believing of the Great Mystery, again talking about land base, talking about the right to govern themselves, the right to whatever people have that constitutes a Nation.

Now, turning specifically to the Sioux Nation, the members of the Sioux Nation, have you talked with them concerning this question? And do you have an opinion, assuming that you have talked to them, as to the belief of the Sioux as they entered into these treaties with regard to this question of the right of self-government?

Not on specific treaties, but on a very broad way. I have talked with them about things, about the kind of mind or the kind of way in which they understand the treaties, but I have never specifically sat down to discuss about certain treaties and what was, what we people, or that the Sioux people were giving up or what they were retaining for themselves. Never have I sat down specifically for those kind of things. But in a broad sense we have spoken.

In that broad sense in which you have talked to them, have there been discussions concerning their oral history as to whether or not they understood they were or were

170

not giving up their right to self-government, their right to control their own lives within the land base they reserved for themselves?

Yes, there was some discussion about that.

Can you tell us what it was, and what the oral history as given to them and as given to you, is?

Some of the discussion, as I remember, not just on one occasion, we came together with the way that it was taught to me about my people's treaties where I come from. Again, when they come to an agreement, there is a way in which people, in this case Sioux people, would sanction their word, which is a Sacred Pipe, where I come from Sacred Tobacco, it is the same understanding.

So when I talk about the sacredness in what they have agreed to, the word speaks for itself when they have made that promise or made that stand, or given their word on that.

I'm asking you specifically about the question of whether or not the signers of the Sioux treaties understood that they were giving up a right of self-government as you understand what they were doing in accordance with the oral history you have discussed with the Sioux People?

No, I do not think they were giving up their right to self-government.

They were not?

In my understanding.

They fit the pattern of the other Native Americans as you understand it?

That's correct.

LAND BASE FOR NATIVE NATIONS
Kirk Kicking Bird

From the expert witness testimony of Kirk Kicking Bird who is Kiowa from Oklahoma.
Mr. Kicking Bird is an attorney, and is Director of the Institute for the Development of
Indian Law. With Karen Ducheneaux he is author of One-Hundred Million Acres.

There is a kind of mythology, partially as a result of Wounded Knee massacre, that people think Indian problems ended with the 1890's. We propose that one of the solutions to current Indian problems is to establish an Indian land base of no less than one-hundred million acres. People think of that amount as rather extraordinary, especially an urban dweller.

When we talk about that one hundred million acres, we are talking about fifty-five million acres that are currently Indian land through individual allotments or as tribal land, and forty million acres of the Alaskan land claim settlement. That is ninety-five million acres. The remaining amount would establish a land base for Native people of the eastern part of the continent who do not have a land base at all.

There are all sorts of problems. The Agriculture Department currently holds land that may have been missurveyed and erroneously placed in national forests or national parks. Terms of treaties may have been just misunderstood. Executive orders were misunderstood and with the error against the Indian.

The Cherokee Nation v. The State of Georgia and *Worcester v. The State of Georgia* cases began the definition by the United States of United States–Native relationship. From those cases came the doctrine of discovery theory.

The other theory to emerge from the cases is the judicial doctrine of interpretation with respect to treaties, statutes, and executive orders affecting Indians—that they must be interpreted in the Indian's favor. The interpretations as conducted by the administration, by bureaucrats, Interior and Bureau of Indian Affairs, is not in favor of the Indians.

One instance of this is the return of the Blue Lakes lands to the Taos. The loss resulted from a series of executive orders which resulted in inclusion of these 48,000 acres of Taos land in a national park. The Taos people brought the suit to the Indian Claims Commission but refused to accept payment and wanted only the land. They had to go through legislative procedure, and they won. The Yakima Tribe regained 21,000 acres of land in the same manner. The land had been lost due to a missing map from the United States Archives.

One of the things that keeps cropping up is that in many of these instances the United States position has been to not allow the return of land but rather require the Indians to take monetary compensation. Of course, this is not what the Indians want. The Indian Claims Commission cannot then solve the type of problem they have. There is some vague, short reference to the possibility of making a land return being within the powers of the Indian Claims Commission, but in actual practice no land has been returned. If there is favorable judgment to the Indians, it is only monetary compensation they receive.

In addition to my studies as a student of law, I have learned through listening to my father and grandfather and our other relatives. During the last two years of Law School at the University of Oklahoma, I talked with the older Kiowa people about various aspects of life. I used, also, all the written reports and documents available to find out more about the Kiowa Tribe and our traditions.

I have pursued the study of treaties, particularly the Papago, Kiowa, Lance Chippewa and the small tribes of western Washington. We just completed the first volume of our treaty series which deals with all the treaties of the continent except the Iroquois. Through my research and through oral history traditions, it is my impression that there is a similar outlook among Indians about their rights to govern themselves.

We see a continuing theme, east or west, the same viewpoint as the Sioux. They see themselves as having the complete jurisdiction over themselves in terms of self government and control over their lands. It is my opinion that the Kiowa and other Indian nations should have sovereignty completely independent of the United States. There is no legal justification for the type of jurisdiction asserted by the United States.

I do not think the United States can properly claim jurisdiction under citizenship laws. I can show you where the court decisions have generally viewed tribal members as having three kinds of citizenship. First and foremost they are tribal members in their own Tribe. Court decisions say they also have a right if they want to assert their state citizenship. Then the 1921 Citizenship Act bestowed citizenship as a privilege. But I don't think the occasion exists in which the Indian has to make any showing of whether or not there is any affirmative acceptance of citizenship with any of the rights, prerogatives, obligations.

I do not believe the Sioux felt they were giving up sovereignty or criminal jurisdiction under the 1868 Treaty. They did not conceive of criminal punishment in the same way that Anglo-American law does. The alternative of not giving over the Indian wrongdoer is accompanied with monetary payments, and this is the only thing the United States would have jurisdiction over. That is the only way they could enforce the provisions by a compensatory mechanism, which would have been closer to the Sioux method of dealing with any kind of injury. I don't believe the Sioux would have understood that they were giving up criminal jurisdiction or jurisdiction or powers at all to the United States.

I don't believe the Sioux acknowledged any kind of power on the part of the United States. They were simply saying that they recognized there might be some problems and agreed to an equitable solution. The United States agreed that it does not have jurisdiction in Indian country, though they have jurisdiction outside of Indian country through an appropriation.

Indian Nations entered into treaties with nations other than the United States— Britain, France, Spain, and with the colonial states before the United States was formed. They also entered treaties with other Indian Nations.

THE PEOPLE CONTINUE
Madeline Red Willow, Pine Ridge Reservation

I have worked in many fields. Now I work with the District Tribal Council and with Save the Children Federation without pay. I work as a part time postal clerk. During the Second World War, I was employed by the United States Government for thirty months, with the WAVES.

I am Lakota. The traditional way of life was embedded in me through my grandparents, and I have been versed since I can remember because I have been close to my grandparents. My maternal grandmother was Cheyenne that had come to the Sioux Nation and was adopted by the Sioux Nation. She was a spiritual grandmother because she was married to a Sioux medicine man. From there I had my instructions in the traditional way of life for an Indian woman.

My paternal grandfater was Cana Se. In his way of life, every time they got together they talked about this Treaty so much. I followed my grandparents around, my grandfather especially. I live according to the traditional way of life of the Lakota people. I have, all my life, passed the tradition to my children.

To my knowledge, I have heard about the 1868 Treaty so many times through my grandparents that I felt that it was the way of life for me when I was small. This land is ours and we can do with it as we please and govern ourselves.

I have three sons who are thirty, twenty-six, and twenty-one. The oldest is an administrative sport superintendent of Pine Ridge at one time. Then the trouble between the tribe and government came and he transferred back to his work as coordinator for the United Sioux Tribes. The middle son is an orator well versed with all the traditional ways of life. He is an athlete and has his own basketball team. He goes to conventions and is president of the Billy Mills organization. My youngest son is in college.

WE CAN TAKE CARE OF OUR OWN
Mario Gonzalez, Chief Judge of the Rosebud Sioux Tribe

Traditionally, there is a way to deal with transgressors, and presently, there are other means. As tribal judge, I have the privilege of going and checking into tribal custom to determine whether an offense has occurred. The traditional method of dealing with offenders may be applied. There is, at the present time, the necessary machinery either under the traditional approach or under the existing Tribal Council, to deal with all offenses.

The Rosebud Sioux Tribal Council has exerted criminal jurisdiction over non-Indian people. I assume that we can handle any crimes we choose. Many offenses, those named in the Major Crimes Act, are referred to the United States attorney first. Many times he declines prosecution. In that event they are referred back to us and prosecuted in Tribal Court.

Many crimes can be federal crime and tribal crime at the same time. For example, an assault with a dangerous weapon, if the United States attorney declines prosecution then we would treat it as assault and battery and prosecute the offender in our Court.

The jurisdiction of our Court is spelled out in the Revised Law and Order Code of the Rosebud Sioux Tribe which was adopted under the provisions of the Tribal Constitution. The Tribal Constitution was adopted under the provisions of the Indian Reorganization Act.

I am an enrolled member of the Oglala Sioux Tribe. I am from the Pine Ridge Reservation and am aware of the set-up at Pine Ridge. The Oglala Sioux Tribal Council enacted a tribal code which spells out the procedure and composition of the Court.

There has always been a way of dealing with transgressors. In 1885, after the Ex Parte Crow Dog case, the Secretary of the Interior created a court for all reservations in the United States termed a Court of Indian Offenses. The Secretary of the Interior established a code for those courts called a Code of Indian Offenses. This code did such things to the Lakota people as abolish the Sun Dance and other religious ceremonies. This was all done by the Secretary of the Interior. When the tribes adopted a constitution under the Indian Reorganization Act, then the Secretarial courts were replaced with the Tribal Courts and these are the courts that we live with today.

Gladys Bissonette of the Pine Ridge Reservation

We look up to the chiefs and headmen of our Oglala Nation. Even though we have a Tribal Chairman under the Indian Reorganization Act we still look to the chiefs and headmen of the elders. The people who are in with the Indian Reorganization Act strip the full bloods of everything. The traditional people are not recognized. Some of them live on their own land but they do not have wells. They use kerosene lamps and little wood stoves.

The Tribal Government gave me a small paying job to move into Pine Ridge into

175

Gladys Bissonette, Lincoln. Photo by Melinda Rorick

the housing. I live in one of these houses with the basement cracked and the floors sagging. Anything that has been done for the Indian is never of good material or quality. It is slopped together.

The sovereignty of the Lakota Nation means that the Indians should govern their own Nation. This is why there are many of us today who uphold our chiefs and headmen and our elders. In signing the Treaty they did not want any other government to govern our sovereign Nation. We did not go to the United States. They came to us because Indians lived on this land long before the white man found the Western Hemisphere.

Traditionally, the Sioux had very strict laws. Our people, our Nation is to be governed by our chiefs and headmen. This was the only way Indians have ever taken care of the people.

If the United States Government had honored our 1868 Treaty, I would think right today we would all live in peace because we the Lakota Nation upheld our treaties. The chiefs and head men, the full bloods of our Nation can run our government.

Any militancy on our part has been provoked by the United States. Anything of violence shows the people of the world that the United States Government has made these laws and not lived up to them. They broke all of them since 1868. We are showing the people of the world that justice must be done.

We have been harassed on our Reservation, Pine Ridge. The United States Government is using Chairman Richard Wilson and his regime of goons to intimidate the Indians. We cannot touch a gun or even keep a .22 in our homes to go hunting. No, they take them away, but the goon squad has highpowered automatic rifles to shoot at people.

Birgil L. Kills Straight, Pine Ridge Reservation

I do many things. I am an organizer in education at the local, tribal, and national level. I have had a lifelong experience of federal and parochial schools and state operated schools.

As an Indian I have received a certain amount of my education through my grandfather and my father and the elders of the Tribe. The book learning education I received helps me to research and analyze and develop ideas and put them into implementation in different forms. But that is only one aspect, a part of a total.

Education is life itself and is based on the value system of the Oglala Sioux Tribe and the Indian people. The value system is derived from religion itself.

I am a member of the board of the Red Cloud School at Pine Ridge. I am a member and official of the Pejuturaka Community College and a member and president of the Coalition of Indian Controlled School Boards. It is a national organization consisting of school boards throughout the United States, Alaska and different parts of the world with around 160 boards participating. All of us who are in this organization have suffered at the hands of a foreign type of domination whose philosophy is based on the Euro-Anglo concept of education.

The Native American form of education includes man and mankind. When you begin to separate the life style of the Lakota, you begin to tear apart what is perfect. Most of us have experiences in Bureau of Indian Affairs schools where we were whipped, flogged, and were taught to learn that the father of this country was George Washington. We have seen in the textbooks ourselves as Indians being savages or heathens out raiding nice innocent people moving across our land, raping. Everything we were taught was completely in contrast to what we are taught as Indians.

Our feeling is that because we do not control the processes involved in education someone else's ideas are being fed into us and we begin to become ashamed of our own Indianness. We find that most of what we have been taught by our elders is not in the history books. We have to go out and develop our own languages from oral history. We talk of oral history as a passing of knowledge from one generation to the next. Our elders are the teachers. Our forefathers are the teachers. We in turn impart that knowledge and wisdom to those that are behind us.

Holy men of the Sioux can tell you that events, incidents, occurrences have always been etched into the minds of the people that lived at that time. A holy man possesses something that is comparable to a doctor of philosophy. He is a doctor of wisdom. He must possess all the virtues of the Lakota People—generosity, fortitude, humility. He must experience all. He must be able to live with himself, be in full control of himself. He must be able to continuously, daily live in that way. The education we receive is from the earth, from our people, from all our life. When one becomes a head man or chief he attains that stature not because of deeds he has done in battle but because he possesses all the virtues. He must understand life and be able to share what he has, must be able to think about the people first and himself last, be able to learn how to counsel and provide. He is a provider, a facilitator. He has to be humble.

From the elders, I know that the 1868 Treaty was an agreement between nations, two separate powers, coming to an agreement and promising each other they will establish and do certain things. The Sioux people today look upon the Lakota Nation as being a nation. The United States has tried to erode this belief. The Secretary of the Interior has ultimate power, veto power over our United States endorsed government since the Indian Reorganization Act of 1934.

The education system that has been imposed on us Indians taught how to be a white man, how to assimilate, how to gather wealth, how to establish savings accounts. The Indian system does not teach the accumulation of wealth nor the sectioning of time. Indian people have always believed in the Hoop, the Sacred Hoop, where everything is around us, everything is now. From the time we enter this world until we re-enter the spirit world, all is one. The four major virtues—humility, fortitude, generosity, and wisdom—are signified by the four cardinal colors.

When I first went to school, I could not speak English. On the wall, it said, "Do not speak Indian." I could not read, so I spoke up and a ruler was broken over my head. That type of punishment and abuse of Indian children is what we are now turning around.

We do not want to be white men. I am Indian. I am Sioux. I am Lakota. I feel the education system has to be changed where we do not read in history books about Indians being rapists and savages. We have to establish an accreditation board that recognizes the 267 different tribes of this land.

177

THE AMERICAN INDIAN MOVEMENT
Faith Traversie of the Cheyenne River Reservation

I attended grade school in a United States Government boarding school in Minnesota. I was transferred to another boarding school for high school in South Dakota. This was a vocational high school. I was a welder for the United States Navy during World War II, then I worked for the Bureau of Indian Affairs for thirteen years until I resigned.

My great grandmother helped raise me until her death when I was ten years old. All my life and ever since I can remember, I always heard of how the Black Hills was taken from us. I always heard how they got the chiefs to sign, that they did not realize what they were signing. They were tricked into signing things. I heard it all my life.

I worked for the Bureau of Indian Affairs at the old agency boarding school on the Cheyenne River Reservation. I was a matron or housemother in the dormitory. Eventually I worked up to a supervisory position. There I learned more about what was being done to our people, what I felt was dishonesty. I did not think that money going for the Bureau of Indian Affairs was being used for our people. I became unhappy because I had a tendency to speak out and take up for the Indian people, the parents. Many times I took up for the people I supervised. I decided to resign.

That is when I found out the whole philosophy, the purpose behind the American Indian Movement. I joined A.I.M. in 1969 because I felt there I could do more for my people. I remember Russell (Means) saying, "Well, we have tried to help and we are helping the urban Indian, but let us concentrate on our grassroots people on the reservation. That is where our people most need help. Let us go back and try to motivate our people. You know they are so downtrodden by the government, by government supervision. Let us go back there and get them interested in doing something." I have diligently done everything I can to do what is right and meaningful and good for our people. I have tried through the American Indian Movement.

My daughter, Madonna Gilbert, is a leader in the American Indian Movement. She has with the help of others organized an Indian cultural learning center for Indian children. It is sponsored by the American Indian Movement.

We believe in the Pipe. A Pipe does not have to be present, be in our hands, but is always with us. It means truth and honesty.

Dennis Banks, Chief Executive Officer of the American Indian Movement

I am familiar with the oral history of the Lakota people, not because I am a leader of the American Indian Movement, but because I am a member of the Sun Dance Religion. I have taken a pledge and vowed to dance four years to the sun each year at the first full moon in August. I have kept that pledge the last three years. During those three years I have listened to chiefs and medicine men and elders speak and I have heard them singing songs. I have heard them tell stories about their way of life.

Dennis Banks, American Indian Movement. Photo by Michelle Vignes

Through this contact I have learned about the ways of the Oglala. I am now married to an Oglala.

From the stories I have been told, the Sun Dance is an act of thanksgiving to the Great Spirit. The Sun Dance itself is a thanksgiving act or thanksgiving ritual whereby Indian men fast for four days and four nights and dance during the day. They dance in the four directions from a cottonwood tree in the center. The cottonwood tree is sacred to the Sioux.

The Sun Dance itself is a reminder to the female of this earth that man is willing to show to his mother or his wife or his grandmother and all females that he is willing to share some of the pain that women go through in giving birth to newborn. The flesh is torn in the dance.

After four days of fasting and receiving spiritual direction from the medicine man and purification from the sweat lodge, there is a traditional piercing of the skin whereby you give thanks to Mother Earth by breaking yourself loose from the cottonwood tree.

The Sun Dance is part of several ways to keep in contact with the Great Spirit. One is to fast and go up to the hills by yourself on a vision quest—four days and four nights. Another way is to go to the sweat lodge every morning and evening and give thanks. You pray with the Pipe at all times, while you are fasting, while you are on the vision quest, while you are in a sweat lodge, while you are in the Sun Dance. That is to me what I have learned from the Sun Dance people. To pray with the Pipe or to say your words with the Pipe is the highest pledge.

I have learned much in three years of sitting around with the drum and I have learned songs. I have listened to Chief Fools Crow, to Kills Enemy, to Young Bear, and Gap. I have heard them talk about the Treaty. From what I have listened to there was an agreement signed and it was to end all war. There were many people at that gathering, then there was gold, and many Indians were killed.

From what I understand the Sioux Nation would control the area they reserved for themselves and that they would allow no one without their permission to reside inside.

They had and still have a very good system of law and order, a traditional form.

I have lived the Lakota way of life. It was around me. However, I was shoved into another kind of life for thirteen years. There was conflict between the foreign way and the traditional way of life. I feel that I am not yet qualified to really speak on the truth of the Pipe. I have been subject to another element or another kind of life. After realizing it was getting me nowhere, I found a family, the American Indian Movement. That family has educated me about the importance and the significance of our way of life.

I was almost to the point of giving up until these beautiful American Indian Movement people of our tribe and our Nation brought that to our attention. Taking an oath on the Pipe, it is automatic. I could never lie.

It is going to take a while because I am coming back to living the beautiful life. I do not feel I am qualified to talk about many things because I am young. The people with full knowledge are the traditional people and the spiritual people.

I really am concerned all my life because of the community and my own experience with this white man's favorite water, alcohol. They brought it into our lives and for many years now the problem has increased. I work as a counselor. The white man has used alcohol against us. A lot of times when the white man wanted some information or wanted something off the Indians, they offered them a bribe. Alcohol has disorganized our communities and our families. People are now beginning to realize that we have this experience. We are working on it now, trying to help. This is why I became involved in the American Indian Movement because this is one of their main goals to overcome the problem and help.

THOSE WHO LEFT ARE RETURNING
Theda Nelson Pokrywka, Pine Ridge Reservation

My great grandmother on my father's side was Chief Red Cloud's sister. She married what is commonly known as a squaw man, John Wyatt Nelson. I received history from my grandmother who is half Sioux and half Cheyenne. They were talking to us ever since we were just little kids. She always told us what happened to them as children, when the treaties were signed and especially the 1868 Treaty, how they were to be taken care of. Then she was left without a husband and Sioux people took her into the Pine Ridge Reservation. The Oglala people took her in and she remained with them the rest of her life.

When I grew up I spoke the Cheyenne language because of my grandmother. Then when she died I began speaking Sioux and then went to school. I had been away from the reservation ever since I was about twelve years old, only going back occasionally, and I never spoke Sioux again.

I went through nurses training and worked off the reservation for the past twenty-six years until just within the last four years, I began to wake up. Many of us who have been away from our people are coming back. Now I can do for my children what was done for me. I can bring my children up the Indian way.

Ted Means, Pine Ridge Reservation

I have been in a learning process for some time now. For me to say that I am a traditional Indian is not easy, because to be a traditional Indian is very hard.

I spent six years in an Episcopal Mission school and attended college for a short time. I was for some time sort of lost. I had been told at an early age by my grandparents on my mother's side about being Indian. But it has been only recently that I have re-identified myself as being proud of what my grandparents passed on to me. Since that time I have been able to learn a great deal from the traditional leaders of the Lakota Nation.

The white education system teaches us that we were savage pigs and heathen people, and that to be Indian is something less than being white. In the experience of traditional education, I have felt the beauty of being Indian, how very spiritual our people are. To be Indian is hard, but it is also very beautiful. Experiencing traditional education has brought about a complete change in my life. Since coming to that, I have been dealing with the white man's educational process and what the United States Government has done to Indian people. I have the sense of accomplishment in the sense of caring for our people.

In the mission school I was taught about living a good Christian life. I was told we must become assimilated, become white. While they talked of being Christian, Indian children were being punished for speaking their own language. They were being beaten because they could not relate to that educational process. They told us we were dirty.

They did not live as Christians in their relations with us.

Indians, just as myself, have come to realize that we cannot be white people. We can only be Indian people and to be Indian is beautiful. The time I spent in the mission schools and the time I spent in the cities and in the bars were part of the process which brought me to this realization. Hopefully, I will be able to pass it on.

During World War II, the United States Government came into the reservations and recruited Indians to go into the shipyards and the military installations to work. My father went to work in a naval shipyard in Vallejo, California. In the 1950's during the Eisenhower administration there was a relocation program. I was part of that program. In two decades of operation, the Relocation Program, designed and operated by the Bureau of Indian Affairs, removed nearly half the Indian population from reservations to urban areas.

Introductory ceremony, always with the Pipe. Photo by Michelle Vignes

THE SACRED HOOP

Hear me, not for myself
but for my people.
Hear me in my sorrow.
I am old.
Hear me that they may once more
go back into the Sacred Hoop
and find the good, red road.
Oh, make my people live.
                        —Black Elk, 1931

Lewis Bad Wound, Pine Ridge Reservation

The sacred hoop. White men refer to things as the circle. The sacred hoop, by its nature signifies truth. Our people are very religious. In theory, in all societies truth is signified by a circle. In our viewing everything in life, we look at overall continuation of life—completeness of a circle.

Events of history we view as coming in the circle. There are things which I could tell which relate to the present history which has the power of learning from the past. Non-Indians would say it is only a coincidence. We view it as completion of the circle.

A hundred years ago a man named Lincoln set the black men free. We come to a city named Lincoln seeking our freedom. Another parallel is that a hundred years ago when we last confronted the United States Government, one of their leaders was Yellow Hair. Today the same thing, one of the leaders is Yellow Hair. We view these overall things. We seek truth in all things in our surroundings. This view of the sacred hoop makes history especially important to Lakota people. It is a continual thing with us.

One of the basic, original instructions we received from great spiritualists is watch and listen. We are more observant and more cognizant of our surroundings than non-Indians. We observe life with nature, observe our surroundings, what is occurring all the time. We listen very attentively to what is occurring around us all the time.

The continuation of life is a complete process. When the man from Europe came to our shores seeking freedom, we granted those freedoms. Subsequent to that time he has reversed positions and denied us our various freedoms. Our people have gone in a great descent in our way of living. But now we believe it is time that we are coming back on the ascent. We are coming back to a position that we had, possessed, at the time of the coming of the man from Europe into our country here.

We believe the Earth is our mother. We are not possessors. We are caretakers for the ones that are following us, our children and their unborn. It is our duty to preserve this for their uses when they come. I can sit here for the next week and expound on the friendship the Indian has for land, Mother Earth, but it is beyond the concept of non-Indians. I have spoken many times to non-Indians and they could not grasp the relationship.

The taking of our lands and these instances where the United States Government offered money, the Indians did not view that as selling land. They do not sell the mother, but permit them to use those lands. It was no outright sale. We have no right to sell these lands.

When the "Pilgrims" landed on our shores, Indians welcomed them in friendship to share what they had with them. One thing that history books invariably fail to reveal is that the people, the ones who greeted the Pilgrims with friendship, within twenty years had to fight for their lives at the hands of these same people who had received their friendship.

Our elders speak of the first three times that our people came in contact with the forces of the United States Government which they are presently known by. Our people were for the family. They did not destroy their language, their culture, or their people. They only told the intruders one thing—try and change the ways, go back and leave us alone. That was not a very hard request, but they would not leave us alone. Yet today we are still repeating the same message.

Our system of government is the exact opposite from what the United States is. I would describe theirs as a pyramid with their heads of state at the top. Ours is the exact opposite. These people tell us what to do. We don't tell them what to do.

The Lakota have never violated the Treaty. Our forefathers have entered into that agreement with the United States Government on the sacredness of the Pipe and we are bound to honor that Treaty. No matter how much cruelty, poverty we must suffer to honor that treaty, we will honor it.

THE PEOPLE WILL STAND AS ONE
Albert Red Bear, Pine Ridge Reservation

Sitting Bull was my great grandfather. From my understanding of the oral history one of the topics discussed was that Oregon Trail and the building of railroads. These were temporary deeds by the white man and whenever they are through using the trail and the railroad they were to leave.

My understanding of the history of the 1868 Treaty is that the land belongs to the Sioux people and that they will live on this land as people. But somehow recently the understanding that I am getting is that the land still belongs to us and for some reason the United States law has been forced upon us and taken a lot of our men away.

The land belongs to us as Sioux people, and that is the only road that we have to travel on. From my understanding the Pipe will govern the people through its sacredness and the people will stand as one.

CONCLUSION

THE CLOCK IS MARKED TWELVE

I thank you, and I thank you, and I thank you. Now,
we have to patch up
or we do no patching.
We have to stand for righteousness at this time.
We come to know our civil rights,
what is civil rights.
                  The keeper up there,
                  equality,
                  equal rights,
                  humanity,
that is never overfilled or never spilled,
it's keeping the same practice
all the time that the people
have to practice
People have to unite together and

                      be one,
                      that no one
                      just only God be with us,

no other country
but ourselves
        right here.

I think those who are anthropologists
and anthropology
                toward Indian,
and I am anthropology toward the white.
                            But they
are all doing that. I am getting all the interpretation.
That's why Abraham Lincoln was to make a good interpretation
and John F. Kennedy
and Martin Luther King.
                  They wanted to get rid
                  of those who want to make
                  a good interpretation.

Your Honor, Judge,
you will be safe.
                You will be long remembered.
So a person

has to speak
                physically
                and spiritually.
That understanding we have to get,
                                those two masters.

I see myself in the water.
I see myself in the death.
They said
            we have some penal institution,
            some people in death row.
                            I ask
poor and rich
to help us want to save
want to be saved in a way,

I said.

The white folks hostile,
                            it's getting stronger.
So that my mind
going to bear a scar.
                    For that, I want this
                    people have to use
                    their word,
                    their life,
                    anything,
to present,
to make
        the people know that we should live.

Maybe it will take a century
or a hundred persons.
They should be single.
                    They have to be
                    in a safe, safe
                    place.
                            And to this time—
my grandfather said that you will come to a time—
Indian time
            is any time,
                        there with God.
But
the white man says
                one thousand nine hundred
                seventy four
                then we come to
                '75.
                    To this time,
we go into another century
about the civilization.

                    A person will be both—
will come to
              at a right age,
              then I'd be the president
              of the United States.
                              And I will say,
You white people,
go back to Europe.
                    How would that sound?
                    How would that look like?
Because you are the garden
and I am the god.
                        So we have to keep the word
                        of God.
                        So I will write the word
                        s-h-a-m-e,
                        shame,
let's put shame away
and put something in place of that.
                              I will tell
my God,
my God,
my spirits,
              talk other things in this world
              like this.
                        Like a snap of the finger.

But we have to tell the world
that we were here,
were here on the right side,
and on the left side,
                        but we were here.
Somebody said that the h-e-a-r,
somebody said h-e-r-e,
                        We are here.
                        Here is here.
                        We get it.
That's why the Indian use this pipe.
                              He stopped
and all like this here.
Until this time, now
                        here I am.
                        I understood.
                              Because
that's why the white folks said in their language,
and that's why they print the law
about the Ghost Dance
and the Sun Dance.

190

Now,
here we are before God.

           So nobody
           couldn't excuse himself.

           If this wasn't so,
this Indian would not be here
or the white folks would not be here.
So,
I am very thankful my voice be heard
in a place like this.
I thank the Great Spirit I was here,
that my word and my sound will cover all
the global world
           as I heard what the white man said
           in the radio and their broadcasting.

Freedom is what,
justice is what,
liberty is what
        we want.

So if anybody wants to shake hands with me
for that, why it's up to them.
           The white folks enjoy
whatever they want in this world,
but we want to have equality and equal rights
of the mankind.
        I thank you.

The clock is marked twelve.
                —Henry Crow Dog

EXCERPTS FROM THE DEFENSE SUMMARY ARGUMENT
John Thorne, Attorney

I will broadly state our position, and it's a simple position. It is as follows: The United States, having been formed as a country, adopted a constitution and under that document certain powers were given to certain branches of the government. One of the powers that is spread equally among the three branches of the government is the power of making treaties—contracts with other nations, agreements; giving promises and receiving promises in return; promises that call for action or inaction, depending upon the promise. It involves all three branches of the government because it involves in the first instance the executive making treaties, negotiating those treaties. It involves the legislative branch, in that the Senate must ratify, and it most assuredly involves the judicial branch, for it is the judicial branch that views those treaties and is mandated by the Constitution to accept them as the supreme law of the land.

Our second position is that the United States did in fact enter into the treaties with various Indian nations across this land; and one of those groups of people with whom we negotiated as a separate sovereign nation were the Lakota—the Sioux as we have come to know them generally.

Our position also is that the time of the entering of the 1868 Treaty, the Lakota people were negotiating from a position of strength. They were protecting their land successfully, and particularly in 1868. The United States that came to these people came because the frontiersmen, the settlers were pressing ever west, moving, moving, moving; and the United States wanted a peace treaty.

By the Fort Laramie Treaty the Sioux agreed to reserve to themselves the particular area of the surface of Mother Earth described in that treaty as their permanent home. We never stop to realize when we use the word "reservation" it comes from the word reserve. What in fact happened is that people were here, the Native Americans, and as the whites and settlers came along and wanted this land, they made treaties with the Native American. The Native American reserved to himself an area for use, and turned over the use of the balance of the land to the United States to its people.

It is interesting to think about the conversation we had about the Louisiana Purchase, and realize that obviously the United States could not think that it acquired any title in the Louisiana Purchase. If it did I would ask why did we have to enter into treaties with the Native Americans following the Louisiana Purchase? We had to enter into treaties because we realized quite clearly that they were in fact the ones who had the title and use of that land.

The Lakota reserved the western half of what is now South Dakota for their absolute and undisturbed use and occupation. It seems clear that those words mean the Lakota have the absolute right to govern themselves, to lead their lives as they desire, to live in accordance with their own culture and their own traditions, and not be disturbed in the use or occupation of that land by the United States, nor anyone else.

If there is any right guaranteed by the "right to govern" it seems to me that right is to make one's own law, because that's what government is. It's the making of rules to guide these interpersonal relationships. And if there is any one body of law that is the base for all of it, it is our criminal law, for it is the criminal law through which we prevent individuals from destroying other individuals, from destroying each other and destroying governments.

Following the Treaty of 1868 every single unilateral act of the United States regarding the Lakota is unconstitutional and illegal because they are unilateral. As an example: Let us assume that the government of Mexico tomorrow passes a law, and in that law it says: "If a citizen of the United States commits the following acts within the United States, the courts of Mexico shall have jurisdiction over those United States citizens for that act within the territorial limits of the United States. We will send our army in and we will arrest them, and we will bring them to Mexico and we will try them, and we will penalize them in accordance with our law." I hesitate to think what would happen when the first Mexican soldier stepped across the border in an attempt to make an arrest. Yet that is exactly what we have done here.

I ask the United States Attorney, can he say, as he looks at all the facts he has seen, that the people who went into Wounded Knee on February 27, 1973, Lakota people, went in there with criminal intent, that they went in to rob or steal or to assault, or that they conspired to commit criminal acts? I don't see how anybody could ever say that. They went in out of the deepest of frustration—a frustration that has gone on and on and on, and on. They said: "Give us our Treaty rights."

The Indian Claims Commission, after admitting the United States acted illegally in taking the Black Hills, says we will now compensate the Sioux. I cannot understand. We admit we stole the property, and as thieves we now say to the people from whom we stole the property, we are not going to give it back, even though you want it, and we shall decide how much to pay you for the land we have stolen!

Let me talk a little bit about where we are in this country today in terms of whether or not we need to look at the 1868 Treaty. If I understand the approach of the prosecution, it is, "Well, those things happened so long ago, they are not of concern today." I would ask this Court to take note of one of our laws. Chapter 1120 of our Public Laws, adopted September 30, 1950, is an enactment authorizing the Chief of Engineers, Department of Army, together with the Secretary of the Interior, to negotiate certain contracts with the Sioux. Interesting language occurs at the end in Section 5(b) and I quote: "No such contract shall take effect until it shall have been ratified by act of Congress and ratified in writing by three-fourths of the adult members of the two respective tribes." This is the clearest recognition of that 1868 Treaty being binding on the United States today, for the requirement that three-fourths of the Sioux must ratify the agreement is directly from the treaty.

We have seen the upheavals in our own country, in our own people, rising up and questioning ourselves and saying, "What are we doing?" The one thing that I keep sensing among the young people of this country is frustration against the system that they see being so destructive to themselves and everything around them. I think what they are really saying is, "We have had it with hypocrisy. Don't tell us we are a nation for peace when we are the only nation who has an army on every continent, and missile bases throughout the world." This questioning is the hope that we are going to survive. We are 6 percent of the world population consuming 45 percent of its non-renewable natural resources. That means there are some people that are not getting their fair share of their own resources. Thus in the mid-east, that great basin of oil, they are saying, "No, you are not going to tell us what we are going to get for our oil.

We are going to tell you, because it belongs to us." It is from the Third World that we take most of the goods.

We have the Palestine Liberation Organization appearing before the United Nations, saying they have a right to exist. And we have Ireland where we are told it's a battle between the Catholics and the Protestants, but that isn't what the fight is all about. It is an economic problem. Always as you look around this world, it's an economic problem.

Look at Chile and the C.I.A. We read our newspapers and find that the C.I.A. has been spying on us in our own homes.

We look at South Africa with the apartheid policy it has, and we still do business there! Your dollars and my dollars are invested there and are maintaining a system such as that.

We look here in the United States and we see organizations like the American Indian Movement and the Black Panther Party, La Raza, and the United Farm Workers. They talk about oppression, and they talk about a better life. They move and they act. In response, we build bigger and better prisons, appoint more and more judges, more police officers, and make more arrests.

We have unemployment and inflation. We have Watergate. Compare the Lakota people who went to Wounded Knee, and their reasons for going there, versus those who were involved in Watergate, and their reasons for doing what they did.

Your honor, it's not you, but it is our law and it is our system, and you speak for that law and that system. I have a hard time when I face this question the prosecution raises, that this is a "political issue" and therefore the courts can't decide it. It has always seemed to me that every issue here is an issue that can be decided by the courts, because that is why courts exist. If it deals with law then it is for the courts to make decisions. And if the courts won't act what is left for them after they have tried everything? They have been to Congress over and over, but what does a Congressman care about a Native American? They don't register, they don't vote. Most Congressmen don't have more than a half dozen registered voters who are Native Americans living in their district. Are they going to listen to them and act in the halls of Congress? No. To say this is a political question and not for the courts is to pass the buck.

Your Honor, I hope you will say: "I, at least, as one person, a citizen of the United States, who has been appointed to serve the people of the United States, say that as a nation we must comply with our obligations to you, the citizens of the Sioux Nation. At least one representative of the people of the United States determines that you are right." This is what you can say.

I want you to be bound by moral law. If you were to suggest that you would be bound by a law passed by Congress that said every third child born to a family shall be put to death, if you were to enforce that law, I don't want you on that bench anywhere. The morality has to be there also.

The Court: *Whence comes my authority? I'm serious. Whence comes my authority?*

Mr. Thorne: To do what?

The Court: *To do anything. I am a judge. Where did I get my authority? Whence cometh it?*

Mr. Thorne: Exactly the same place that the Treaty between the United States and the Sioux Nation gained its status as a solemn agreement.

Now I think it is entirely possible for the courts of this country to say we have a unilateral right to abrogate a treaty, and when we say it, I think what we are saying is

194

"might makes right." We are the strongest, therefore we will do what we want. We will impose on you, the Indian people, anything that we want. We can do that. We are the strongest. But it leaves one alternative and one only, and that is war. That is the only right they have left. And the frustration, I am sure, can't go on forever.

We could do it, Judge, there is no question about that. We have done it. We've been doing it all these years. We've imposed our will on them by might. We can go on doing that, but if we are going to, at least let's not fool around any longer and dodge the issue, say this is a political question, it's up to Congress, when we know good and well Congress isn't going to do anything about it.

The Native Americans in this country have not resorted to violence. They haven't issued any declaration of war and gone out to do violence anywhere. They have continued to try to use the halls of Congress and these courts to seek a redress of grievances. Frankly, I think that a decision saying this court does not have any jurisdiction would begin to build within the Sioux a feeling that might be different than from what Russell Means indicated in his testimony when he said "we have waited a long time to see this integrity and honesty come forth," and that he is going to die fighting for those Treaty rights.

Sioux Not Sovereign, Says Court

LINCOLN, Neb. (UPI) — A federal judge Friday dismissed a claim that the United States government has no jurisdiction on Indian reservations and ruled the Sioux Indian people are not fully sovereign and have not been for many years.

U.S. District Court Judge Warren K. Urbom rejected an Indian claim that federal agents had no business on the Pine Ridge Indian Reservation during the 71-day armed occupation of Wounded Knee, S.D., by members and sympathizers of the American Indian Movement in 1973.

"The conclusion that Indian tribes do not have complete sovereignty is irresistible if I am to follow an unbroken line of decisions of the United States Supreme Court extending from the early 19th Century until the year before last," he said.

Urbom said, "White Americans may retch at the recollection" of the way Indians were treated during the westward expansions of whites across the United States. But he added, "Feeling what is wrong does not describe what is right."

Whether the Sioux will ever again be fully sovereign, the judge said, will be up to Congress and the President and is not a decision that will come from the courts.

Urbom's decision climaxed a special hearing at which members of the Oglala Sioux tribe argued the tribe had never surrendered its jurisdiction over Indian lands set aside for their forebears in an 1868 treaty between the Sioux Nation and the United States.

The hearing was held on the contention of about 65 defendants, accused of criminal acts during the AIM occupation of Wounded Knee, that the U.S. government lacked jurisdiction on the reservation.

During the long hearing last month, lawyers for the Indians claimed the 1868 pact had never been abrogated and the Sioux people are sovereign in a territory encompassing roughly the western half of South Dakota.

Urbom ruled that jurisdiction is not a matter of treaties alone but also of legislation. And he said the 1868 treaty has been modified several times by congressional legislation.

The judge said that when Congress granted U.S. citizenship to all American Indians in 1924 it by implication transferred criminal jurisdiction over Indians to the U.S. government.

Urbom said Supreme Court decisions have never been based on the concept that Indians had complete sovereignty but rather looked upon them as members of dependent nations, subject to treaty making and laws of Congress.

EXCERPTS FROM THE DECISION
Judge Warren Urbom

... From as objective and earnest an evaluation of the testimony, briefs, evidence and law as I can make, I conclude that the broad proposition advanced by the defendants cannot be accepted and that this court has jurisdiction over the pending charges.

The Sioux people were once a fully sovereign nation. They are not now and have not been for a long time. Whether they ever will be again is dependent upon actions of the Congress and the President of the United States and not of the courts. There is a residue of sovereignty, however, a part of which reserves for the Sioux partial criminal jurisdiction. . . .

The defendants recognize that the developed law is squarely in opposition to their legal position here. They therefore attack that law and the reasoning behind it as being arrogant and unjust, insofar as it holds that sovereignty of an Indian tribe or nation may be diminished by anything except a treaty, and they ask that this court repudiate that law.

It cannot be denied that official policy of the United States until at least the late 19th century was impelled by a resolute will to control substantial territory for its westward-moving people. Whatever obstructed the movement, including the Indians, was to be—and was—shoved aside, dominated, or destroyed. Wars, disease, treaties pocked by duplicity, and decimation of the buffalo by whites drove the Sioux to reservations, shriveled their population and disemboweled their corporate body. They were left a people unwillingly dependent in fact upon the United States.

It is an ugly history. White Americans may retch at the recollection of it.

They may also ask themselves these questions: How much of the sins of our forefathers must we rightly bear? What precisely do we do now? Shall we pretend that history never was? Can we restore the disemboweled or push the waters of the river upstream to where they used to be?

Who is to decide? White Americans? The Native Americans? All, together? A federal judge?

Who speaks for the Sioux? Those traditional people who testified here? Those Sioux of a different mind who did not testify? The officials elected by the Sioux on the eight reservations?

Feeling what *was* wrong does not describe what *is* right. Anguish about yesterday does not alone make wise answers for tomorrow. Somehow, all the achings of the soul must coalesce and with the wisdom of the mind develop a single national policy for governmental action.

I feel no shirking of duty in saying that formulation of such a national policy should not be made by a federal judge or the handful who may review his decision on appeal. Four reasons press me to that conclusion.

First, a strength of the elective process is that the citizenry may choose those who mirror their thoughts, and an amalgam of many thus elected is more likely to reflect the conscience and wisdom of the people than a few who are appointed.

Second, legislative bodies have investigative tools for listening to a wider community than do courts for ferreting out the deeper consciousness of the body politics.

Third, *relations with American Indians are rooted in international relations (and would pointedly be so governed if the defendants' position were adopted), including the laws of conquest and of treaties developed over centuries, not by courts, but by executive heads of nations through negotiations.* (Author's emphasis.) The United States in its early history accepted in its dealings with other nations the European concepts. Perhaps it should not have done so in its relations with the American Indians. But it did. Changing now, after nearly two centuries, is a matter of massive public policy for broader exploration than courts are able to provide. Essentially, the issues here have to do with the methods of shifting power from one group to another—by war, threat of war, economic pressure or inducement, verbal persuasion, election, agreement, or gradual legislative encroachment. The acceptability of each method should be decided by the citizenry at large, which speaks directly or through its elected representatives.

Fourth, the people of the United States have not given me or any other judge the power to set national policy for them. By the Constitution the people have assigned governmental powers and have set their limits. Relations with Indian tribes are given exclusively to the executive and legislative branches. Perhaps it should be otherwise, but it is not. When and if the people amend the Constitution to put limits on the executive and legislative branches in their affairs with Indian tribes, the federal courts will uphold those limits, but in the meantime the courts cannot create limits. In short, a judge must hold government to the standards of the nation's conscience once declared, but he cannot create the conscience or declare the standards.

The defendants, then, are addressing the wrong forum for gaining relief in their sovereignty grievances.

If it be thought that the Supreme Court nevertheless *did* decide the policy issues of Indian sovereignty in such decisions as *United States v. Kagama* and *Worcester v. Georgia*, even though it thought it was not, and therefore could again, it must be answered that if it did, every lower federal court is bound by the pronouncement. When the Supreme Court speaks clearly, I must honor the statement or be as unfaithful to my duty to the law as the United States has been to its promises to the American Indians.

In the event the Supreme Court concludes that it can and should change the law regarding sovereignty of and treaties with Indian tribes, the record made in this hearing will assist in providing a basis. For example, one of the grounds of justification used by Chief Justice Marshall for reducing the sovereignty of the Indians was the assertion that the Indians were "fierce savages, whose occupation was war . . ." The record made here should go far to dispel that assertion. The Sioux, and undoubtedly many other tribes as well, had a highly developed governmental system, a religion proclaiming the sacredness of all nature and life, and a disposition toward peacefulness at least as effective as that of the white intruders.

It may also be that the hearing just concluded will serve to make the citizenry of the United States more aware and more willing to grapple with the hard decisions that need to be made. If nothing else, perhaps it can help us learn to listen. . . .

There remains the question of this court's jurisdiction under the Treaty of 1868 to try Indians accused of violating general federal criminal laws. This is a question of no small moment, since almost all the remaining indictments charge a violation of Title 18, U.S.C. 231, which is a statute that applies to anyone anywhere. I conclude that I have jurisdiction to try such indictments. . . .

198

IT DOES NOT
END HERE

DECLARATION OF CONTINUING INDEPENDENCE
BY THE FIRST INTERNATIONAL INDIAN TEATY COUNCIL
AT STANDING ROCK INDIAN COUNTRY JUNE 1974

A long time ago my father told me what his father told him. There was once a Lakota Holy man called Drinks Water, who visioned what was to be; and this was long before the coming of the Wasicus. He visioned that the four-legged were going back into the earth and that a strange race had woven a spider's web all around the Lakotas. And he said, "When this happens, you shall live in barren lands, and there beside those gray houses you shall starve." They say he went back to Mother Earth soon after he saw this vision and it was sorrow that killed him.

Black Elk, Oglala Sioux Holy Man

PREAMBLE

The United States of America has continually violated the independent Native Peoples of this continent by Executive action, Legislative fiat and Judicial decision. By its actions, the U.S. has denied all Native people their International Treaty rights, Treaty lands and basic human rights of freedom and sovereignty. This same U.S. Government which fought to throw off the yoke of oppression and gain its own independence, has now reversed its role and become the oppressor of sovereign Native people.

Might does not make right. Sovereign people of varying cultures have the absolute right to live in harmony with Mother Earth so long as they do not infringe upon this same right of other peoples. The denial of this right to any sovereign people, such as the Native American Indian Nations, must be challenged by *truth* and *action*. World concern must focus on all colonial governments to the end that sovereign people everywhere shall live as they choose, in peace with dignity and freedom.

The International Indian Treaty Conference hereby adopts this Declaration of Continuing Independence of the Sovereign Native American Indian Nations. In the course of these human events, we call upon the people of the world to support this struggle for our sovereign rights and our treaty rights. We pledge our assistance to all other sovereign people who seek their own independence.

DECLARATION

The First International Treaty Council of the Western Hemisphere was formed on the land of the Standing Rock Sioux Tribe on June 8-16, 1974. The delegates, meeting under the guidance of the Great Spirit, represented 97 Indian tribes and Nations from across North and South America.

We, the sovereign Native Peoples recognize that all lands belonging to the various Native Nations now situated within the boundaries of the U.S. are clearly defined by the sacred treaties solemnly entered into between the Native Nations and the government of the United States of America.

We the sovereign Native Peoples charge the United States with gross violations of our International Treaties. Two of the thousands of violations that can be cited are the "wrongfully taking" of the Black Hills from the Great Sioux Nation in 1877, this sacred land belonging to the Great Sioux Nation under the Fort Laramie Treaty of 1868. The second violation was the forced march of the Cherokee people from their ancestral lands in the state of Georgia to the then "Indian Territory" of Oklahoma after the Supreme Court of the United States ruled the Cherokee treaty rights inviolate. The treaty violation, known as the "Trail of Tears," brought death to two-thirds of the Cherokee Nation during the forced march.

The Council further realizes that securing United States recognition of treaties signed with Native Nations requires a committed and unified struggle, using every available legal and political resource. Treaties between sovereign nations explicitly entail agreements which represent "the supreme law of the land" binding each party to an inviolate international relationship.

We acknowledge the historical fact that the struggle for Independence of the Peoples of our sacred Mother Earth have always been over sovereignty of land. These historical freedom efforts have always involved the highest human sacrifice.

We recognize that all Native Nations wish to avoid violence, but we also recognize that the United States government has always used force and violence to deny Native Nations basic human and treaty rights.

We adopt this Declaration of Continuing Independence, recognizing that struggle lies ahead—a struggle certain to be won—and that the human and treaty rights of all Native Nations will be honored. In this understanding the International Indian Treaty Council declares:

The United States Government in its Constitution, Article VI, recognizes treaties as part of the Supreme Law of the United States. We will peacefully pursue all legal and political avenues to demand United States recognition of its own Constitution in this regard, and thus to honor its own treaties with the Native Nations.

We will seek the support of all world communities in the struggle for the continuing independence of Native Nations.

We the representatives of sovereign Native Nations united in forming a council to be known as the International Indian Treaty Council to implement these declarations.

The International Indian Treaty Council will establish offices in Washington, D.C., and New York City to approach the international forces necessary to obtain the recognition of our treaties. These offices will establish an initial system of communications among Native Nations to disseminate information, getting a general consensus of concerning issues, developments and any legislative attempt affecting Native Nations by the United States of America.

The International Indian Treaty Council recognizes the sovereignty of all Native Nations and will stand in unity to support our Native and international brothers and sisters in their respective and collective struggles concerning international treaties and agreements violated by the United States and other governments.

All treaties between the Sovereign Native Nations and the United States Government must be interpreted according to the traditional and spiritual ways of the signatory Native Nations.

We declare our recognition of the Provisional Government of the Independent Oglala Nation, established by the Traditional Chiefs and Headmen under the provisions of the 1868 Fort Laramie Treaty with the Great Sioux Nation at Wounded Knee, March 11, 1973.

We condemn the United States of America for its gross violation of the 1868 Fort Laramie Treaty in militarily surrounding, killing, and starving the citizens of the Independent Oglala Nation into exile.

We demand the United States of America recognize the sovereignty of the Independent Oglala Nation and immediately stop all present and future criminal prosecutions of sovereign Native Peoples. We call upon the conscionable nations of the world to join us in charging and prosecuting the United States of America for its genocidal practices against the sovereign Native Nations; most recently illustrated by Wounded Knee 1973 and the continued refusal to sign the United Nations 1948 Treaty on Genocide.

We reject all executive orders, legislative acts and judicial decisions of the United States related to Native Nations since 1871, when the United States unilaterally suspended treaty-making relations with the Native Nations. This includes, but is not limited to, the Major Crimes Act, the General Allotment Act, the Citizenship Act of 1924, the Indian Reorganization Act of 1934, the Indian Claims Commission Act, Public Law 280 and the Termination Act. All treaties made between Native Nations and the United States made prior to 1871 shall be recognized without further need of interpretation.

We hereby ally ourselves with the colonized Puerto Rican People in their struggle for Independence from the same United States of America.

We recognize that there is only one color of Mankind in the world who are not represented in the United Nations; that is the indigenous Redman of the Western Hemisphere. We recognize this lack of representation in the United Nations comes from the genocidal policies of the colonial power of the United States.

The International Indian Treaty Council established by this conference is directed to make the application to the United Nations for recognition and membership of the sovereign Native Nations. We pledge our support to any similar application by an aboriginal people.

This conference directs the Treaty Council to open negotiations with the government of the United States through its Department of State. We seek these negotiations in order to establish diplomatic relations with the United States. When these diplomatic relations have been established, the first order of business shall be to deal with U.S. violations of treaties with Native Indian Nations, and violations of the rights of those Native Indian Nations who have refused to sign treaties with the United States.

We, the People of the International Indian Treaty Council, following the guidance of our elders through instructions from the Great Spirit, and out of our respect for our sacred Mother Earth, all her children, and those yet unborn, offer our lives for our International Treaty Rights.

GLOSSARY

TREATY. "An agreement made by negotiation or diplomacy; specifically, an agreement, league, or contract, between two or more states or sovereigns, formally signed and usually ratified." *Webster's New Collegiate Dictionary.*

SOVEREIGN. "Independent of, and unlimited by, any other; possessing, or entitled to, original and independent authority or jurisdiction." *Webster's.* Only a state or sovereign can enter into a treaty. The U.S. government made 371 treaties with various Native American nations, all of which considered themselves sovereign and fully capable of making treaties. They still so consider themselves and are desirous of claiming the authority and jurisdiction thereof.

NATION. "1. A people connected by supposed ties of blood generally manifested by community of language, religion, customs, etc. 2. Any aggregation of people having like institutions and customs and a sense of social homogeneity and mutual interest. 3. The body of inhabitants of a country united under a single independent government; a state." *Webster's*. Although it seems self-evident to Native American people that their groupings are defined by all three dictionary choices, *Webster's* further states as another choice: "One of a group of Indian tribes; as the Six Nations."

TRIBE. One of the reasons *Webster's* makes a special separation of Native American nations from others becomes apparent on reading its definition of TRIBE: "Any aggregation of people, especially in a primitive or nomadic state, believed to be of a common stock and acting under a central authority, as a chief." Native American nations prefer not to be referred to as "tribes."

BAND. In common usage, it means a sub-group, such as the Oglala band of the Sioux Nation. A band might be considered somewhat comparable to a state of the United States, in that bands live together and have a headsman or council somewhat under the authority and somewhat autonomous of the headsman or council of the nation. Many bands have sub-bands, such as Geronimo's group, the Bedonkohes Band of the Chiricahua Apache Nation. (BAND would also seem to carry the same derogatory connotation of primitiveness as TRIBE. It is another European designation for terms in native languages which do not carry the same connotations in the original language.)

CONFEDERACY. In Native American usage, a group of nations bound together by mutual agreements of aid and cooperation, usually having similar customs and modes of government, as in the Iroquois Confederacy.

RESERVATION. A piece of land reserved by a Native American nation for its own use, when ceding other parts of its native territory to the U.S. government in a treaty. Now the word is synonymous with PRISON or ZOO to many people who live in squalid conditions on their pitiful portions of land, eroded by sales under the Allotment Act, leased out under BIA supervision or stolen outright. Nevertheless, by the present generation it is often considered better to remain on the reservation with one's own culture and family than to cut the life-giving ties and try for a better economic situations among strangers.

TRADITIONAL. A word used much by Native Americans and which is often misinterpreted by whites. It does not mean returning to the lifestyle of four-hundred years ago—an obvious impossibility—nor does it mean denying the real benefits of Western technology. It *does* mean retaining and strenghening our cultural and political integrity, our vision of the world and humanity's place in the world; retaining and developing the values which have made us great nations, and which can be our real contribution to world affairs. Traditionalism implies for us a unity and inter-relatedness of all the areas of human endeavor, *i.e.*, religion, science, medicine, politics, etc. Further, it means that we hold the earth to be sacred, not to be bought and sold, and that use of certain areas of land belongs to those people who are part of that land. All other forms of life that are part of an area of land have equal rights with humanity. Agreements over land rights and usage are considered sacred by traditional Native Americans, who are the majority of our people.

BIA (Bureau of Indian Affairs). A U.S. government agency under the authority of the Department of the Interior (originally created under the auspices of the War Department); its declared purpose is to oversee the affairs of all Native Americans within the borders of the U.S.A. The Indian Preference Act (ordering preferential hiring and promotion of Native Americans within the BIA) notwithstanding, the BIA is and always has been run mainly by white people who have looked after Indian's interests by forcing them to lease most of their minuscule remaining lands and by other atrocious means trying to guide them in the direction of becoming "good U.S. citizens" (*i.e.*, assimilation).

TERMINATION. A 145-year-old policy of the U.S. government; for the purpose of "civilizing" Native Americans by destroying their tribal governments and forcing them to take a place in the mainstream of white society as individuals rather than as co-existing separate national cultural groups. The Choctaws, terminated in 1830, were the first tribe to be dissolved by a unilateral act of another sovereign state. A new, more sophisticated effort at this policy began in the 1940's, culminating in an act in 1954 which ordered the termination of the Menominee Tribe in Wisconsin, the first of many such directives to tribes to take on total responsibility for education, health, welfare, taxes (local, state, and national). Although entirely willing to get out from under the thumb of resented BIA supervision, the tribes were in all cases completely unprepared to cope with these crushing financial burdens, all the more mentally crushing to people who had for a century been treated as wards of the government (*i.e.*, not-too-bright children). By almost all accounts now available, the U.S. government's policy of termination has been an absolute disaster for *all* parties concerned.

DEPENDENT DOMESTIC NATIONS. Chief Justice John Marshall, in the case of *Johnson and Graham's Lessee v. McIntosh* (1823), declared Indian nations to be quasi-sovereign, complete sovereignty being diminished by "the original principle that discovery gave exclusive title to those who made it." In the case of *Cherokee Nation v. Georgia* (1831), Marshall ruled that the former was a "domestic dependent nation."

INDIAN APPROPRIATION ACT (1871). Section 2079 of this act declared that: "No Indian nation or tribe within the territory of the United States shall be recognized or acknowledged as an independent nation, tribe or power with whom the United States may contract by treaty." Although guaranteeing that all previous treaties would be honored, this act closed the 93 years of more or less equal negotiations and brought an end to treaty-making between Native American nations and the U.S.

ALLOTMENT ACT (The Dawes Act, 1887). An act of the U.S. Congress providing for the compulsory allotment of reservation lands to Native Americans in severalty (*i.e.*, the lands could be held by individuals only, not collectively), with the explicit purpose of allowing the government to buy Indian lands without resorting to cumbersome individual Congressional procedures in the case of each sale. The act made Native Americans holding patents to allotments subject to the laws of the state by which their lands were surrounded. It also graciously declared all such Native Americans, who would have "taken up . . . residence separate and apart from any tribe of Indians, and has adopted the habits of civilized life" to be citizens of the U.S.

CITIZENSHIP ACT (1924). An act of Congress conferring U.S. citizenship on all "non-citizen Indians born within the territorial limits of the United States," provided it did not interfere with rights to tribal property. Having been deprived of nationhood, Native Americans were by this act drawn into the U.S. "body politic" and given a citizenship to replace their usurped citizenships.

IRA (Indian Reorganization Act, 1934). An act of Congress which was supposed to conserve and develop Indian lands and resources and to grant certain rights of home rule to Indians, and many other things. It is now known primarily to Native American people as the act which was used to force them to abandon traditional forms of government and adopt "majority rule democracy," which today means a tribal council set up, organized, engineered and overseen by the BIA. This act also gave supreme powers to the U.S. Secretary of the Interior in many areas of the lives of Native Americans.

INDIAN CLAIMS COMMISSION. A special adjudicating body created in 1946 for the special purpose of hearing, investigating and ruling on claims for compensation for land losses during the treaty period. Since the Claims Commission was founded, it has ruled against Native American claims more often than it has granted them. Even when it has ruled in their favor, Native Americans have been offered money instead of restitution of land. No matter how the Claims Commission rules, it costs the plaintiffs thousands of dollars in lawyers' fees and years of waiting; the Black Hills claim of the Great Sioux Nation has been before the Commission for 19 years.

International Indian Treaty Conference, Standing Rock Sioux Reservation, June, 1974. Photo by Michelle Vignes.

INDIAN SOVEREIGNTY—IT'S ALIVE

Larry B. Leventhal

Mr. Leventhal was one of the attorneys for the Defense at Lincoln. He wrote this article in January 1977 to clarify the legal aspects of Indian sovereignty.

The legal relationship between the United States and the respective Indian tribes is unique. Unlike all other political entities within the borders of the United States, Indian tribes derive their powers not solely through delegation, but also through their sovereign existence, past and present.

One attempting to derive some logic from Constitutional provisions,[1] 371 treaties,[2] periodic agreements, numerous statutes, an entire volume of the United States Code,[3] federal regulations governing an over-inflated Bureau of Indian Affairs and other agencies, and often contradictory case law, must start with the proposition of initial sovereignty of the various tribes. Tragically, the development of United States Indian Law is drenched in blood (usually Indian), stolen lands (always Indian), and broken promises.[4] Yet despite removal,[5] allotment,[6] and termination,[7] the tribes remain as viable political and cultural entities.

It is well to keep in mind that a review of federal Indian law principles, through which Indian sovereignty has been diminished, should not preclude consideration of principles of Indian traditional law, international law, and inherent justice. The following, extracted from *A History of Indian Jurisdiction* prepared by the Institute for the Indian Training Program, provides such expression:[8]

> Indian traditional law usually gives complete jurisdiction to the Indian government to rule Indian territory, to manage Indian national affairs, to settle disputes and so on, all without outside interference. On the other hand, if you go by United States law, actual Indian jurisdiction is much less than the inherent, sovereign jurisdiction which each nation has or had under its own law. Of course, each Indian nation must be looked at individually in light of its own history and law.
>
> Almost everything written on Indian jurisdiction has looked only at the federal law (the laws applied in the United States courts and the decisions of these courts). Naturally, the United States courts are one-sided. If Congress passes a law saying that a particular Indian nation has no government and no jurisdiction at all, then the United States court must accept that as law. According to Indian law and international law, however, Congress has no power to terminate another nation's government. United States law is especially important because, in one way or another, many important cases end up in federal courts, and the federal government may enforce its decisions by force if necessary. So, it is useful to know what the United States law is concerning jurisdiction, no matter how wrong or ridiculous it may be compared to Indian law, international law, or common sense.

Indian tribes have inherent powers deriving from a sovereign status. "Their claim to sovereignty long pre-dates that of our own government." *McClanahan v. Arizona*

Tax Commission, 411 U.S. 164, 36 L.Ed. 2d 129 (1973). The basic sovereign power of the Indian tribes is still existent, but subject to restrictions which have developed through their relationship with the United States. *Iron Crow v. Oglala Sioux Tribe*, 231 F.2d 89 (8th Cir. 1956).

Felix S. Cohen, in his authoritative and extensive work entitled *Federal Indian Law* (U.S. Department of Interior, 1944),[9] explains the nature of the residual sovereignty of Indian Tribes:

> Perhaps the most basic principle of all Indian law supported by a host of decisions . . . is the principle that *those powers which are lawfully vested in an Indian tribe are not, in general, delegated powers granted by express acts of Congress, but rather inherent powers of a limited sovereignty which has never been extinguished.* Each Indian tribe begins its relationship with the Federal Government as a sovereign power, recognized as such in treaty and legislation. The powers of sovereignty have been limited from time to time by special treaties and laws designed to take from the Indian tribes control of matters which, in the judgment of Congress, these tribes could no longer be safely permitted to handle. The statutes of Congress, then, must be examined to determine the limitations of tribal sovereignty rather than to determine its sources or its positive content. What is not expressly limited remains within the domain of tribal sovereignty. (emphasis contained in original source)

The current status of the Indian nation has been variously described as "quasi-sovereign tribal entities" *Morton v. Mancari*, 417 U.S. 535 (1974); "quasi-sovereign nations" *Iron Crow, et al. v. Oglala Sioux Tribe*, 231 F.2d 89 (8th Cir. 1956); "dependent nations" *Colliflower v. Garland*, 342 F.2d 369 (9th Cir. 1965); "residual sovereignty" *Long v. Quinalt*, No. C75-677 (W.D. Wash., Sept. 2, 1975); and "semi-sovereign existence" *Quechan Tribe of Indians v. Rowe, et al.*, No. 72-3199 (9th Cir. Feb. 2, 1976).

The international concept of nationhood and its attendant sovereignty can be generalized in the language of *Montoya v. United States*, 180 U.S. 261. In summary, *Montoya, supra*, specifies that a Nation is a group of people with an organized society in a specific geographical area, bound by common language and customs. Such is in accord with classical definitions.[10] The various Indian tribes quite clearly satisfy such conditions of nationhood. Internally, each had an identifiable language, culture, and social organization. The geographic extent of their dominion was recognized by their neighbors. They had the capacity to govern themselves, to make war, to establish peace, and to form alliances with other nations.

The first known legal document relating to the American Indian was written at the behest of the Emperor of Spain by Franciscus de Vitoria in the mid-sixteenth century. In his work,[11] which was influential throughout Europe and generally incorporated into the then developing international law, Father Vitoria stated that "the aborigines in question were the true owners" of lands in the new world. Thus, he found that "discovery" could convey no title upon Europeans; even the Pope had no right to partition the property of the Indians. Rather, a treaty conveying such rights to which the Indian sovereign was agreeable, was seen as the prerequisite to land acquisition.

Early relationships were established and treaties entered into between the Indian nations on the East Coast of North America and the various European powers, including Great Britain, France, Belgium, and the Netherlands. In addition, the colonies, prior to the formation of the Federal Union which was to become the United States, individually entered into treaty relationships with the Indian nations.

Under the United States Constitution, Article VI, Section 2, treaties entered into by the President and the Senate as mandated by Article II, Section 2, Clause 2, are considered to be "the supreme law of the land." As such, "judges in every state shall be bound thereby."

Under this Constitutional authority, the United States entered into approximately 371 Indian treaties with the various Indian nations. The Constitutional authority employed is the same as that which enabled the federal government to enter into other international treaties.[12] Indian treaties represented agreements at law between two sovereigns—the respective Indian nation and the United States of America.

The method of dealing with Indians by treaty was abandoned with the passage of the Appropriations Act of March 3, 1871.[13] The prohibition of the use of the treaty form in dealing with the Indian nations arose out of a jealousy on the part of members of the House of Representatives that they, unlike Senators, could play no part in the formation and approval of a treaty. The legislation expressly provides that treaties ratified prior to the date of the cut-off would have continuing validity.

Many of the treaties with the respective Indian nations served to limit the sovereignty, rights, and independence of the respective tribes. However, what is important is that there is a residue of sovereignty which remains inherent in these Indian nations which is exercised, not through powers delegated to Congress, but through the inherent power of the sovereigns. In other words, such treaties are "not a grant of rights to the Indians, but a grant of rights from them—a reservation of those not granted." *U.S. v. Winans*, 198 U.S. 371, 381 (1905); *Winters v. U.S.*, 207 U.S. 564 (1908); *U.S. v. Ahtanum Irrigation District*, 236 F.2d 321 (9th Cir. 1956).

The treaties between the United States and the respective Indian nations and those between the United States and European nations are similar in form.

The first treaty entered into by the Continental Congress was with the Delaware Indians in 1778.[14] It recognized boundaries and provided for the formation of a military alliance; no land cession was involved. Increasingly, however, the United States used the treaty process as a means of justifying and institutionalizing land appropriation by force and the threat of force.

For their part, Indian nations were frequently anxious to secure promises from the United States honoring tribal control of unceded lands, respecting self-government, pledging non-interference with tribal society and law, guaranteeing hunting and fishing rights, etc. These guarantees, unless specifically abrogated by Congress, remain good law today, and have formed the foundation upon which many successful lawsuits have been instituted for the purpose of protecting Indian rights.

The meaning of the Sioux Treaty of 1868 (the last treaty between the United States and the Sioux) and the inherent guarantee relative to sovereignty, was aptly summarized by the United States Supreme Court in *Ex Parte Crow Dog*, 109 U.S. 556 (1883). The Court found that the Treaty of 1868, in the context of both tribal sovereignty and United States law, constituted a

> pledge to secure to these people with whom the United States was contracting as a distinct political body, an orderly government, ... [which] necessarily implies, ... that of self-government: The regulation by them-selves of their own domestic affairs; the maintenance of order and peace among their own members by the administration of their own laws and customs.

This, the Court specified, was "the highest and best of all" of the "arts of civilized life." Because of such guarantees, the Court ruled that the United States did not have jurisdiction on the Sioux reservation to prosecute an Indian on charges of murder of another Indian.

The limited character of the independence of the Indian nations found its classic expression in the judgments of Chief John Marshall, who described them as "domestic dependent nations." Their rights, he said, had never been entirely disregarded, but had been impaired by colonialization. Specifically, they had lost their right to sell their lands to whomever they chose. *Johnson v. McIntosh*, 8 Wheat. 543 (1828); *Worcester v. Georgia*, 6 Pet. 515 (1832).

The limitation of external sovereignty and the limitation of rights to sell land were the earliest of the legal detractions from the independence of the tribes or nations; there have been many others since. To a degree, the history of Indian law in this country has been a history of the gradual abolition of the elements of Indian independence. What is of fundamental importance in understanding this specialized area of law is that the basic framework has never been abandoned and that Indian tribes still possess a degree of sovereignty recognized by law.

The status of the Indian nations was initially given expression by Chief Justice John Marshall in several cases.

In *Cherokee Nation v. Georgia*, 5 Pet. 17, 8 L.Ed. 25 (1831), Chief Justice Marshall considered the application of the words "nation" and "treaty" to the various Indian people:

> The very term 'nation,' so generally applied to them [Indians] means 'a people distinct from others.' The Constitution, by declaring treaties already made, as well as those to be made to be the supreme law of the land, has adopted and sanctioned the previous treaties with the Indian nations, and consequently admits their rank among those Powers who are capable of making treaties. The words 'treaty' and 'nation' are words of our own language, selected in our diplomatic and legislative proceedings by ourselves, and have a definite and well-understood meaning. We have applied them to the other nations of the earth. They are applied to all in the same sense.

In the next year, in *Worcester v. Georgia, supra*, Chief Justice Marshall spoke more directly to the question of Indian status. In that case, the Court held that a clergyman had been wrongfully imprisoned by the State of Georgia for attempting to interfere with the state's removal of the Cherokees. The Court ruled that the Cherokees were entitled by sovereign treaty rights and, as a distinct independent political community, to occupy its own territory:

> . . . and the settled doctrine of the law of nations is, that a weaker power does not surrender its independence—its right to self-government—by associating with a stronger, and taking its protection. A weak state, in order to provide for its safety, may place itself under the protection of one more powerful, without stripping itself of the right of government, and ceasing to be a state. Examples of this kind are not wanting in Europe. 'Tributary and feudatory states,' says Vattle, 'do not thereby cease to be sovereign and independent states, so long as self-government, and sovereign and independent authority are left in the administration of the state.' At the present day, more than one state may be considered as holding its right of self-government under the guarantee and protection of one or more allies.

> The Cherokee nation, then, is a distinct community, occupying its own territory, with boundaries accurately described, in which the laws of Georgia can have no right to enter, but with the assent of the Cherokees themselves, or in conformity with treaties, and with the acts of Congress. The whole intercourse between the United States and this nation is, by our Constitution and laws, vested in the government of the United States. The act of the State

of Georgia, under which the plaintiff in error was prosecuted is, consequently void, and the judgment a nullity.

The lack of state jurisdiction relative to the conduct of Indian affairs was made evident in *Worcester v. Georgia, supra*. The Court's enunciation that "the Cherokee nation is under the protection of the United States of America, and no other sovereign whatsoever," along with the Court's enunciation of the tribe's sovereignty, revealed at an early date that jurisdiction relative to Indian people on tribal lands was shared by two sovereigns—the tribe and the United States. The tribe was seen as retaining internal sovereignty over its affairs, with external sovereignty (relations with other powers) being submerged in favor of the protection of the United States.

Indian people have often found that when courts speak to protect their interests, the courts are not always heeded. The Supreme Court's determination that Georgia's attempted removal of the Cherokee was illegal, only briefly delayed the troops. The long, deadly "Trail of Tears" of the Cherokee to the Oklahoma Territory followed President Andrew Jackson's declaration that "John Marshall has rendered his decision, now let him enforce it." [15]

The principles set forth in *Worcester, supra*, have fared better than the native lands of the Cherokee. These principles can be summarized as follows: (1) the federal government has plenary authority to regulate Indian affairs; 2) an Indian tribe does not lose its internal sovereign powers by becoming subject to the power of a stronger nation; and 3) Indian country is separate and distinct from the state in which it is located, and within its boundaries, state laws do not apply.

Relative to the principles stated above, it is perhaps not surprising that the first principle (i.e., the plenary power of the United States) has been applied by Congress and interpreted by the courts in such a manner as to partially erode the vitality of the other two principles (*i.e.*, internal sovereignty and lack of state jurisdiction).

The concept that the United States possesses plenary power over Indian tribes developed from cases in which the courts have refused to question executive or Congressional action on the ground that such was seen as being a "political question." [e.g., *Johnson and Graham's Lessee v. McIntosh*, 8 Wheat. 543 (1823)] This has meant that official abuses toward Indian people largely went unreviewed.

This plenary power has also been justified as having been derived from the power of Congress to "regulate Commerce . . . with the Indian tribes." [16]

Early Congressional legislation directed toward Indians was cautious to speak to external relationships. The Northwest Ordinance (1787) [17] proclaimed that "the utmost good faith shall always be observed toward the Indians." The Indian Non-Intercourse Act of 1790 [18] limited trading prerogatives and restricted land cessions and treaties by the Indian tribes with any party other than the federal government. [19] The General Crimes Act, enacted in 1817, [20] while providing for federal court criminal jurisdiction in Indian Country, expressly precluded such jurisdiction where the matter concerned Indians only, the tribe had acted, or such provision for jurisdiction would be contrary to treaty provisions.

The internal sovereignty of the tribes later came to be compromised through such legislation as the Major Crimes Act (1885) [21] which, following a public outcry resulting from the decision in *Ex Parte Crow Dog, supra*, extended total federal jurisdiction over specified major crimes (initially seven in number, presently fourteen). The General Allotment Act of 1887 [22] authorized federal subdivision of reservations in an effort to "break up the tribal mass," to encourage "civilized" farming, and, of course, to provide for federal assumption of "excess" lands beyond the individual allotments selected.

210

State laws have generally been held to be inapplicable within the boundaries of an Indian reservation, based upon the rationale of infringement upon tribal self-government and federal pre-emption.[23]

Public Law 280,[24] enacted in 1953, departs from the traditional principle that a state has no jurisdiction on an Indian reservation, by conferring upon six specified states general civil and criminal jurisdiction within reservations. Public Law 280 did, however, by its terms, specify that it did not authorize the "alienation, encumbrance, or taxation of any real or personal property," nor was it to be applied in such a manner as to deprive an Indian tribe or group "of any right, privilege, or immunity afforded under federal treaty, agreement, or statute with respect to hunting, trapping, or fishing, or the control of licensing or regulation thereof." The extension of civil jurisdiction under Public Law 280 is limited to the availability of state courts to hear civil causes of action arising upon Indian reservations. *Bryan v. Itasca County* (No. 75-5027, June 14, 1976).

The concept of Congressional plenary power over Indian affairs has been judicially extended to the point that Congress is recognized as possessing the power through legislation to abrogate (*i.e.*, change or nullify) an Indian treaty. *Lone Wolf v. Hitchcock*, 187 U.S. 553 (1903).

The abrogation of portions of a treaty or of an entire treaty by statute is usually justified by viewing both statutes and treaties as being on the same footing. In Article VI of the United States Constitution, both are part of the "supreme law of the land." The conclusion is therefore usually reached that the latest in time prevails. *Lone Wolf, supra.* Since the United States has terminated its entering into Indian treaties, however, legislation is inevitably the latest in time, in matters of current interest to Congress.

Abrogation cannot, however, be by implication, but must be specifically stated. The courts have continually stated that "[T]he intention to abrogate or modify a treaty is not to be lightly imputed to the Congress." *Menominee Tribe of Indians v. United States*, 391 U.S. 414 (1968); *Pigeon River Company v. The Cox Company*, 291 U.S. 138 (1934); *Squire v. Capoeman*, 351 U.S. 1, 100 L.Ed. 883, 76 S.Ct. 611 (1956).

In *United States v. Consolidated Wounded Knee Cases*,[25] the defendants in indictments arising out of the Wounded Knee siege of 1973, sought dismissal of the various charges on grounds of the lack of jurisdiction of the United States on a Sioux reservation, due to guarantees, inherent in the Sioux Treaty of 1868, of internal tribal sovereignty and of tribal ability to deal with Indian wrongdoers on the reservation. The court, while noting the existence of "residual" sovereignty, found that such criminal jurisdiction had been properly asserted by the United States, due to statutory provisions enacted subsequent to the U.S. Supreme Court's decision in *Ex Parte Crow Dog, supra.*[26] The court's summary of history is both shocking and accurate:

> It cannot be denied that official policy of the United States until at least the late 19th century was impelled by a resolute will to control substantial territory for its westward-moving people. Whatever obstructed the movement, including the Indians, was to be—and was—shoved aside, dominated, or destroyed. Wars, disease, treaties pocked by duplicity, and decimation of the buffalo by whites drove the Sioux to reservations, shriveled their population and disemboweled their corporate body. They were left a people unwillingly dependent in fact upon the United States. It is an ugly history. White Americans may retch at the recollection of it.

Yet, despite this acknowledgement, the court relied, without terming it such, on the old political question doctrine. It specified that "relations with Indian tribes are given exclusively to the executive and legislative branches," and concluded that "[t]he

211

defendants, then, are addressing the wrong forum for gaining relief in their sovereignty grievances." The court noted judicial precedents supporting federal criminal jurisdiction on a reservation, stating:

> When the Supreme Court speaks clearly, I must honor the statement or be as unfaithful to my duty to the law as the United States has been to its promises to the American Indians.

While the concept of Indian sovereignty continually reappears in case law, distortions relative to even the identity and origin of the tribes can be found, particularly in the era of westward expansion. See, for example, *Markey v. Coxe*, 59 U.S. 100 (1855), wherein an Indian tribe was referred to as "a territory which originated under our constitution and laws."

In *Talton v. Mayes*, 163 U.S. 376 (1896), the U.S. Supreme Court, however, citing its "repeated adjudications," specified that the sovereign powers of the Cherokee Nation, although recognized by the federal government, were not created by the federal government; and that, therefore, the judicial authority of the Cherokees was not subject to the limitations imposed by the Bill of Rights.[27] The Court explained that "... the existence of the right in Congress to regulate the manner in which the local powers of the Cherokee nation shall be exercised, does not render such local powers federal powers ..."

In recently assessing the status of the Indian nations, the Ninth Circuit has characterized their status as being higher than that of states:

> Indian tribes are, of course, not states; they have a status higher than that of states. They are subordinate and dependent nations, possessed of all powers as such, and limited only to the extent that they have been expressly required to surrender their powers by the superior sovereign, the United States. *Colliflower v. Garland*, 342 F.2d 369 (1965).

The status of the sovereign powers of an Indian tribe, as interpreted by federal law,[28] are concisely summarized by Felix Cohen, in his *Handbook of Federal Indian Law:*[29]

> The whole course of judicial decision on the nature of Indian tribal powers is marked by adherence to three fundamental principles: An Indian tribe possesses, in the first instance, all the powers of any sovereign State. Conquest[30] renders the tribe subject to the legislative power of the United States and, in substance, terminates the external powers of sovereignty of the tribe, *e.g.*, its power to enter into treaties with foreign nations, but does not by itself affect the internal sovereignty of the tribe, *i.e.*, its powers of local self-government. These powers are subject to be qualified by treaties and by express legislation of Congress, but save as thus expressly qualified, full powers of internal sovereignty are vested in the Indian tribes and in their duly constituted organs of government.

There is a temptation in the minds of many to consider concepts of Indian sovereignty to be solely of historical interest. Such an assumption is misguided. During the past several decades, the United States Supreme Court and other federal courts have applied principles of Indian sovereignty in the resolution of questions relating to such diverse areas as taxation, criminal jurisdiction, extradition, authority of tribal courts, licensing, and sovereign immunity.

In *McClanahan v. Arizona Tax Commission, supra*, the United States Supreme Court found that state taxation[31] of the income of an Indian whose entire income was derived from reservation sources, was impermissible. The court explained the special status of an Indian tribe.

It must always be remembered that the various Indian tribes were once independent and sovereign nations, and that their claim to sovereignty long pre-dates that of our own Government ... '[T]he relation of Indian tribes living within the borders of the United States [is] anomalous one and of a complex character ... They were, and always have been, regarded as having a semi-independent position when they preserved their tribal relations; not as States, not as nations, not as possessed of the full attributes of sovereignty, but as a separate people, with the power of regulating their internal and social relations ...' *U.S. v. Kagama*, 118 U.S. 375, 381-382, 30 L.Ed. 228, 6 S.Ct. 1109 (1886).

In *Morton v. Mancari*, 417 U.S. 535 (1974), the United States Supreme Court upheld the Indian preference in employment practiced by the Bureau of Indian Affairs, against both statutory and constitutional challenges. The Court noted that "the preference is political, rather than racial, in nature." It explained that "[t]he preference, as applied, is granted to Indians not as a discrete racial group, but, rather, as members of quasi-sovereign tribal entities."

The "jurisdiction in the Navajo Tribe over intersovereign rendition" was found, by the Ninth Circuit in *Arizona ex rel. Merrill v. Turtle*, 413 F.2d 683 (1969), to be sufficient to defeat the agreement of the State of Arizona to extradite an Indian, sought by Oklahoma, from the Navajo reservation located within the State.

The authority of tribal courts has been upheld on the basis of the inherent rights of sovereignty. The Eighth Circuit spoke eloquently to this effect, in *Iron Crow v. Oglala Sioux Tribe*, 231 F.2d 89 (1956):

[F]rom time immemorial, the members of the Oglala Sioux Tribe have exercised powers of local self-government, regulating domestic problems and conducting foreign affairs, including in latter years, the negotiation of treaties and agreements with the United States.

We hold that Indian tribes, such as the defendant Oglala Sioux Tribe of the Pine Ridge Reservation, South Dakota, still possess their inherent sovereignty excepting only where it has been specifically taken from them, either by treaty or by Congressional act.

It would seem clear that the Constitution, as construed by the Supreme Court, acknowledges the paramount authority of the United States with regard to Indian tribes but recognizes the existence of Indian tribes as quasi-sovereign entities possessing all the inherent rights of sovereignty excepting where restrictions have been placed thereon by the United States itself.

Speaking to the same effect, the Ninth Circuit has recently stated:

[A]s a matter of general Indian law, tribal courts are residuals of each tribe's semi-sovereign existence, having criminal jurisdiction over all persons and offenses within the tribes' domains, to the extent that such jurisdiction is not inconsistent with treaties, agreements or federal enactments. *Quechan Tribe v. Rowe*, No. 72-3199 (9th Cir., February 2, 1976.)

In recently upholding tribal criminal jurisdiction over non-Indians, the Ninth Circuit noted that "[t]he proper approach to the question of tribal criminal jurisdiction is to ask first, what the original sovereign powers of the tribes were, and, then, how far and in what respects these powers have been limited." *Oliphant v. Schlie*, No. 74-2154 (August 24, 1976). The court further declared that the various Indian tribes "retain those powers of autonomous states that are neither inconsistent with their status nor expressly terminated by Congress."

Indian tribes have been uniformly held to possess sovereign immunity,[32] in the sense that they are immune from suit in the absence of express congressional waiver of

213

such immunity.[33] *United States v. United States Fidelity and Guaranty Co.*, 309 U.S. 506 (1940).

The Fifth Circuit, in *Maryland Gas Co. v. Citizens National Bank of North Hollywood*, 361 F 2d 517, 520 (1966), explained the origin of this concept:

> Indian nations, as an attribute of their quasi-sovereignty, are immune from suit, either in the federal or state courts, without Congressional authorization . . . From the beginning of our government, Indian Nations or tribes have been regarded as dependent political communities or nations; and as possessing the attributes of sovereignty, except where they had been taken away by Congressional action. They are quasi-sovereign nations.

In *United States v. Mazurie*, 419 U.S. 544 (1975), the U.S. Supreme Court noted that "the independent authority over matters that affect the internal and social relations of tribal life" was a sufficient basis on which to support the delegation of Congressional authority to the tribe relative to the control of liquor licensing on non-Indian owned land within the reservation. The Court stated:

> Thus it is an important aspect of this case that Indian tribes are unique aggregations possessing attributes of sovereignty over both their members and their territory, *Worcester v. Georgia*, 6 Pet. 515, 557, 8 L.Ed. 483 (1832); they are 'a separate people' possessing 'the power of regulating their internal and social relations . . .' (citing cases).

Recent statutory enactments, such as the Indian Self-Determination Act[34] and the Indian Education Act,[35] are directed toward restoring tools to Native Americans to regulate their internal and social relations.

We are now at a crossroads in our dealings with the Indian nations within our borders. The United States has always prided itself on its cultural diversity and its federal system of division of powers. Surely, within our midst, there is room for those native to this continent to exist and grow within their tribal structures. Sadly, our national honor has been repeatedly blemished by our failure to live up to our word and to extend a fragment of the human respect that first greeted visitors to these shores. The tribal structures have, however, survived, and sovereignty, in a real, although diminished, form has continually been acknowledged by the courts. Such sovereignty must be encouraged; for it is by the strengthening of tribal bonds and culture that not only Indian people will be served, but our national honor as well.

REFERENCES

1. United States Constitution: Article VI, Section 2; Article I, Section 8, Clause 3; Article II, Section 2, Clause 2.
2. 371 is the total number of treaties signed by both parties, subsequently ratified by Congress, and proclaimed by the President. Additional treaties were signed by the United States and Indian nations that were thereafter not ratified, or if ratified, not proclaimed.
3. Volume 25.
4. A follower of Red Cloud, the Great Sioux Chief, stated that "[t]hey made us many promises, more than I can remember, but they never kept but one; they promised to take our land and they took it."
5. The Indian Removal Act, 4 Stat. 411 (1830); similar legislation followed.
6. The General Allotment Act, 24 Stat. 388 (1887); further legislation provided for allotment of specific reservations.
7. See H. R. Con. Res. 108, 83d Cong., 1st Sess., 99 Congressional Record 9968, 10815 (1953).
8. "A History of Indian Jurisdiction," *American Indian Journal*, vol. 2, no. 4, April 1977, pp. 2-15.
9. Felix Cohen, *Handbook of Federal Indian Law* (1942), p. 122. The 1958 "revision," issued by

the U.S. Department of Interior, is an unreliable reference, since it was "updated" (not by the original author, then deceased) to provide support for the termination policies then in vogue.

10. Perhaps the oldest non-biblical definition of national sovereignty is offered by Cicero:
    Every nation that governs itself, under whatever form, without dependence on any foreign power, is a sovereign state. Nations or states are body politic, societies of men united together for the purpose of promoting their mutual safety and advantage by joint efforts of their combined strength.
    The continued modern day sovereignty of the Indian tribes also finds support in Cicero:
    We ought to include as sovereign states those who have united themselves with another more powerful by an unequal alliance, in which, as Aristotle says, to the more powerful is given more honor, and to the weaker more assistance ... Provided the inferior ally reserved to itself the sovereignty, or the right of governing its own body, it ought to be considered as an independent state that keeps up an intercourse with others under the authority of the law of nations."

11. Franciscus de Vitoria, *De India et De Jure Belli Reflectiones*, circa 1539.

12. United States Constiution: Article VI, Section 2; Article II, Section 2, Clause 2; Article I, Section 8, Clause 3.

13. 25 U.S.C. § 71.

14. 7 Stat. 13, Sept. 17, 1778.

15. Greeley, *American Conflict* (1864), Vol. 1, p. 106.

16. United States Constitution, Article I, Section 8, Clause 3.

17. 1 Stat. 50 (1787).

18. Act of July 22, 1790, Ch. 33, 1 Stat. 137.

19. Interestingly, the Indian Non-Intercourse Act is now providing ammunition to a few small Eastern tribes which had ceded land to the state by a treaty following 1790. The Non-Intercourse Act precluded treating with Indian tribes by all but the federal government. If these state treaties are illegal, state claim to the lands ceded is in doubt. In the context of land area, the most significant claim is that of the 3,000 Passamaquoddy and Penobscot Indians of Maine, who now claim 58% of the state. Because of the claim, bond counsel to municipalities, school boards, and state units have refused to certify a number of proposed bond issuances.

20. 18 U.S.C. § 1152.

21. 18 U.S.C. § 1153.

22. 24 Stat. 388 (1887).

23. See *McClanahan v. Arizona*, 411 U.S. 164 (1973); *Williams v. Lee*, 358 U.S. 217 (1958); *Kennerly v. District Court of Montana*, 400 U.S. 423 (1971).

24. 25 U.S.C. § 1321 et seq. as amended (1953).

25. *United States v. Consolidated Wounded Knee Cases*, 389 F. Supp. 235 (D. Neb. W.D. S. D., 1975); aff'd in major part, 8th Circuit Court of Appeals, No. 75-1173, No. 75-1398, No. 75-1483, July 15, 1976; Petition for Writ of Cert. pending before U.S. Supreme Court.

26. 109 U.S. 556, 3 S. Ct. 296, 27 L.Ed. 1030 (1883).

27. The Indian Civil Rights Act, 25 U.S.C. § 1301-1303 (1968), guarantees specified rights against infringement by Indian tribes. These constitute some but not all the rights specified in the Bill of Rights.

28. Another interpretation of the effect of the power of the United States on Indian sovereignty is contained within the "Red Paper," issued by the International Treaty Council, following the second International Indian Treaty Conference held on the Yankton Sioux Reservation on June 13-20, 1976. The International Treaty Council proclaimed sovereignty for the respective Indian nations, and views the actions of the United States as colonial:
    The United States has imposed a foreign form of government on the Indians and recognizes that government ... not a traditional, legitimate government. The United States maintains that no Indian nation's law is effective without United States approval. It imposes its criminal law, foreign trade, currency, postal service, radio, television, and air transport regulations on reservations.... An Indian nation is not even allowed to sign contracts or to hire a lawyer without the permission of the United States. Any self-government left to Indian nations by the United States is, it is made clear, left only by the grace of the United States Congress. The United States maintains it has a right to, at any time, pass a law and make it applicable to Indians on their reservations whether or not the laws conform to treaties with Indians, to international law, or to the United Nations Charter.

29. Cohen, *Handbook of Federal Indian Law* (1942), p. 123.

30. It should be noted that some tribes such as the Chippewa and Sioux (native to Minnesota), have never been conquered, but entered into treaties with the United States from a position of strength.
31. In *Bryan v. Itasca County*, Minnesota, (No. 75-5027, June 14, 1976), the Supreme Court defeated attempts to tax Indian-owned, reservation-based property within Minnesota. The Court stated that *McClanahan, supra* was applicable, despite Public Law 280 which provided for the delegation of certain civil and criminal authority on Indian reservations in six states, including Minnesota. The Court stated that Public Law 280, in the context of civil jurisdiction constitutes "a reaffirmation of the existing reservation Indian-Federal Government relationship in all respects" except for "the conferral of state court jurisdiction to adjudicate private civil causes of action involving Indians."
32. See *Turner v. United States*, 248 U.S. 354 (1919); *Hamilton v. Nakai*, 453 F.2d 152 (9th Cir. 1971); *Greene v. Wilson*, 331 F.2d 769 (9th Cir. 1964); *Cherokee Nation v. State*, 461 F.2d 674 (10th Cir. 1972); *Twin Cities Chippewa Tribal Council v. Minnesota Chippewa Tribe*, 370 F.2d 529 (8th Cir. 1967); *Maryland Casualty Co. v. National Bank*, 361 F.2d 517 (5th Cir. 1966); *Iron Crow v. Oglala Sioux Tribe*, 231 F.2d 89 (8th Cir. 1956); and *Barnes v. United States*, 205 F. Supp. 97 (D. Mont. 1962).
33. In Indian Civil Rights Act (25 U.S.C. § 1301 et seq.), enacted in 1968, guarantees specified rights against infringement by Indian tribes. Courts have held that the Act manifests a waiver by Congress of the sovereign immunity of an Indian tribe as to actions alleging violation of the specified civil rights.
34. 25 U.S.C. § 450 (1975).
35. P.L. 92-318, P.L. 92-380.

Selected Bibliography

I. THE GREAT SIOUX NATION

Anderson, Harry H. "The Controversial Sioux Amendment to the Fort Laramie Treaty of 1851." *Nebraska History*, XXXVII: September 1956, 201-20.
———. "Indian Peace-Talkers and the Conclusion of the Sioux War of 1876." *Nebraska History*, XL: December 1963, 223-54.
Bland, T. A. *A Brief History of the Late Military Invasion of the Home of the Sioux.* Washington: n.p., 1891.
Bordeaux, William J. *Conquering the Mighty Sioux.* Sioux Falls: n.p., 1929.
Brininstool, E. A. *Fighting Red Cloud's Warriors.* Columbus: The Hunter-Trader-Trapper Company, 1926.
Clough, Wilson O., ed. *Fort Russell and Fort Laramie Peace Commission in 1867.* Sources of Northwest History, No. 14, State University of Montana.
Colby, L. W. "The Sioux Indian War of 1890-91." Nebraska State Historical Society, *Transactions and Reports*, III (1892), 144-90.
Deland, Charles E. "The Sioux Wars." *South Dakota Historical Collections*, XV (1930), 8-730.
Eastman, Charles A. *Indian Heroes and Great Chieftains.* Boston: Little, Brown, and Company, 1920.
Green, Charles Lowell. "The Indian Reservation System of the Dakotas to 1889." *South Dakota Historical Collections*, XIV (1928), 307-416.
Hafen, LeRoy R. and Young, Francis M. *Fort Laramie and the Pageant of the West, 1834-1890.* Glendale: Arthur H. Clark Co., 1938.
Hans, Fred M. *The Great Sioux Nation.* Chicago: M. A. Donohue and Co., 1907.
Hassrick, Royal B. *The Sioux: Life and Customs of a Warrior Society.* Norman: University of Oklahoma Press, 1964.
Hoig, Stan. *The Sand Creek Massacre.* Norman: University of Oklahoma Press, 1961.
Hyde, George E. *Red Cloud's Folk.* Norman: University of Oklahoma Press, 1937, 1957.
———. *A Sioux Chronicle.* Norman: University of Oklahoma Press, 1956.
Johnson, W. Fletcher. *Life of Sitting Bull and History of the Indian War of 1890-91.* Edgewood, S.D.: Edgewood Publishing Company, 1891.
Johnston, Sister Mary Antonio. *Federal Relations with the Great Sioux Indians of South Dakota, 1887-1933, With Particular Reference to Land Policy Under the Dawes Act.* Washington, D.C.: The Catholic University of America Press, 1948.
Lamar, Howard R. *Dakota Territory, 1861-1889.* New Haven: Yale University Press, 1956.
Lassen, Arthur J., ed. "The Black Hills Gold Rush." *North Dakota Historical Quarterly*, VI (1931-1932), 302-18.
McGregor, James H. *The Wounded Knee Massacre.* Baltimore: Wirth Brothers, 1940.
Olson, James C. *Red Cloud and the Sioux Problem.* Lincoln: University of Nebraska Press, 1965.

Pennington, Robert. "An Analysis of the Political Structure of the Teton-Dakota Indian Tribe of North America." *North Dakota History*, XX (July 1953), 143-55.

Report of the Special Commission Appointed to Investigate the Affairs of The Red Cloud Indian Agency, July, 1875. Washington, D.C.: Government Printing Office, 1875.

Sandoz, Mari. *Crazy Horse.* New York: Alfred A. Knopf, 1942.

Standing Bear, Luther. *My People the Sioux.* Boston: Houghton Mifflin Co., 1928.

Utley, Robert M. *The Last Days of the Sioux Nation.* New Haven: Yale University Press, 1963.

Voices From Wounded Knee: The People Are Standing Up. Roosevelttown, N.Y.: Akwesasne Notes, 1975.

Wemett, W. W. "Custer's Expedition to the Black Hills in 1874." *North Dakota Historical Quarterly*, VI (July 1932), 292-301.

Wissler, Clark. "Societies and Ceremonial Association in the Oglala Division of the Teton-Sioux.." *Anthropological Papers of the American Museum of Natural History*, IX (1916), 1-99.

Zimmerman, Bill. *Airlift to Wounded Knee.* Chicago: Swallow Press, 1976.

II. COLONIALISM IN NORTH AMERICA

Adams, Howard. *Prisons of Grass: History of Canada From The Native View.* Toronto, 1975.

Brady, Cyrus Townsend. *Indian Fights and Fighters.* Garden City, N.Y.: Doubleday, Page and Co., 1940.

Brown, Dee. *Bury My Heart at Wounded Knee.* New York: Holt, Rinehart, and Winston, 1971.

Cahn, Edgar S., and Hearne, David W.., *Our Brothers Keeper: The Indian in White America.* New York: New American Library, 1969.

Cohen, Felix. "Americanizing the White Man." *The American Scholar*, XVI, No. 2, Spring 1952, 177-91.

Collier, Peter. *When Shall They Rest? The Cherokees' Long Struggle with America.* New York: Holt, Rinehart, and Winston, 1973.

Deloria, Vine Jr., *Custer Died for Your Sins.* New York: Macmillan Publishing Co., 1969.

———. *We Talk, You Listen.* New York: Macmillan Co., 1970; Dell, 1974.

DeRosier, Arthur H., Jr. *The Removal of the Choctaw Indians.* Knoxville: University of Tennessee, 1970.

Folsom, Franklin. *Red Power on the Rio Grande: The Native American Revolution of 1680.* Chicago: Follett Publishing, 1973.

Foreman, Grant. *Indian Removal.* Norman: University of Oklahoma Press, 1953.

Forbes, Jack. *Frontiers in American History and the Role of the Frontier Historian.* Desert Research Institute, No. 21. Reno: University of Nevada Press, July 1966.

———. *Apache, Navajo, and Spaniard.* Norman: University of Oklahoma Press, 1960.

Horseman, Reginald. *Expansion and American Indian Policy.* East Lansing: Michigan State University Press, 1967.

Jacobs, Wilbur R. *Dispossessing the American Indian.* New York: Charles Scribner's Sons, 1972.

Josephy, Alvin, Jr. *Patriot Chiefs.* New York: Penguin Books, 1976; Viking, 1961.

Jorgensen, Josephy G. *The Sun Dance Religion: Power for the Powerless.* Chicago: University of Chicago, 1972.

Leckie, William H. *The Military Conquest of the Southern Plains.* Norman: University of Oklahoma Press, 1963.

McNickle, D'Arcy. *They Came Here First.* Philadelphia: J. B. Lippincott, 1949.

Meyer, William. *Native American: The New Indian Resistance.* New York: International Publishers, 1971.

Murphy, Lawrence R. "The United States Army in Taos, 1847-1852." *New Mexico Historical Review* 47, No. 1 (January 1972), 33-49.

Nammack, Georgiana C. *Fraud, Politics, and the Dispossession of the Indians: The Iroquois Land Frontier in the Colonial Period.* Norman: University of Oklahoma Press, 1969.

The Navajo Nation: An American Colony. Report of the United States Commission on Civil Rights. Washington, D.C.: September 1975.

Reno, Phillip. "Rebellion in New Mexico, 1837." *New Mexico Historical Review* XL: No. 3 (1965), 197-213.

Robertson, Heather. *Reservations Are for Indians.* Toronto: James Lewis and Samuel, 1970.

Rogin, Michael Paul. *Fathers and Children: Andrew Jackson and the Subjugation of the American Indian.* New York: Alfred A. Knopf, 1975; Vintage, 1976.

Sandoz, Mari. *Cheyenne Autumn.* New York: Hastings House Publishers, 1953.

Steiner, Stan. *The Vanishing White Man.* New York: Harper and Row, 1976.

Spicer, Edward H. *A Short History of the Indians of the United States.* New York: D. Van Nostrand Company, 1969.

———. *Cycles of Conquest: The Impact of Spain, Mexico, and the United States on the Indians of the Southwest, 1533-1960.* Tucson: University of Arizona Press, 1962.

Sutton, Imre *Indian Land Tenure Bibliography Essays and a Guide to the Literature.* New York and Paris: Clearwater Publishing Company, Inc., 1975.

Traders on the Navajo Reservation: A Report on the Economic Bondage of the Navajo People, Southwestern Indian Development, Inc. Window Rock, Arizona: 1968.

Van Every, Dale. *The Disinherited.* New York: Avon Books, 1966.

Vogel, Virgil, ed. *This Country Was Ours: A Documentary History of the American Indian.* New York: Harper and Row, 1972.

Wallace, Anthony F. C. *The Death and Rebirth of the Seneca.* New York: Alfred Knopf, 1970; Vintage Books, 1972.

Young, Mary E. *Redskins, Ruffleshirts, and Rednecks: Indian Allotments in Alabama and Mississippi, 1830-1860.* Norman: University of Oklahoma Press, 1961.

III. OTHER READINGS: INDIAN CULTURE

Browne, C. A. "The Chemical Industries of the American Aborigine." *ISIS* XXIII (1935), 406-24.

Burchard, John, and Bush-Brown, Albert. *The Architecture of America.* Boston: Little Brown and Co., 1961.

Collier, John. *Indians of the Americas.* New York: W. W. Norton, 1947.

Cook, Sherburne F. and Borah, W. W. *Essays in Population History.* Berkeley: University of California, 1972.

Cook, Sherburne F. *The Conflict Between the California Indian and White Civilization.* Berkeley: University of California, 1976.

Griffin, James B., ed. *Lake Superior Copper and the Indians.* Ann Arbor: University of Michigan Press, 1961.

Josephy, Alvin M., Jr. *The Indian Heritage of America.* New York: Bantam Books, 1968.

Levine, Stuart, and Lurie, Nancy O. *The American Indian Today.* Baltimore: Penguin Books, 1965.

Sauer, Carl O. *Early Spanish Main.* Berkeley: University of California, 1966.

Stone, Doris, and Balser, Carlos. *Aboriginal Metal Work of Lower Central America.* Chicago: Field Museum of Natural History, 1967.

Verrill, A. Hyatt. *Food America Gave the World.* Boston: C. C. Page, 1937.

Vogel, Virgil. *American Indian Medicine.* New York: Harper and Row, 1975.

IV. ORAL TRADITION: ORAL HISTORY

Bobbi Lee: Indian Rebel: Struggles of a Native Canadian Woman. Vancouver, B.C.: Liberation Support Movement Press, 1975.

Crashing Thunder, the Autobiography of a Winnebago Indian. Paul Radin, ed. New York: Appleton-Century, 1926.

Lame Deer, John Fire, and Erdoes, Richard. *Lame Deer: Seeker of Visions.* New York: Simon and Schuster, 1972.

Momaday, N. Scott. "The Man Made of Words." *Indian Voices: The First Convocation of American Indian Scholars.* San Francisco: Indian Historical Press, 1970.

————. *The Way To Rainy Mountain.* Albuquerque: University of New Mexico Press, 1969; New York: Ballantine, 1970.

Mountain Wolf Woman. Nancy Oestreich Lurie, ed. Ann Arbor: University of Michigan Press, 1974.

Neihardt, John G. *Black Elk Speaks.* New York: William Morrow, 1932; Lincoln: University of Nebraska, 1961; New York: Pocket Books, 1972.

Ortiz, Alfonso. *The Tewa World.* Chicago: University of Chicago Press, 1969.

Ortiz, Simon. "Song and Poetry: Perception and Expression." *Suntracks* (Tucson), Vol. 3, No. 2 (Spring 1977).

Stands in Timber, John, and Liberty, Margot. *Cheyenne Memories.* New Haven: Yale University Press, 1967.

Sun Chief: The Autobiography of a Hopi Indian. New Haven: Yale University Press, 1942.

Wroth, Lawrence C. "The Indian Treaty as Literature." *The Yale Review,* Vol. XVII, No. 4 (July 1928).

The Zunis: Self Portrayals. New York: New American Library, 1972.

V. LEGAL STUDIES

Casner, A. James. *American Law of Property: A Treatise on the Law of Property in the United States.* 7 vols. Boston: Little, Brown, 1952.

Cohen, Felix. *Handbook of Federal Indian Law.* 1942. Reprinted Albuquerque: University of New Mexico, n.d.

————. *The Legal Conscience.* New Haven: Yale University Press, 1958.

Deloria, Vine, Jr. *Behind the Trail of Broken Treaties: An Indian Declaration of Independence.* New York: Dell, 1974.

Higgins, Frank B. "International Law Consideration of the American Indian Nations by the United States." 3 *Arizona Law Review* 74: 1961.

Kappler, Charles J., compiler and editor. *Indian Affairs, Laws and Treaties,* Vol. 1-2: 57th Cong., 1st Sess., S. Doc. 452; Vol. 3: 63d Cong., 2d Sess., S. Doc. 719.

Kickingbird, Kirk, and Ducheneaux, Karen. *One Hundred Million Acres.* New York: Holt, Rinehart, & Winston, 1974.

Llewellyn, K. N., and Hoebel, E. Adamson. *The Cheyenne Way.* Norman: Univeristy of Oklahoma Press, 1941.

Moynihan, Cornelius J. *Introduction to the Law of Real Property.* St. Paul, Minn. West Publishing Company, 1962.

Nielson, Richard Allen. "American Indian Land Claims." *University of Florida Law Review* 25, No. 2 (Winter 1972), 308-26.

Price, Monroe E. *Law and The American Indian: Readings, Notes and Cases.* New York: Bobbs-Merrill, 1973.

Restatement, Second, Foreign Relations Law of the United States. American Law Institute, 1965.

Trennert, Robert A., Jr. *Alternative to Extinction: Federal Indian Policy and The Beginnings of the Reservation System, 1845–1851.* Philadelphia: Temple University Press, 1975.

Washburn, Wilcomb E. *Red Man's Land: White Man's Law.* New York: Charles Scribner Sons, 1971.

Treaties and Agreements of the Sioux Nation. Washington, D.C.: Institute for the Development of Indian Law, 1972.

VI. CASES AND STATUTES
((listed chronologically)
(See "Indian Sovereignty—It's Alive," *infra,* for more complete case listing.)

Northwest Ordinance of 1787. U.S.C. (1934 ed.) p. III, 1 Stat. 50, 1 Stat. 106.

Johnson and Graham's Lessee v. McIntosh. 8 Wheat 523 (1823).

Cherokee Nation v. State of Georgia. 30 U.S. 1 (1831).

Worcester v. State of Georgia. 315 U.S. 515 (1832).

Treaty of Peace, Friendship, Limits, and Settlement with the Republic of Mexico. February 2, 1848 (Treaty of Guadalupe Hidalgo), U.S. Statutes at Large, 1859, pp. 922-43.

Fort Laramie Treaty of 1868. 15 Stat. 635.

Appropriations Act of March 3, 1871. 25 U.S.C. 71.

Ex Parte Crow Dog. 109 U.S. 556 (1883).

Major Crimes Act. 35 Stat. 1088, 47 Stat. 336, 18 U.S.C. 1151-53.

General Allotment Act of 1887 (Dawes Act) 24 Stat. 388.

Indian Reorganization Act of 1934. 48 Stat. 984, cf. 25 U.S.C. 1461-75.

Indian Citizenship Act. Act of June 2, 1924, 43 Stat. 253; 8 U.S.C. 3.

Choctaw Nation and Cherokee Nation v. State of Oklahoma. 397 U.S. 620 (1970).

United States v. Consolidated Wounded Knee Cases. 389 F. Supp. 235 (D. Neb. W.D.S.D., 1975): aff'd in major part, 8th Circuit Court of Appeals, No. 75-1173, No. 75-1398, No. 75-1483, July 15, 1976; Petition for Writ of Cert. before U.S. Supreme Court denied.

VII. BIBLIOGRAPHIES: NORTH AMERICAN INDIANS

A Chronological List of Treaties and Agreements Made by Indian Tribes with the United States. Washington, D.C.: The Institute for the Development of Indian Law, 1973.

Dobyns, Henry. *Native American Historical Demography: A Critical Bibliography.* Bloomington: Indiana University Press, 1976.

Edwards, Everett E. *A Bibliography on the Agriculture of the American Indians.* Washington, D.C.: Misc. Publications No. 447, 1942.

Heizer, Robert F. *The Indians of California: A Critical Bibliography.* Bloomington: Indiana University Press, 1976.

Helm, June. *The Indians of the Subarctic: A Critical Bibliography.* Bloomington: Indiana University Press, 1976.

Henry, Jeanette. "Our Inaccurate Textbooks." *The Indian Historian* I, No. 1 (December 1967), 21-24.

Iverson, John. *The Navajos: A Critical Bibliography.* Bloomington: Indiana University Press, 1976.

Stensland, Anna Lee. *Literature by and about the American Indian: An Annotated Bibliography.* Urbana: National Council of Teachers of English, 1973.

Swadesh, Frances Leon. *20000 Years of History: A New Mexico Bibliography.* Santa Fe: Sunstone Press, 1973.

Tanner, Helen Hornbeck. *The Ojibwas: A Critical Bibliography.* Bloomington: Indiana University Press, 1976.

Vogel, Virgil J. *The Indian in American History.* Chicago: Integrated Education Associates, 1968.

Whiteside, Don. *Aboriginal People: A Selected Bibliography Concerning Canada's First People.* Ottawa: National Indian Brotherhood, 1973.

VIII. PERIODICALS
(Continental in Scope)

American Indian Law Review (annual). Norman: University of Oklahoma, College of Law.

American Indian Quarterly (quarterly). Hurst, Texas: Southwestern American Indian Society.

American Indian Journal (monthly). Washington, D.C.: Institute for the Development of Indian Law.

Akwesasne Notes (bi-monthly newspaper). Roosevelttown, New York: Mohawk Nation.

Bulletin: An Independent Journal on Native Affairs (quarterly). Ottawa: Canadian Association in Support of the Native Peoples.

Indigena (quarterly newspaper). Berkeley, California.

The Indian Historian (quarterly). Journal of the American Indian Historical Society, San Francisco.

Spirit of the People (bi-monthly). St. Paul, Minn.: Native American Solidarity Committee (NASC).

Sun Tracks (quarterly). Tucson: An American Indian Literary Magazine.

Treaty Council News (monthly). San Francisco, New York: Official Bulletin of the International Indian Treaty Council, published by the American Indian Treaty Council Information Center, San Francisco.

Wassaja (monthly, newspaper). San Francisco: Indian Historical Press.

IX. PRIMARY SOURCE

Transcript of The Trial on the Motion to Dismiss for Want of Jurisdiction before the Honorable Warren K. Urbom, Chief Judge United States District Court for the District of Nebraska, Lincoln, Nebraska. United States (Plaintiff) v. Consolidated Wounded Knee Cases (Defendants). CR. 73-5019, December 1974.
Full transcript also available from Native American Rights Fund, Boulder, Colorado.